From Workshop to Toy Store

A Fascinating Inside Look at How Toy
Inventors Develop, Sell, and Cash In
on Their Ideas

RICHARD C. LEVY AND
RONALD O. WEINGARTNER

A Fireside Book Published by Simon & Schuster
New York, London, Toronto, Sydney, Tokyo, Singapore

FIRESIDE
Simon & Schuster Building
Rockefeller Center
1230 Avenue of the Americas
New York, New York 10020

First Fireside Edition 1992
Published by arrangement with Henry Holt & Co., Inc.

FIRESIDE and colophon are registered trademarks
of Simon & Schuster Inc.

Manufactured in the United States of America

10 9 8 7 6 5 4 3 2 1 Pbk.

Library of Congress Cataloging in Publication Data

Levy, Richard C.
  [Inside Santa's workshop]
  From workshop to toy store: a fascinating inside look at how toy inventors
develop, sell, and cash in on their ideas/Richard C. Levy and Ronald O.
Weingartner.—1st Fireside ed.
      p. cm.
  Reprint. Originally published: Inside Santa's workshop. New York: H. Holt,
© 1990.
  "A Fireside book."
  Includes bibliographical references and index.
  1. Toy industry.   I. Weingartner, Ronald O.   II. Title.
[HD9993.T692L48   1992]
338.4'768872—dc20   91-31691
                                                              CIP

ISBN 0-671-74738-X Pbk.

This book was previously published under the title *Inside Santa's Workshop*.

Permissions on the Following Page

Contents

Acknowledgments

As authors of a book of this nature we are essentially reporters, and as such heavily dependent on the cooperation and assistance of many people. During the course of our year and a half of research, we contacted at least 125 professional toy and game inventors, and more than ninety corporate executives and industry observers, many of whom racked their brains on our behalf for story and fact. Their warm reception, patience, interest, hospitality, generosity, and understanding helped to make this project enjoyable, enlightening, and one we will both fondly remember always.

Many of our colleagues from the inventing community and corporate corridors filled out our comprehensive questionnaire, accepted our lengthy telephone calls, placed lengthy telephone calls back to us, invited us to their homes, visited our homes, and tolerated having tape recorders shoved into their faces during Toy Fair, product presentations, and, on some occasions, while trying to enjoy a quiet lunch or dinner.

We owe a special debt of gratitude to the following executives who gave of their time and shared their feelings with us in individual interviews on one or more occasions: **Buddy L:**

David R. Berko, vice president for marketing. **Cadaco Games:** Waymon Wittman, president; Barbara Allen, director of marketing. **The Ertl Company:** George B. Volanakis, president and CEO; James Walsh, vice president of licensing and premium sales; Richard Knight, director of product development. **Fisher-Price:** Charles S. Riter, vice president for research and development (R&D); Peter Pook, director of infant toy product. **Lewis Galoob Toys:** David Galoob, president; Saul Jodel, executive vice president of marketing and R&D; Gary J. Niles, senior vice president; Patricia Ann Tura, product manager. **The Games Gang:** Brian J. Cornacchia, sales manager; Lee Gelber, national sales manager. **Hasbro:** Alan Hassenfeld, president; Steve D'Aguanno, senior vice president of R&D; Kate Stanuch, associate director of market research. **International Games:** Jeff Conrad, vice president of R&D. **Kenner:** Howard Bollinger, senior vice president of advanced concepts. **Lego Systems:** Dick Garvey, vice president of marketing. **Mattel U.S.A.:** Robert Sansone, president; Bob Rao, vice president of marketing and product development. **Mayfair Games:** Darwin P. Bromley, president. **Milton Bradley:** George R. Ditomassi, president; Mike Meyers, senior vice president of R&D; George H. Merritt, vice president of public relations; Joe Gullini, senior vice president of operations; Dale Siswick, vice president of marketing. **Monogram/Kidstar:** Randy Karp, senior vice president of sales and marketing; Dwain Dial, director of product development. **Nasta International:** Loren T. Taylor, senior vice president for marketing. **The Ohio Art Company:** William C. Killgallon, president; Lowell T. Wilson, vice president of product development. **Parker Brothers:** Chris Campbell, director of product acquisition. **Playskool:** John Hall, vice president for R&D. **Revell/Monogram:** Pat Ruhl, vice president of marketing. **Spearhead Industries:** James Kubiatowicz, director of product development. **Tiger Games:** Bill Dohrmann, senior vice president for marketing and sales. **TSR:** Michael H. Cook, vice president of new product development; Jack Morrissey, vice president of sales. **Tyco Toys:** Dick Grey, president; Jim Alley, senior vice president of marketing; Michael Lyden, vice president of business development; Neil Tilbor, vice president of marketing; Woody Browne, vice president of marketing; Neil Werde, director of marketing; David O'Neill, director of marketing; Harold Frankel, director of marketing; Mike Hirtle, vice president for R&D; Warren Bosch, director of product development. **View-Master/Ideal:** Jill Ottinger, vice president of marketing; Anne Pitrone, director of product development. **Western Publishing:** Barrie Simpson, senior director of creative development; George Propsom, manager of product development (games and puzzles). **Worlds of Wonder:** Josh Denham, president and CEO.

We owe as great a debt to the inventors who responded to our seemingly endless queries and to those who took the extra effort to fill out our "Santa Survey." The names can be found throughout this book. One and all gave us their time and advice most generously.

Thanks also to Judy Ellis, chairman, Toy Design Department, Fashion Institute of Technology; George Dunsay, president, Total Toy; Jerry Houle, president, Bliss House; Bonnie M. Limbach, manager of external communications, The Society of the Plastics Industry; Patricia A. McGovern, manager, public relations, Parker Brothers; David M. Lafrennie, manager, public relations, Lego Systems; Mary Terdiman, account executive, Ruder-Finn; Wayne Charness, associate vice president, public relations and promotions, Hasbro; Paul Vanasse, administrator, Intellectual Properties, Hasbro; David Dubosky, counsel, Hasbro; Carol Prestidge, Tonka Corporation; Dennis M. Wesolowski, corporate counsel, Tyco Toys; Mel Taft, president, Mel Taft & Associates; Stan Weston, chairman, Leisure Concepts; Bernie Loomis, president, Bernard Loomis, Inc.; Paul B. Beatty, publisher, *Toy & Hobby World;* Paul Valentine, toy industry analyst, Standard & Poor's; David Leibowitz, senior vice president, American Securities Corporation; Lisa Laganella, licensing coordinator, Royalty and Property Management; and Professor (and pal) Warren Greenberg, George Washington University, for giving this book his time, his sage suggestions, and its first reading.

A special thanks to: Diane P. Cardinale, assistant communications director, Toy Manufacturers of America, who opened her heart and clip files to us, and without whose assistance this book would not have begun as easily as it did; Toy Manufacturers of America for its literature and research; Hasbro, Inc., and its associate vice president-legal, Cynthia S. Reed, for permitting us to reproduce Hasbro's Product Development Overview line chart; and to all the companies that generously supplied line art for our cover and chapter openers.

In closing, a couple of personal notes:

To my wife and collaborator, Sheryl, and to our daughter and constant inspiration, Bettie, no amount of thanks or love could ever repay you two for tolerating my writing yet another book and the erratic work schedule it required. I could not have accomplished it without your help. I am indebted to Sheryl, who unselfishly gave of her excellent organizational skills, advice, and encouragement, and to Bettie for the quintuple swirls, warm hugs, and *besos grandes* when they were needed most.

To my coauthor, Ron, a creative and insightful pro with whom I have worked closely for almost two years on this project, thanks for a great idea, an enjoyable partnership, and what I know is a lifelong friendship.

To those very clever fellows in the inventing community with whom I have collaborated over the past thirteen years, and the courageous and imaginative executives who have put their confidence in me and our products, an enormous thank you and my deepest appreciation. Any plaudits that this book may receive are due in large part to your contribution.

—R. C. L.

As with any collaborative work, this book is the result of shared thoughts, perceptions, and efforts, and I thank all who have shared their insights into the subject of toy inventing. No greater thanks is due to anyone more than my coauthor, Richard Levy, who gave his boundless enthusiasm, creative thinking, and diligence to our book—many of the qualities that have made him a force in the toy-inventing community. Also, a most special thank you to my wife, Leslie, a full-time professional marketer and developer, who helped immeasurably with the story that unfolds on the pages that follow.

I am grateful to many colleagues at Milton Bradley with whom I have experienced many of the events woven through the book. I am fortunate to have had the opportunity to be exposed to many of the creative inventors highlighted herein and to have a career where each day is filled with so many new opportunities.

—R. O. W.

Preface

*F*rom *Workshop to Toy Store* is written first and foremost as a tribute to the talented men and women who form what is properly known in the toy industry as the "inventing community." Comprised of seasoned, innovative, full-time professionals, it is this small core of gifted inventors *cum* designers *cum* engineers *cum* developers *cum* marketers that satisfies the voracious appetite of America's over $13 billion toy market with amusing and refreshingly new and novel product year in and year out.

These independent "idea people" work outside the confines of any single toy or game manufacturer yet rely totally on those companies to take their creations to market. As a group, they survive on their ability to generate the sparks for new forms, fantasies, and fun that often become items on Christmas wish lists.

We use the terms *inventory*, *developer*, and *creator* interchangeably, as does the industry, to signify one or more of the independent creative forces behind a product, usually a signatory to the agreement between inventor (licensor) and manufacturer (licensee), and, as such, a participant in any advances and royalty income.

We make no attempt to recognize any coinventing credits,

for this would be an impossible task, as anyone familiar with this business knows. Throughout our book you will notice that two or more inventors often take credit for the same product. This is normal in a business where many diverse and specialized talents are required to bring an idea from the embryonic stage to the retail stage. It was never our aim to attempt to pinpoint which associate or partner was responsible for a particular key idea, or the contribution and/or enhancement that caused a concept to be bought by a manufacturer. The process of innovation is not easy to analyze. Perhaps Paul Saffo, a research fellow with the Menlo Park, California–based Institute for the Future, put it best when he told *Newsweek* that trying to understand innovation is like shoveling smoke.

When we use the term *toy industry*, we mean to encompass all categories, such as games, dolls, action figures, ride-ons, and so forth. The same is true when we call someone a *toy inventor*; that is, he or she could be a creator of a wide range of playthings, including games and dolls.

By focusing on the independent inventor, we have no wish to imply that there is any lack of creativity or inventiveness at the corporate level. Just the opposite is true. Many outstanding concepts come from in-house sources. And the contributions made by corporate research-and-development (R&D) and/or marketing executives to outside submissions can often make the difference between success and failure of a product. It should be also noted that many of today's most accomplished and respected independents came from the corporate ranks. But without the work of the inventing community, the industry as we know it would not exist.

Through our combined experiences in product development, we are aware that cross-pollination and synergism of many forces produce the ultimate success. Product development to subsequent sale is such a delicate, complex, and serpentine chain of egos, events, whims, technologies, designs, and marketing skills that if any link were to break, an entire project could flag. In the end, the whole is more powerful than any of its individual parts.

The professional developers mentioned in our book fully understand that it is one thing to have an idea, another thing to design and engineer an idea, and yet another thing to polish, package, position, and negotiate the sale of an idea for manufacture. They know—luck being a given—that it takes teamwork to make anything happen. It is rare when one person has an idea, prototypes it himself, shows it to a manufacturer, and walks away with a check.

We made every effort to interview as many independent developers and corporate executives as possible. Some of those contacted did not wish to participate. Others missed our deadlines. We cross-checked our lists of professional inventors with numerous corporate vice presidents of R&D in an attempt not to overlook any prolific concept sources.

Omissions were unintentional and an absentee inventor may be no less talented and productive as a product source than the contributors who opened their workshops to us.

Just as in any business, toy executives do change jobs or affiliations. All executives are credited with the positions held at the time of our original interviews. The fact that Bernstein, Daniels, Friedman, Gatto, Kalinske, Langieri, Miller, Orbanes, and Schwartz no longer occupy the desks from where they shared their perceptions in no way diminishes their views of the toy business. Interestingly they have all moved to new stations in the same arena—the arena where their wits and wisdom will likely make them participants in one of the next big toy hits.

It is our hope that *From Workshop to Toy Store* will intrigue, inform, entertain, and turn over a rock or two for even the most seasoned toy-industry veterans. We have designed the book to provide insights about how the selection and development of new product works and how the creative forces inside and outside a company interact and think.

We blended our words and interviews into a flavor that we

feel accurately reflects the industry and its personalities. We have stocked it with a wide-ranging and colorful cast of characters, a bit of hyperbole, a dash of dreams, the crackle of the irresistible fire of imagination, inspiring and exciting stories of success, and the hard troubling realities of one of the toughest businesses there is. We accept the full responsibility for the point of view, the people selected for interviews and profiles, and the conclusions drawn from our research.

Introduction

Once upon a time, we came very close to not having a night before Christmas. It was a year that the Grinch nearly got away with the holiday; that children's letters to the North Pole stood a chance of going unanswered; that stockings could have gone unfilled. In the immortal poem by Clement Clarke Moore, "A Visit From St. Nicholas," the "right jolly old elf" arrives at every home with a sleigh full of toys for all girls and boys. However, one year Santa almost didn't show.

It happened more than seventy years ago, in 1917. The United States, under the leadership of President Woodrow Wilson, had entered World War I. The U.S. Council for National Defense, called by one news service "a committee of bureaucratic Scrooges," proposed the introduction of an embargo on the purchase and sale of Christmas gifts as a way to conserve the nation's resources and direct the economy toward the war effort. Toymaking was looked at as a frivolity. Uncle Sam threatened to close Santa's workshops.

Empty stockings? Broken hearts? Disappointed children? Not if A. C. Gilbert, inventor of the Erector Set, had anything

to say about it. As president of the one-year-old trade association, Toy Manufacturers of the U.S.A., he went to the nation's capital, accompanied by a bevy of fellow toymakers,
prepared to do battle on behalf of his industry, his colleagues,
and American kids. Fortified with an assortment of products,
they set out to persuade the men on the council that most toys
would not sap the war effort of raw materials or manpower.

According to a report in the *Boston Post*, inventor Gilbert
and his colleagues at first were so intimidated by the dignified
atmosphere of the council's offices, and the serious demeanor
of its members, that they stashed their toy samples behind a
couch; but Gilbert went on to present a powerful argument for
the importance of toys in the building of national pride and
readiness among American youth.

It didn't take long for the council to reverse its position. A
toy inventor had saved Christmas. As the *Boston Post* reported,
from the moment he opened his bags of samples, "the Secre-
taries were boys again. Secretary [of the Navy] Daniels was as
pleased with an Ives submarine as he could be with a new
destroyer. . . . He kept fast hold of it. . . . 'Toys appeal to the
heart of every one of us, no matter how old we are,' said another
cabinet member. And it was because they did . . . that the boys
and girls of the United States are going to awake this Christmas morning upon a day as merry as Christmases in the past."

Switch to a December 22, any year. The Christmas shopping countdown is in the red zone of single digits. Time ticks
with great frenzy. Colorful advertising inserts in extra-heavy
newspapers announce red tag specials, round-the-clock sales,
and slashed prices on goods for all ages. Only infants and tod-
dlers are insulated from the slick mail order catalogs, sublimi-
nal media messages, and storefront billboards screaming super
savings on sophisticated do-all playthings, twenty-first century
abracadabra, electronic toys and games, and the latest whirl-
ing, screaming gizmos.

To children, the next forty-eight hours are filled with great anticipation and last-minute plans to ensure an array of brightly bowed rectangles and squares wrapped in metalized paper and pyramided under The Tree. To the besieged moms and dads, and their moms and dads, bathed in unselfishness, the final hours are filled with choices, selections, and expenses that build the pyramid of gifts for the seasonal showplace. They know their task.

It is December 22, any year. Cars are double-parked and idling in fire lanes at suburban malls. The sprawling multi-tiered bazaars are resplendent with a near-endless array of gewgaws, bric-a-brac, curios, and vitals. Mountains of merchandise stand ready to satisfy the seasonal esprit of consumer generosity.

Against the backdrop of booming, nonstop Muzak, millions of Christmas-hearted parents play out the role of the legendary plump, scarlet- and fur-clad, all-knowing, ever-giving, timelessly loved holiday cherub known as Santa Claus.

Central to these mind- and eye-boggling wintry fairylands, at the end of mall avenues, is the epicenter of holiday fantasy, the huge candy-cane throne. Artificial gingerbread cutouts and twinkling gumdrop lights line pathways to the red-and-white perch befitting only the most revered royalty. Among papier-mâché elves and bridled, plastic molded reindeer is an endless procession of youngsters anxious for a brief chat with the celebrity of the season.

At that special moment, each child delivers a message with varying degrees of confidence, but with consistent intent. Every youthful visitor enumerates a lengthy list of most desired playthings. And as the children chatter to their bearded friend, adoring parents strain to overhear the desires and dreams. They listen for clues and hints that separate happiness from disappointment. It may be the Santa figure who probes, questions, and teases to learn the prized toys and games; but it will be up to the loving onlookers to see that the visions of the season are delivered.

It is December 22, any year. The heavy gray skies forecast a late-December storm. The season of buying may be all around, but inside a workshop an independent, professional toy inventor stands at his model-making table casting urethane parts for a product he hopes will be in kiddie demand not forty-eight hours away, but rather a full year or two in the future.

The center of his concentration is a novel concept, the prototype of which he hopes will someday debut at an annual American International Toy Fair in New York City. He isn't waiting for Santa to discover his exciting new toy opportunity. His plan is to license it to a toy company, and, with the right marketing, his item may be high on children's "I want" lists for some future Christmas.

The inventor has alerted his established network of toy-industry contacts that his labors may yield the next Weebles, a once-very-successful line of characters that wobbled but didn't fall down. He has set up appointments with executives from Fisher-Price, Playskool, and Mattel and penciled them into his diary.

There will be no interference in this inventor's tasks by bell-ringers, twinkling lights, and mistletoe (well, maybe mistletoe!). He turns aside the hype of the season, and even though he is still part kid and part industrial designer, he is also a businessperson who operates Santa's real workshop.

When Santa wants his sleigh filled with new toys and games each year, he gets plenty of help. Nothing about the pile of playthings to deliver or the helpers who create the cherished gifts is elfin by any measure. And certainly not one helper lives even close to the North Pole. You are more likely to catch helpers in Northridge, California; St. Paul, Minnesota; Kennelon, New Jersey; or Chicago, Illinois.

Santa's real helpers are on the job far more than the final two weeks in December. Every day, year after year, you will find the inventors, developers, and concept people behind Santa's bounty on the job. Their minds and skills never shut down.

Their genius is being tested constantly; their creations are in demand by toy and game users not just at year's end but all year long.

Santa doesn't make toys. They start in the workshops of real people who have committed their talents to originating the next megahit of children's playthings. In the kiddie world, Santa may get credit for the sugar plum, but in the adult world, highly talented people compete ferociously to create the hot-selling plums. This book is their story.

1 Toys Are Us

NAMES IN THE GAME

DONNER, DANCER, DASHER, BLITZEN, COMET,
CUPID, PRANCER, VIXEN, AND, O.K., RUDOLPH

Everyone knows what these legendary names mean to Santa
Claus. Once a year, on a most significant and magical night,
Ol' St. Nick calls on these trusted reindeer to pull his sleigh,
laden with toys, to homes of children everywhere.

BARLOW, BRESLOW, GOLDFARB, GRUEN,
JONES, REILING, REINER, AND, O.K., WEXLER

Few outside the toy industry know what these names mean
to Santa Claus. Throughout the year, these people are called
upon to create the toys and games that will be in demand
during the Christmas season. Nary an elf among them; they
represent some of the greatest talents who invent the goodies
that stuff the stockings, cover the floors around Christmas trees,
and entertain and delight millions of kids while generating in
excess of $13 billion in retail sales in 1990.

Many people know the stories of such inventors as Robert ("Steamboat") Fulton, George ("Air Brake") Westinghouse, Edwin ("60-Second Camera") Land; King ("Safety Razor") Gillette, and Clarence ("Packaged Frozen Food") Birdseye. But few people know of Gordon ("Mouse Trap") Barlow; Jeffrey ("Simon") Breslow; Eddy ("Stompers") Goldfarb; Paul ("Payday") Gruen; Larry ("Cricket") Jones; Vic ("Hit Stix") Reiling; Larry ("G.I. Joe") Reiner, and Howard ("Connect Four") Wexler.

What Makes Them Special

Like all inventors, toy inventors share a sense of adventure, a discontentedness with the status quo, and a courage to continually meet new challenges head-on. They know that there is no future in believing something cannot be accomplished. The future is in making it happen. They spend much of their lives as a minority of one, on the edge, pushing the envelope, and, of course, dreaming. Sure, lots of people dream, but toy creators spend time with their dreams. As Edgar Allan Poe once observed, those who dream by day are cognizant of many things that escape those who dream only by night.

The professional independent toy inventors do easily what others find difficult. The most inventive do what others have not done. These product developers can make people fall in love with their creations before they exist. They can fan their ideas into flames that illuminate but don't burn. And, like all artists, they speak to the human capacity for amusement and amazement.

The imaginations of professional toy and game inventors are fired not only by compensation and commendation, but as much or more by curiosity and challenge. They are people to whom the elves still whisper. Their talents are special creative gifts broadened by the acquisition of business experiences. They operate in a kind of never-never land where pumpkins turn into coaches and mice into horses; cows jump over moons and dishes run away with spoons.

Toy and game inventing is a profession in which few outside the industry recognize the requirements for excelling. When one talks about the need to fix an exotic automobile, build a house, play a professional sport, cure an illness, or program a computer, experts are summoned. But it seems people everywhere tend to feel a natural ability to be able to develop toys and games. Yet just as some jobs require a highly skilled mechanic, carpenter, athlete, physician, and computer programmer, so it takes a person experienced in toy and game development to create new playthings.

In this highly specialized profession, there is no edge given to those whose experiences include childhood, fatherhood, or motherhood. Nor does the act of dating or marrying a professional creator of toys and games give one claim to this esoteric ability or talent. For it is only in the seasoned professional that creativity and imagination are guided and tempered by hard business realities and historical perspective. Toy inventing isn't brain surgery, but it is far from child's play.

The pros in the inventing business are not so much *rational* animals in the Aristotelian sense as *doing* animals, agents of action who see variation as the raw material of evolution and nonconformity as acceptable. They think in degrees and believe in taking their own chances and not those of others. They seek opportunities, not guarantees. This group of self-actualizing, "you-ain't-seen-nothing-yet" artists lives to experience what Ralph Waldo Emerson called the "delicious awakenings of the higher powers."

The most successful toy inventors are those who share and practice the tenet that thinking is a form of doing, and not vice versa. If creative thinking is a very important prerequisite to their profession, initiative and strong motivation to do something with ideas are also vital to the inventing specialist. Nine out of every ten professional inventors surveyed for this book gave highest ratings to both creativity and initiative/strong motivation as key attributes for success.

The Chosen Few

While many thousands of would-be inventors every year attempt to submit ideas to the major toy companies in hopes of selling them, our research reveals that fewer than 150 professional toy and game inventors are "recognized" by the likes of a Galoob, Hasbro, Kenner, Mattel, Milton Bradley, Parker Brothers, Tonka, Tyco Toys, and other market heavyweights. Within this group, between fifty and seventy-five inventors are recognized as "long-ball hitters" and perennial originators of future hot-selling products.

Consider this fact. According to Toy Manufacturers of America, the industry trade association, over 5,000 new playthings are introduced at the annual American International Toy Fair in New York City. The professional inventors interviewed for this book assert that they conceive on average 100 to 150 original concepts each year. If this is the case, this group of inventors alone could generate twice as much product as the industry introduces each year.

Another measure of the pros' annual productivity is the percentage of total new products that comes from them. Company executives credit the inventing community with originating 50 to 75 percent of their lines annually. At these levels, professional inventors can be credited with several thousand new playthings each year.

An amazingly close-knit fraternity, toy and game manufacturers refer to it as "the inventing community." Members of the community are people whose idea packages are never returned unopened by manufacturers. They don't receive boilerplate rejection letters (at least not often!). Their previous credits give them access to the highest levels of corporate management. An appointment to show new product is just a phone call away. Why? Because the manufacturers count on these pros to fill their pipeline year in and year out with innovative, well-executed, fresh product.

There is a trust and respect between these outside idea sources and the corporate executives. Exchanges on concepts are valued and confidential. Most inventors maintain active relationships, both business and personal, with key corporate contacts. In many cases, if inventors cannot make it to a manufacturer's headquarters, the company will dispatch executives to inventors' offices, studios, workshops, and homes. The executives know that the time and money spent dealing with these inventors can lead their company to its next runaway bestseller and help maintain the firm's sales momentum.

More Than Just a Hobby

Toy and game inventors are, after all, in the full-time business of conceiving, defining, formulating, and selling ideas. To create for this industry, inventors cannot work in an isolated, sheltered laboratory. They cannot be caught with their trends down. They originate ideas for a specialized segment of the consumer market, in itself a multibillion-dollar annual business.

They do their homework. They know the history of playthings. They know their product. They know the manufacturers. They know the market. They know the odds. They know how to sell their product visions. They know it isn't easy. And as much as luck plays a factor in the business of originating new toys and games, the pros leave nothing to chance. Like top prizefighters, when they get knocked down, they're up at the count of eight and back in the fight again.

Far more than creativity, sweeping visions, and model-making skills separate the pros from thousands of amateurs and second-tier product designers and developers. The major asset the full-time professional possesses is a profound understanding of and feel for the toy industry as a business—its personalities, the realities of its marketplace, and the changing needs of the consumer and the trade. The pros are also sensitive to lead times, buying and selling cycles, tool and die costs, margins, play value, packaging, telegenics, perceived values, nicheman-ship, focus testing, and the internal evaluation process at toy and game companies. They understand and appreciate the powerful and changing forces behind every detail of product evolution and execution.

The pros are accustomed to seeing UPS, Federal Express, Purolator, and DHL trucks gridlock in their driveways deliv-ering rejected prototypes. They know that rejection is part of the game and that new concepts rarely sell the first time out. They don't take rejection personally. It's part of the business. It's part of the game. And it's why their most important trait is raw perseverance. They are like the salesperson who will drive the extra miles at 4:15 P.M.; the actor auditioning for the hundredth time; and the writer facing a typewriter every day, turning out twenty-five sheets of paper to get two or three us-able passages. Toy inventors don't quit on their dreams, and they often love the ideas in their closets no less than the ones on retail shelves.

Many inventors like to say that it is the glamour of the industry more than the money that drives them. But the pros also know the kinds of financial rewards a hit item can pro-duce. The professional toy inventor is a self-employed owner and operator of a business, a business that runs on profits and one that chases the big return.

A lot of these inventors, but far from all of them, have been professionally trained to generate ideas. They are graphic art-ists and designers who can illustrate and sketch ideas. They are industrial designers and model-makers who can dimensionalize and sculpt ideas. They are mechanical engineers who can mock up and schematize ideas. They are electronics experts bringing state-of-the-art to toyland. And they are marketers with a keen sense of product and the marketplace.

In describing Marvin Glass, perhaps the most celebrated independent developer of toys and games the industry has ever seen, Jeffrey Breslow says, "Marvin wasn't necessarily hands-on, but he was very creative, very stimulating, and very imaginative. He didn't have the skills and dexterity to make something per se, but he certainly had the vision and imagination for concepts."

It is interesting that when asked to define what they do for the industry, many inventors tend to sound very much alike:

"We are people who recognize unfilled needs in the toy and game marketplace and have the vision and skill to create something of value to fulfill those needs," says Paul Lapidus of The Together Group. Independent inventor Leonard Israel believes an inventor is "a person who sees a need for an item and then creates it." Mike Ferris says toy inventors are people who put together a "creative assembly of unlike things." But Perry Grant perhaps best sums up the independent toy and game developer: a person with free time and an itch.

The anatomy of the inventors' inspiration and creativity is complex. Ideas can come to them anywhere at any time. The best products have come through observation. A walk through a shopping center, amusement park, gaming arcade, or hardware store. A relaxing afternoon at the movies. Paging through magazines. Scanning newspapers. Viewing television. Or just watching kids kicking stones.

Elliot A. Rudell, inventor of UpWords (Milton Bradley), sometimes gains inspiration through prayer: "Several major ideas have just been given to me." And Mike Ferris, whose Mickey Mouse Telephone for AT&T was the first personalization of a Bell box, gets ideas "usually from skuszoos of past failures."

Life on the Edge

Most full-time independent developers receive no weekly pay-checks, annual vacations, sick days, or coffee breaks. Financial rewards, when they arrive, come in the form of advances and/or royalties. Advances come with a signed agreement; royalties, if any, after the close of each calendar quarter.

The insecurity and fear of rejection that hinder the casual inventor give birth to wisdom and creativity in their full-time professional counterparts. The pros have only the security provided by their wits, drives, instincts, and whichever of their products are currently being marketed and bought by a "prove-it-to-me" trade and demanded by fickle consumers. Most assuredly, a career in toy inventing is not for the faint-of-heart.

Independent toy developers have deserted traditional thought and structured work for spontaneity and unrestricted creative license. They ask, "Why not?" and "What if?" Whether market pulled or technology pushed, their highly intellectual work is not a pursuit but a passion.

These are men and women who stay fresh by living in the current idiom but whose minds dip into the future and back to the past for inspiration. In fact, for all intents and purposes, there is no "now." Although independent developers compete with each other as well as against R&D groups, they are paced against the march of time. In the toy industry, everyone is betting on and working toward future product introductions.

The most talented independents combine a knowledge of what's happening in the culture with their own concepts, flights of fancy, and fascination with the odd and extravagant deviations of the human experience. They are always on duty and alert for clues and impressions, notepad or tape recorder at hand. "An inventor is very knowledgeable about what is going on in the world regarding changing fads, the family unit, technology, and educational changes that affect children's ephemeral needs," says George B. Volanakis, president and chief operating officer of The Ertl Company and a twenty-two-year industry veteran.

Toy inventors are people who, like little Susan in the holiday classic film *Miracle on 34th Street*, keep on believing even when common sense tells them not to. And that extra ounce of believing can make the difference between success and failure.

No matter how seasoned and businesslike today's professional toy inventors, they—like Pinocchio's kindly old woodcarver, Geppetto—also feel a sense of magic when they embrace their ideas or see something special created by a competitor.

Eddy Goldfarb is one of America's most prolific and successful toy inventors with more than 500 products sold, including such favorites as Battling Tops and Kerplunk (Ideal), Quiz Wiz (Coleco), and Shark Attack! (Milton Bradley). He says emphatically that before originating an abundance of great ideas, one needs a keen sense of what's in vogue. Says Arthur Albert, inventor of Dress 'n Dazzle (Tonka), "A toy inventor is a Renaissance man who is currently aware of what's happening and applies it to a toy or device for children."

"It takes a lot of fortitude, . . . a lot of drive, . . . steadfastness and the ability to recover from rejection after rejection after rejection," says Howard Wexler, inventor of the classic Connect Four (Milton Bradley). "Talent must be there," Wexler continues, "but it takes perseverance . . . and luck too. You could have talent and perseverance and not get anywhere if your timing is wrong."

Charlie Girsch, who with his wife, Maria, directs Girsch Design Associates, says that he reflects on the words of two "contemporary philosophers" when he thinks about what it takes to make it as a professional inventor in the toy industry. The first is Bud Grant, former coach of the Minnesota Vikings, who said, "You work and practice hard so in case the ball bounces your way on Sunday you'll know what to do with it."

The other is Ronald McDonald, who says, "Keep your eyes on the fries."

The power to create resides in the process of transition from the "I've got an idea" stage to the "Look at my idea" stage. Idleness destroys inventiveness just as that proverbial little fly affects the ointment. Hence, professional toy and game developers must be self-starters by nature. They must be as can-do as the kids for whom they invent. They may slow down on occasion to go over a speed bump, but there is no obstacle so great that it can keep them or a great concept down for the count.

Several years ago, Dr. Erno Rubik was asked how young children were able to solve his puzzle cube in no time flat and adults could not. Responded the Hungarian professor, "Because no one ever told the child it could not be done."

The pros know that creating toys is serious business. It is big business. It can be a cutthroat business. It is also a very risky business—part fun house and part chamber of horrors. Too many amateur inventors think that all one has to do is sell a product and, voilà!, a cash cow is born that's destined to become another Cabbage Patch Kids or Trivial Pursuit. No way. More often than not, the inventor is told, "Your ideas will not pass 'Go.' Do not collect $200."

Products are subjected to numerous and critical manufacturer line reviews (aka "shoot-outs") that go on right up until Toy Fair. New concepts constantly are flowing into review. Although the pace has accelerated in recent years, toy development remains essentially a filtering process. With the thousands of proposals submitted each year—not to mention concepts generated by their own internal R&D groups—manufacturers' priorities are flexible and products get dropped, often in spite of substantial corporate financial commitments. At any time, a chief executive may say to his team, "If I told you that one product had to be cut, which one would it be?"

Everything is on a life-support system until it can survive on its own at retail. Items are in one day, out the next. Every toy inventor has felt the loss through the axing of a concept or the dropping of a product; or, worse yet, a line of products. The pros have learned to live with the reality of high product burn-out.

The most experienced independents know not to pop the bubbly when a product is optioned for a cash advance and a signed contract. They may be told, after months of internal development, that the trade does not like it. Even after it reaches retail, it might be a ''stiff'' and languish on the shelves, rejected by the consumer, the ultimate judge. As Murphy's first corollary goes, Nothing is as easy as it looks. And Murphy's second corollary says, Everything takes longer than you think.

No Easy Money

It is a misconception that there is an easy dollar to be made developing and licensing product to toy manufacturers. In an industry with legends of instant millionaires such as Dr. Erno Rubik (Rubik's Cube), Xavier Roberts (Cabbage Patch Kids), and Robert Angel (Pictionary), very few inventors actually make a lot of money. Most independent toy and game developers grind it out on a day-to-day basis. Only the strong survive. In this way, it is on a par with the most highly competitive businesses.

''Even when you're doing well—I mean we've done pretty well in the past five or six years—there are days when you are so down because it is rejection after rejection. One day you have fifteen concepts out; the next day you have three,'' muses Mike Satten, inventor of Sweet Secrets (Galoob), a line of some seventy-five transforming toys for girls. But would he rather be doing something else? ''Oh, please, no way.''

The toy and game industry is a business where losers far outnumber winners. So many are called, so few are chosen. The rejection rate for games is reported to be around 97 percent. And of the games that finally make it to retail, most of them last no longer than a year or two in toyland. Toys do not fare much better. Now you see them, now you don't. If a company gets two to three years out of an inventor's product, it is doing well. Remember Inhumanoids (Hasbro) and Visionaries (Hasbro)? Captain Power (Mattel)? Dinosaucers (Galoob)? All missed major sales expectations. No manufacturer is exempt from failure. No inventor is exempt from a manufacturer that will fail.

Although the toy market is huge, the number of companies supplying product is declining. Mergers have consolidated former competitive manufacturers/marketers into larger corporate entities. Bankruptcies have stripped many brand names from toy shelves. This turmoil has netted fewer companies buying ideas from professional inventors. Many ex–R&D staffers at dissolved companies gravitate toward the ranks of the independent inventing community either as "associates" or as competitive startups.

When asked to characterize the current climate for selling ideas, inventing pro Ben Kinberg says, "Very simply, there are less people, less companies with whom to do business. As some toy companies become larger, their procedures become more complex with more people becoming involved in the selection process. Should one single member in the selection chain fail to sign off on a new product, that product is effectively killed."

Another threat to inventors is the flood of imported toys and games, greater now than ever before in our nation's history. TMA estimates that 70 percent of the toys sold in the United States are manufactured in whole or in part, overseas. In 1989 the United States imported $5.567 billion worth of toys. The more entrepreneurial developers are forming alliances with foreign manufacturers to merge their inventiveness and connections with sources of supply. They then are able to approach U.S. marketers not only with unique concepts but also with product completely manufactured.

Today the most popular plaything in America is the Japanese-produced Nintendo Entertainment System, which commands a whopping 25 to 30 percent share of U.S. toy and game sales. In 1990, Nintendo sold $3.4 billion in video-game systems and cartridges and projects $4.0 billion in 1991. Its products can be found and heard in over thirty million American homes. Long-established toy companies are in a battle to recapture market share from this offshore video-game producer.

The impact of a product such as the Nintendo Entertainment System is not limited to the video-game category. Shock waves are felt throughout all product categories because consumers spend tightly budgeted dollars on toys and games. For example, the child who acquires a $50 Nintendo game cartridge will not be permitted to spend another $50 on items such as a remote-control car or any combination of other products. Sales of major boys' toys have been significantly eroded by the Nintendo craze.

Inventors who are not originating Nintendo games must produce concepts that can compete head-to-head for their dollars. Market share is controlled and expanded one way and one way only—through the introduction of fresh, exciting, imaginative product. So the pros with something special have an edge. There's always room for a super item, especially when the manufacturers want to make leadership moves.

"It takes a special talent to survive in an industry like this that's ever-changing, faddish, transitory, sometimes whimsical, sometimes volatile," says George R. Ditomassi, president of Milton Bradley, the world's largest game company and a division of Hasbro.

Jeffrey Breslow has seen many crazes dominate toy purchases in his twenty-plus years in the business. He comments,

"Nintendo has a life cycle to it. Obviously, Nintendo hurts the overall toy business, but things come and things go. There's always next year and new product."

"I would be frightened to death if I was put into a room and told, 'Look, here's some capital, be a toy inventor.' It's a terribly tough thing," says Bill Dohrmann, senior vice president for marketing and sales at Tiger Games. "You can make a lot of money. You can get very rich in this business. But it's like going to Hollywood, working in the car wash and hoping you're going to be the next Tom Cruise. Inventors own a decaying asset. A product goes in and two years later, if they sit still and go to sleep, it's gone. Unless you build up a list of perennials, which is very hard to do, by the way, you gotta push the rock up the mountain every year," concludes Dohrmann, a twenty-year industry veteran.

"There are fewer companies for independents to present products to with all the mergers and bankruptcies," says Lowell T. Wilson, vice president for product development at The Ohio Art Company. "Also, many companies today are so large that they are not interested in one- or two-million-dollar products anymore, but need items that will generate $10 million and up. For such companies to make a commitment and develop an advertising program around a product, it must be a very special product that is capable of performing in such an arena." He suggests that they are few and far between.

"The guys that are doing best are really clever guys who are calling on new technologies . . . nuances in the psychology in our lifestyles. The guy that just brings the product in that is a wrinkle off something that was done five years ago isn't going to make it," he concludes.

"It's a crapshoot," Pong inventor Nolan Bushnell tells a reporter from "The McNeil/Lehrer Report." The man who is credited with putting games on video monitor says, "The toy business is very, very difficult to predict. . . . You have to make your commitment far in advance."

"Some years it's a great living, some years it's a good living, some years it's a horror," admits independent pro Neal Kublan, head of The Knack Group. Ben Kinberg, creator of Glo-Doodler (Colorforms), feels that the independent development business is "fraught with monstrous hazards and bottomless chasms."

Hank Atkins, creator of the 1981 game Razzle (Parker Brothers), says, "For the average game inventor, the odds of making it financially are next to impossible." Ron Milner, inventor of A. G. Bear (Axlon), agrees with the tough odds in the business: "To make it as an independent inventor, you have to have uncommitted time and money you don't mind throwing away. You have to do some of it just for the fun of it, realizing the chances of selling a toy are one in a million."

But It Can Happen

On the other hand, independents experience what few outside the artistic community do, and that is freedom—personal freedom and, if they get lucky, financial freedom. Freedom provides not safety so much as opportunities, the most satisfying of which is the opportunity to use their talents. While their careers are fraught with turns, precipices, and pitfalls, they can also make a fortune if the right products are a hit.

"My goal was to make $50,000 a year and stay home with my kids; anything after that is gravy," Kathy Rondeau, inventor of such games as Girl Talk (Western Publishing) and Encore! (Parker Brothers), told reporter Charles Osgood in an interview for "48 Hours." "How's it going?" he asked. "Lots of gravy," she responded.

In that same CBS program, filmed at the eighty-sixth annual American International Toy Fair, doll inventor Hank Garfinkel was asked by Osgood how much he stood to make if his electronic Suzie Scribble, a doll that holds a pen and scribbles, became a success. "The potential on this is many millions of dollars," he replied, saying he had no apologies for his lack of modesty.

Toy & Hobby World magazine reported that the inventors of Teddy Ruxpin, the animatronic teddy bear with a tape recorder in its belly, earned more than $21 million in royalties between 1986 and 1989.

When asked if he had earned a million dollars in the toy business, inventor Eddy Goldfarb once told *Parade* magazine, "Actually, it's closer to several million."

"Toy inventing has given us a nice lifestyle," says Arthur Albert, who together with his wife, Judy, designed the first Cabbage Patch Kids dolls for Coleco. "We have a studio attached to the house. We live on three and a half acres in the country overlooking the water. We travel. We have financial independence."

"We are in a business where you could wake up with a dream and that dream can become a reality. There are enough stories in our industry where you know you can become a multimillionaire in literally one year," says Howard Wexler.

Robert Angel, a Seattle waiter, did it with Pictionary, after he licensed it to The Games Gang. Pictionary has sold approximately fourteen million sets worldwide since 1986, spawning its own industry: Pictionary Junior; Pictionary Junior Play It with Clay; Bible Pictionary; Hip-Pocket Pictionary; Travel Pictionary; numerous foreign editions; and a syndicated TV show. It has also earned classic status, which means fresh income to its inventor and perhaps even his grandchildren's grandchildren.

Cleveland, Georgia, artist Xavier Roberts did it with his megahit, Cabbage Patch Kids. The homely, latex-faced, sixteen-inch dolls brought in more than $1.5 billion (sales of $540 million in 1984 and $600 million in 1985) and have become an entire industry for their inventor, with all the different dolls, their accessories, and licensed products that carry CPK images. Cabbage Patch Kids has since been acquired by Hasbro.

A group of young Canadians created Trivial Pursuit, and, at a reported astronomical royalty of 15.7 percent (industry average is 5 percent), each coinventor made a personal fortune. In its first year, Selchow & Righter, the game's original U.S. manufacturer, sold twenty-two million sets at retail prices ranging as high as $40. To date, Trivial Pursuit has sold more than sixty million games worldwide, and the story of its origin was immortalized in the Canadian Broadcasting Corporation's made-for-television movie *Breaking All the Rules*. Trivial Pursuit has since been acquired by Parker Brothers.

Dr. Erno Rubik, a creative Hungarian engineer and mathematician, saw his Rubik's Cube go atomic. The deceptively innocent-looking two-and-a-quarter-inch puzzle, with more than forty-three quintillion possible combinations but only one true solution, became such a craze that it made the inventor a household name and one of his country's wealthiest individuals. The Cube, during a three-year run, generated sales of an estimated 100 million authorized copies, plus fifty million knockoffs and at least ten million books explaining how to solve it.

Tonka's adoptable Pound Puppies made their designer, Mike Bowling, a factory worker at the Ford Motor Company near Cincinnati for seventeen years, a multimillionaire. What began as a Christmas present to his wife has sold more than fifty million units in fifty countries since he signed on with Tonka in 1984.

In 1983, Teenage Mutant Ninja Turtles were born in the fertile imaginations of two struggling Northampton, Massachusetts, cartoonists, Peter Laird and Kevin Eastman. The now celebrated, so-called Heroes on a Halfshell lived in obscurity for five years on the pages of cult comic books until a savvy marketer by the name of Mark Freedman recognized their potential and led the Turtles from the sewers of New York City to stardom.

Teenage Mutant Ninja Turtles' 1990 earnings were approximately $400 million. In 1991, the Teenage Mutant Ninja Turtles' creators will reportedly earn for themselves $30 million from their hot property.

Says Larry Jones, president of Cal R&D, who lists among his creations Microvision (Milton Bradley) and Star Rider (Playskool), "The toy business has more turnover than any business. But I think it probably still is and always will be one of the best opportunities for entrepreneurs."

The Butcher, the Baker, the Candlestick Maker

Such an unconventional profession as that of toy inventor requires faith and belief in oneself. Like their ideas, these men and women are naturals, people whose entry into the fluid and egalitarian business of toy and game development just happened, at the appropriate time, through a variety of circumstances rarely planned but that seem somewhat destined when looked at in retrospect.

Charlie Girsch came to the toy industry with what he calls "stellar qualifications that the business was clamoring for at the time: a master's degree in theology, a strong minor in philosophy, and just short of credits for a second minor in Gregorian chant." Team Windsor became Girsch Design Associates when his wife, Maria, a former nun, joined the effort. Together they have created a wonderful array of product such as Funwich Factory (Playskool), Wrist Racers (originally by Knickerbocker and reintroduced by The Ertl Company in 1990 using the Batman license), People Magazine Game (Parker Brothers), and Fun House Game (Pressman), while raising a family of six children.

Ed Holahan was invited by Charlie Girsch to join his product development company back in 1972. "He thought I had good hands and a sense of humor," Ed recalls. "It seemed to make sense for a person trained in writing, photography, and film." Since then, Ed has been responsible for a string of hit games, including Trap Door (Milton Bradley) and Dino Bones (Warren), as well as assorted Parker Brothers Nerf items.

Judy Blau wrote and illustrated the children's book *The Bagel Baker of Mulliner Lane* for McGraw-Hill in 1976. As a result of the publicity and licensing of the characters from the book into children's apparel and home furnishings, a toy manufacturer called her to ask whether she would consider designing toy concepts. "I gave it a try and sold my first plush concepts," explains the president of J. Hope Designs, Ltd. "I then discovered that two talented electronic toy inventors lived in my neighborhood [Greg Hyman and Larry Greenberg], and we got together. With their help and encouragement and introductions, I found myself working both independently and with other inventors," adds the inventor of Sweetie Pops (Playskool) and the holder of ten patents, twenty trademarks, and 110 copyrights.

Elliot A. Rudell—president of Rudell Design, a prolific innovator, and holder of some thirty patents—lays claim to many hit toys and games, including Wethead (Mattel), Weebles (Playskool), and the Mickey and Minnie Sidewalk Bikes and Trikes (Roadmaster). He says he got into the inventing business through the most basic of drives: "I needed to eat."

A Pratt Institute industrial design graduate, Rudell studied under General Motors, New York State Regents, and Pratt scholarships and then landed a job with Mattel (first part time, then full time), on the East Coast. After a five-year stint there and in the company's Hawthorne, California, offices, he went solo, as a consultant/freelance designer then as an inventor.

"I took my father's phonograph apart and made a baseball game in which the players ran bases on the turntable," says Julie Cooper, a forty-three-year veteran of the toy industry, holder of thirty-two patents, and a partner in the development firm of Cooper & Kunkel. The former senior vice president for product development and marketing at Ideal, he adds, "I loved toys and games as a child far beyond what I today consider normal."

After World War II, the company for which he was working fell on hard times, having lost its defense contracts. "I invented a game using surplus military parts called Home Stretch. The company made and sold the game, which put them back in business." And this put Cooper in business as well. In 1949 he sold his first item to Milton Bradley, a detective game called Intrigue.

"The first toy I sold was myself to Marvin Glass in 1967," jokes Jeffrey Breslow. "I had to convince him that I could design and invent games. That was the hardest job, getting through the door at Marvin Glass & Associates." Marvin Glass is a legend in the toy business, the man responsible for a seemingly endless string of hit toys and games, among them Mr. Machine, Mouse Trap, Kissy Doll, Electronic Simon, Hands Down, Masterpiece, Rock'em Sock'em Robots, Operation, and Lite Brite.

Breslow knew he wanted to do toy development as a career after graduating with a degree in industrial design from the University of Illinois. But he worked first for two years designing medical equipment and a mobile field hospital for Vietnam while designing toys in his off-hours. Then, when he had enough "off-hour inventions" to show the then-undisputed king of toy development, he sought the interview. Jeffrey was at Marvin Glass & Associates for twenty-two years, ultimately becoming a senior partner.

"I started in the toy business coming out of school as a designer with Child Guidance before moving on to Knickerbocker Toys," says Mike Satten. "I was in the middle of the best job I ever had when Knickerbocker was sold to Hasbro and suddenly I found myself unemployed." He landed at Determined Productions, a San Francisco manufacturer of plush and gift items. The company's president, Connie Boucher, permitted him to do his own products as long as they were noncompetitive with her company.

"It's the miracle toy," says Paul L. Brown, referring to WIZ•Z•ZER, his stringless gyroscopic top that since its introduction by Mattel in 1970 has sold more than twenty million units. "Its success has surpassed my wildest expectations, but the greatest reward has been watching kids enjoy the magic." From a broken home, sixth in a family of nine, Brown grew up in the Clark County Children's Home in Springfield, Ohio, where he began building model airplanes and crystal radio sets in an attic space above his living quarters. He dropped out of school after the eleventh grade to join the Civilian Conservation Corps (CCC) and completed his high-school education by correspondence. Later, lacking the funds to fulfill his dreams of becoming a mechanical engineer, he took technical courses at numerous trade schools. It was while he was employed by the U.S. Army's Corps of Engineers, at age thirty-seven, that he created, with simple hand tools, the model for what would become WIZ•Z•ZER.

In 1957, ten-year-old Greg Hyman issued a hand-printed flier to the third and fourth graders at his New Rochelle, New York, elementary school. It read, in part, "Learn to invent, learn all about electricity [and] how electric motors work. . . . There are lessons every Monday, Wednesday, and Friday. Make your own shop. That's what I did. . . . Three lessons FREE! Yours truly, Greg the Inventor."

Now president of Greg Hyman Associates, he no longer teaches inventing to kids; instead, he invents toys and games for them. Greg was an electronics engineer doing readouts, lockouts, buzzers, and bells for Ron Greenberg Productions in New York City, a production company that specialized in TV game shows. One day he backed into the game industry in partnership with Greenberg's brother, Larry (aka "The Colonel"). A special sound-effects device he had designed for a pilot show became, through a series of serendipitous events, a toy called Major Morgan (Playskool). Hyman/Greenberg also hit with Alphie and Alphie II (Playskool), a child's first electronic learning toy.

Professional toy and game developers genuinely appear to love what they do for a living, and too few people can say that. Sid Sackson, America's undisputed "game guru" and inventor of Can't Stop (Parker Brothers), tells aspiring inventors, "Love it very, very much, or forget it!"

"We are searching for a little magic, a touch of abracadabra, something that will stop executives in their tracks like a red light stops traffic," says Sheryl Levy, creator of Adver-*teasing* (Cadaco). "And I love every minute of it."

"I looked at many industries," says Andrew Bergman, the brains behind the PXL2000 Camcorder (Fisher-Price), "but was attracted to the toy business after seeing men in suits pulling ducks down a hallway." Bergman, a former employee of Buckminster Fuller, enjoys making a worthwhile contribution to children's playtime.

A Force of One or More

Professional toy and game inventors understand that ingenuity is just a first step, not an end in itself. Inventors need help. It often takes teamwork to create a concept that is salable to a manufacturer. Few inventors work alone. Garry Donner, inventor of Uno Dice (International Games), says, "You can no longer work alone. You need to be an expert in too many areas.''

It is not unusual for the more prolific developers to find themselves working simultaneously on projects that require expertise in areas ranging from gearing, hydraulics, levers, and electricity to plastics, fabrics, refractors, and microelectronics. It is also common to see the highly technical developer join forces with a sculptor, an illustrator, or a gaming theorist. A marketer who smells an opportunity may seek a developer (and associates) to make a concept come alive. In the toy and game inventing business, it is a daily survival skill to know how, to know who: ''Whatever it takes'' is the rule.

''I think there is a wonderful brotherhood between inventors, and I am talking about successful people, because they realize how difficult this business is. . . . I wish very well for any of my fellow inventors,'' says Howard Wexler.

''I think it is very hard to invent successfully in a vacuum,'' notes Greg Hyman. He believes that even when you can build a model to describe a great concept, you still need input from other sources because it is hard to be objective about your own creation. This airing of the concept, he explains, may take the form of a partnership with another professional developer.

A lack of experience in one area, however, should never be a reason for an idea to go undeveloped. The pros will merge talents at the drop of a marble, the tick of a timer, or the roll of a die. They understand the big picture. They know that there is always a need for good product, and a hit generates enough reward for everyone. This is why a single product often has several parents; it is truly the creation of multiple talents. The objective is to get points on the product scoreboard. Touchdowns are desired, but field goals are equally valuable. A shared spotlight is better than no spotlight. For example, the headline inventors of such recent hits as Pictionary, Scruples, Cabbage Patch Kids, Win, Lose or Draw, Girl Talk, Rubik's Cube, and Pound Puppies share or have shared portions of their lucrative royalties with others—without whose assistance, either financially or creatively, their items might never have come to market.

The Anonymous Elves

Professional toy and game inventors can walk up and down the aisles of a toy store and tell you who invented what, as if the products were books with authors' names emblazoned across their covers. Mike Satten's Army Gear (Galoob) is merchandised near Marty Abrams's Power Glove (Mattel). Jim McMurtry's Oreo Cookie Factory Game (Cadaco) is down the shelf from Gordon Barlow's Gnip Gnop (Tiger Games) and Fred Kroll's Hungry Hungry Hippos (Milton Bradley). Reuben Klamer's roller skates (Fisher-Price) are a few giant steps from the Alberts' Dress 'n Dazzle (Tonka). On the wall, Pat MacCarthy's Ribbon Yo-Yo (Imperial) hangs to the right of some blister cards offering Jim Becker's Sliders (Milton Bradley) and just under Jim Routzong's Spit Balls (LJN).

Of all creative endeavors, perhaps the one least recognized for individual achievement is toy invention. This is an odd phenomenon, because toys and games touch us all from our earliest days and make as great an impression as other forms of popular entertainment. From a commercial standpoint, some toys and games earn more money than best-selling books, records, or films. A few toy developers collect royalties that put them in the same league as rock stars, athletes, movie idols, and TV celebrities.

Books are bought for their authors, not publishing houses; records for recording artists, not labels; and feature films for actors, not production companies. Though there are no popularly known "stars" billed on toys and games, there is a known group of professional inventors on whom manufacturers rely for the blockbusters of the toy shelves.

And So, Who Can I Turn To?

In surveying the industry for this book, we have found that
executives at the highest levels know the value of outside professional developers, and that, *ipso facto*, the most successful
manufacturers license the greatest number of concepts from
this valued resource. When looking for significant sales dollars
from new products each year, corporate officers go looking for
the latest ideas from the pros.

"Toyland would be a much duller place without the independent inventor," says Standard & Poor's toy-industry analyst Paul Valentine. "When you go down the list and look at
the megahits that have emerged in the past ten years, lines that
have done more than $50 million each, they are primarily com-
ing from the independent inventor, with the exception of licensed properties."

Hits such as Cabbage Patch Kids, Pound Puppies, Teddy
Ruxpin, Trivial Pursuit, Glo Friends, Pictionary, Monopoly,
Etch-A-Sketch, Mr. Potato Head, Stompers, Puffalumps, and
Nerf are just a few from a list of thousands of items created by
outside developers. It is the colossal sweep of the independents'
genius, the web of interlinking ideas that they spin, and their
varied artistic gifts that weave a plexus of unsurpassed product
and business opportunities for manufacturers who buy their
concepts.

In an industry that says product is king, independent inventors are about as close to the throne as anyone. Executives
are unanimous in their praise for and appreciation of the independent developer. Mike Meyers, senior vice president of
R&D at Milton Bradley, when asked where his company would
be today without the input of the independent inventing community, answers, "Well, first of all you begin by rattling off a
bunch of products that are our classics, that have sustained this
company. Candy Land. The Game of Life. Chutes and Ladders. Operation. Bed Bugs. Mouse Trap. Twister. Electronic

Battleship. Stratego. Simon. What do you have left? When you take a look at a list like that, that's very impressive. It's the backbone of the company. These items all came from the outside.''

George R. Ditomassi, president of Milton Bradley, maintains that the independent is absolutely essential. He says that in any particular year, more than half of the new line could be made up of outside submissions. ''They give us a fresh view from the outside looking in. . . . We need independents,'' he adds.

Tony Miller, senior vice president of R&D at Tonka, finds that most toy companies focus on what they do best, which can only lead to a limited number of conclusions. The outside inventor, he says, is coming from beyond internal management and marketing parameters, which leads to ideas that would be totally unpredictable. ''The main value of the outside inventor to the company is to produce the wild card,'' Miller notes.

Miller explains that Tonka, a maker of steel trucks, would never of its own volition have decided to make a line of stuffed dogs. But Mike Bowling, the man who brought stuffed dogs to Tonka, put something on the table that looked like a solid business opportunity for the company. Low investment. Fresh idea. A track record in some foreign markets. ''In its best year, our Pound Puppies did $140 million, which was more than all the company's other business combined,'' Miller notes.

William F. Dohrmann, senior vice president for marketing and sales at Tiger Games, recalls the time in 1969 when he was Parker Brothers' director of marketing and product development and a couple of men from Minneapolis walked through his door with what he describes as ''a sort of beer-drinking game where you put a little net up in your living room and bounced around a ball cut from foam.''

At the time, he wondered why anyone would bring a novelty ball to Parker Brothers, a manufacturer of board games. ''We must have been way down the line, because as the in-

ventor of Milton Bradley's hit game Twister, Reynolds Guyer
had access to every company," he figured. Upon seeing the
foam ball, Dohrmann recalls saying to himself, "My God,
that's it, the world's first indoor ball. I even wrote that line
down and it wound up on the first package of what would
become Nerf." According to Dohrmann, Nerf has been a $25
to $30-million-a-year category for Parker since the item's in-
troduction in 1970.

"Without independent inventors, the business would be
colorless and predictable," says Phil Orbanes, a senior vice
president for R&D at Parker Brothers, a company working
very aggressively these days with some 125 idea sources in the
United States.

Howard Bollinger, senior vice president of advanced concepts at Kenner, maintains that independents are important
because they "bring a keen awareness of how to put things
together in such a way that it gives kids goose bumps. . . .
They mix current awareness with a lot of traditional things,
stir the pot, and visualize what will happen. They can always
feel the magic. They've never had the kid programmed out of
them."

Corporate executives know that there is no limit to the distance that the minds of professional independent inventors can
stretch, nor a boundary to their efforts, discoveries, or successes. Just when it might seem impossible to top the current
crop of magical playthings, a new cycle for the coming year
brings inventors through the door with even more innovative
product. These inventors are vital to companies in an industry
that, like large businesses everywhere, requires its employees
to do something as a form of thinking more than allowing time
for thinking as a form of doing.

The independent inventors, on the other hand, see it as
their birthright to be different, usually alone against a whole
cry of voices. They tinker with the abstract, impose design

upon experience. The best and brightest have a multivalued orientation; a fresh, schooled, and inquiring eye; and a sophisticated innocence that permits them simultaneously to have one foot in childhood and one foot in the corporate world. Toy executives value the imprints of those feet on their annual product plans.

Toy manufacturers benefit by getting independent toy and game inventors to provide what amounts to speculative external research and development. The inventing community, on a continuing basis, shows an endless array of innovative product concepts, unencumbered by corporate dogma. Further, the passion that independent professionals bring with their submissions often becomes a catalyst to stimulate internal corporate creativity. At the same time, the outside developers obtain what every artist seeks, an audience for their work and a rich patron who can afford to buy and *commercialize* it to the artist's advantage.

"The quality of product ideas submitted to Fisher-Price by the design community has been excellent and has encouraged us to put even greater emphasis on externally developed concepts in all of our product groups," says Charles S. Riter, vice president for R&D at the world's leading manufacturer of preschool toys. "New product ideas are very important to Fisher-Price, and having the ability to select concepts from either our talented internal staff of designers and engineers or from the top creative efforts of outside inventors has provided us with short-term success as well as building a line of classic performers that make the retailer and the consumer happy."

Josh Denham, president and CEO of Worlds of Wonder, maintains that the independent is essential. "I don't think any really earthshaking, innovative product can survive at the larger companies because of the committee approach they take in reviewing product. Things get squashed in the early stages." Denham, the former president of Mattel Electronics, adds that many corporate marketing people tend to look at the wake instead of the bow of the ship, while independent inventors look to the future.

"The most valuable thing I possess is my list of inventors," says Bill Dohrmann of Tiger Games. Peter Pook of Fisher-Price agrees with him: "It's [a Rolodex with developers' names and addresses] the only thing sitting here on top of my desk."

Saul Jodel, executive vice president of marketing and R&D at Lewis Galoob Toys, could not be more resolute when he says to the interviewer, "I'm the person who's going to tell you this the strongest. . . . I depend on the independent inventor as the most important thing I have. That is my single most important resource."

Jodel's associate, Gary J. Niles, senior vice president at Lewis Galoob, adds that "without independent toy inventors, the industry would be 25 to 30 percent less in gross volume." Extrapolating Niles's estimate from 1989 retail sales suggests that $3.5 to $4 billion of retail sales come from the ideas generated by independent inventors.

The Pro Advantage

"They [professional independent inventors] give us the food upon which this business feeds," says Andy Gatto, president of Matchbox Toys (USA) Ltd., a company best known for die-cast vehicles. "We are very, very dependent upon ideas and we like to have as many minds and fresh approaches come to us with concepts as possible."

"You naturally want to do as much development inside as possible when you have an R&D staff," says David R. Berko, vice president for marketing at Buddy L, a manufacturer of steel trucks for more than seventy-five years. But he feels that the outside people serve industry well because they're generally off in their own corner of the world thinking differently from the rest of the business in the mainstream. Adds Berko, "The home runs in this business have been things that weren't done yesterday—like ugly dolls."

George B. Volanakis, president and CEO of The Ertl Company, says the independents are important because they are not restricted to the projects they believe their bosses will be receptive to, current company product direction, line extensions, and so forth. "They do not suffer from inbreeding," he exclaims.

Neil Friedman, senior vice president for marketing at Hasbro, notes that more than 50 percent of his company's line comes from outside sources. "The professional independent inventor is the lifeblood of our business," he says. Agreeing very closely with Friedman is Waymon Wittman, president of Cadaco Games, who states, "Independent inventors are the plasma supply line to our industry."

Michael Cook, vice president of new product development at TSR, the manufacturer of Dungeons & Dragons, says that the independent inventors provide 50 to 70 percent of his product. With TSR's Lake Geneva, Wisconsin, location outside major consumer centers, inventors are also important as the company's eyes and ears to the industry. "We wouldn't be in business without them," he adds.

For years there has been running debate at the corporate level as to how much pure R&D a company can afford to fund. While a few of the larger companies operate advanced planning groups—i.e., designers and engineers charged with consulting crystal balls and dreaming up way-out concepts for two to five years into the future—most find it more profitable to depend upon the pros for left-field concepts. Creative staffs within R&D departments are assigned instead to engineer and design outside products as well as to extend existing product lines or licensed character merchandise.

Mike Meyers of Milton Bradley says, "Using internal staff

or external sources is a numbers game. I have X amount of staff time to develop thirty or more internally generated products a year as well as redevelop other ideas from outside sources. I see from the outside in excess of two thousand opportunities. The talents of my staff are brought into hundreds of those ideas. They are left with little time for pure invention. To invent you need time to fail. We really don't have the luxury to fail very often."

Meyers also notes: "The outside concept really has the advantage because with the inside one, you have the option of waiting. The outside product is looked at with much more intensity. There's always that paranoia that you'll make a mistake and turn down something great. With the inside product, if you don't do it, you can't make a mistake. It might have been great, but who knows?"

Doing It the Company Way

Independent inventors have choices, whereas corporate employees, no matter how creative, do not. No one dictates how the independents should look at something, or when and if they should work on something. They are not burdened by corporate standard operating procedures.

George B. Volanakis of The Ertl Company says that because of the "day-to-day drudgery of in-house development and company bureaucracy," the outside inventor has become an important element to a company's product development process.

"Without them [independent inventors], we would not be nearly as successful at satisfying the demands of our young consumers," states William C. Killgallon, president of The Ohio Art Company.

Loren T. Taylor, senior vice president for marketing at Nasta International, feels that independent inventors are incredibly important. "Without independent inventors you are not going to get a lot of fresh ideas, and let's face it, without strong new products we're nothing. It has really been the influx of fresh new inventor products that has helped us grow very quickly."

Our survey of key R&D executives, normally the people in closest liaison with external product sources, shows just how strongly the toy and game makers rely on a core group of professional inventors.

Michael Lyden, vice president for business development at Tyco Toys, says, "There are probably fifty people that we know enough that every time they call I'll pick up the phone, if I can, and speak with them." He hastens to add that there are another thirty toy developers who are persona non grata.

Jack Daniels, senior vice president of R&D at Matchbox Toys (USA), prefers to deal with a few prominent pros. He estimates that he has ongoing relationships with some seventy-five inventors in the United States and another fifty overseas.

"I personally have a closed list," says Saul Jodel of Galoob, "but the overall Galoob list is longer than mine." His personal list, pros he will see routinely about once a month or chat with on the phone once a week, is in the neighborhood of ten to twelve people.

Jeff Conrad, vice president of research and development at International Games, personally deals with only twenty developers, half of them constantly. Steve D'Aguanno, senior vice president for product development at the Hasbro toy division, figures he deals with approximately 100 inventors.

The Amateur Disadvantage

Outside inventors are divided into two categories—the professionals (the known quantity) and the amateurs (the unknown quantity). When toy executives talk about the value of the independent inventing community, they refer to the full-time professionals whom they can rely upon and work with, day in and day out, to create innovative product. On the other hand, manufacturers receive thousands and thousands of unsolicited ideas every year from amateur inventors. Most companies, especially the larger ones, return packages unopened if the sending party is not on a list of known inventors.

"The main single problem I have with amateur submissions is that they're rarely fresh. They are usually the reinvention of some wheel that has been seen ten times in the history of the industry, or not sufficiently novel to warrant a big company making a serious investment in it," explains Tony Miller of Tonka. "I have actually been shown a stick and hoop by two so-called inventors . . . who thought that the world was waiting for another stick and hoop.

"The time that it takes to say to them, gently, 'This really isn't a new idea,' or 'It really isn't an important idea,' or 'It really is a terrible idea,' and then to soothe their bruised egos and to assure them that we're not going to rip them off and all that kind of stuff, the conversation inevitably takes an hour or so. Spending an average of one hour on one thousand poorly executed unsolicited ideas can easily consume a third to half the time of an R&D manager—time that leads to no new product.

"The best guys don't leave anything to chance. Their ideas are executed in a 'looks-like, works-like' sample that is so professional that it will survive not only the first screening by the R&D guy who can see past the quality of the sample, but in each of the successive presentations. These are the meetings that have to happen with the marketing staff, the sales organization, the chief executive, or whoever else is involved at a large company in endorsing a product before a contract is actually written. The guys who are at the top of the stack usually execute those samples so that they look great and knock everybody out."

Anne Pitrone, View-Master/Ideal's director of product development, says that amateurs don't understand how things are marketed. "What holds them back," she observes, "is that they have no concept of issues such as manufacturing processes, prototyping, and costing."

Woody Browne, vice president for marketing at Tyco Toys, echoes this sentiment, saying that even when amateurs have a great idea, they never think about the business side, such as how to market the product or what it's going to cost to produce. His Tyco Toys colleague Michael Lyden adds that some people come in, put a product on the desk, and wait for a reaction. He says it's almost like a con game; they want the company to get so excited that it will do the market research, costing, and other exercises that the inventor should have done. "Or they'll bring you something and you'll say, 'Can we contract with you to develop this?' and they say, 'Well, no, I don't know how to do it.' "

Dwain Dial, director of product development for Monogram/Kidstar, says that nonprofessionals tend to develop product in a shotgun approach and don't really know what industry, let alone what company, they're targeting.

Darwin P. Bromley, president of Mayfair Games, says that 99 percent of the items he sees are "somebody's notion of a variant on a game that they enjoyed last night. Or the game they always wanted to design because they've played ten games and they think they have something great." He adds that the pros who do the good games are thoughtful creators and know and can execute what will be truly different.

Barrie Simpson, senior director of creative development at Western Publishing, a company that sees about a thousand products a year and ultimately produces six, states, "Everybody thinks that their idea is the next best thing to sliced bread, and in many instances we have already seen thirty things exactly like it." She says that the amateur's ego is also a problem, "because they are not very humble." She adds, "Amateurs do not deal with rejection as a piece of reality. They are too intent on chasing the dream of big royalties."

It seems that the more successful a company becomes, the harder it is for amateurs to get through the door. A few years ago, one of the most approachable game companies was Western Publishing. But since the huge success of Pictionary (in association with The Games Gang), Girl Talk, and Outburst, the atmosphere has changed dramatically. "It has been as if an atom bomb went off" is how George Propsom, Western Publishing's manager of product development (games and puzzles), describes the influx of new products. Barrie Simpson says, "We're going to have a closed list. It takes too much time and the legal issues are immense . . . to deal with the total universe of inventors or would-be inventors."

"It is very time-consuming to work with an amateur who really doesn't know how to work efficiently with a major company. And very often the ideas of an amateur are redundant; they've been done ten times before," says Phil Orbanes, senior vice president for R&D at Parker Brothers.

Mixed Attitudes

While almost every promotional toy company works with the professional inventing community, the remaining manufacturers vary in their use of the pros. Manufacturers of nonpromoted products such as plastic beach pails and what the industry calls "plastic-by-the-pound" usually do not buy designs from independents. Their lines are so basic and profit margins so thin that products will not support a royalty load. Staff engineers and designers or offshore sources create their lines on a nonroyalty basis.

An exception is Lego Systems, a promotional company that does not presently deal with outside developers. "Early on they came and knocked on our doors, but we turned them away," explains Dick Garvey, vice president of marketing. If the company were to solicit ideas, he feels 90 percent would already have been thought of and "the other 10 percent is probably something we already have on the drawing boards in one way or another." However, he admits, "It's controversial. We've thought maybe we should open the door."

For decades Mattel had a reputation for not making outside developers feel welcome. Even among the best and most successful pros, it was known as a difficult penetration. According to several former Mattel executives, much of this attitude came from in-house design managers who felt their people could do anything better than the inventing community could deliver. It isn't hard to see where the company got its confidence. With such lines as Barbie, Hot Wheels, and assorted other powerful brands, the company expanded its own design staff rather than rely on inventors to place it in a leadership position.

But alas, the mighty Mattel, which lost its number-one standing to an aggressive and acquisitions-oriented Hasbro several years ago, is now trying to foster significant work with independents. Mattel's current leadership realizes that one of the company's problems has been not having enough give-and-take with the professional inventing community. "We need to nurture and revitalize a spirit of creativity and openness to ideas," Robert Sansone, president of Mattel and a former General Foods executive, told a group of inventors being courted by the company at a Toy Fair reception. Sansone, sold on the contribution that independents can make, is out to alter his company's past image: "We clearly understand that we have no monopoly on creativity. We have no monopoly on wonderful ideas. What we need to be is open and smart enough to accept your wonderful ideas."

Perhaps a manufacturer can survive without the contribution made by inventors, but there will be no growth, and growth is evidence of life. Manufacturers tend to get stuck on plateaus, and only explosive products can move them to a higher level. Sales records indisputably support that much of such product emanates from the creatives in the independent inventing community.

The demand for toys begins within the first weeks of life. Parents look to "first playthings" to give babies amusement, pleasure, and discovery. Clutch balls. Mobiles. Rattles. Busy boxes. This demand for unique and different playthings only increases as the child grows. Tricycles. Dolls. Die-cast vehicles. Board games. Electronic musical instruments. Even teens and adults enjoy sophisticated playthings. Adult social interaction games. Seasonal outdoor games. Novelty puzzles. Video games. To satisfy the marketplace demand for new toys, manufacturers respond with calls to the pros for more and more new ideas.

COOPER, FUHRER, GIRSCH, KLAMER, LAPIDUS,
MILLER, PHILLIPS, RUDELL, AND, O.K., WOLF

Without Santa Claus, Christmas would be just another holiday. Without the professional independent toy and game inventor, a toy and game manufacturer would be just another injection molder or marketer. It is indeed the creative input from the inventing community that breathes life into both the Yule season and the manufacturers. Few people exhibit a greater diversity of skills or touch more lives with their work than the inventors who fuel the industry workshops with the toys we adults know don't come from Santa.

2 Maple Seeds to Microchips

A HISTORY OF TOY INVENTION

On the Eighth Day, He created the toy inventor. . . . Even though we may not be able to trace this egalitarian profession to such a divine origin, we do find the imprint of playthings all the way from antiquity. Since historical evidence records the existence of toys, we can only surmise that some individuals toiled, if not for royalties, then to exercise their imaginative gifts and varied talents to create things for amusement and for play.

It is a fact that toy inventors have played an important role in children's lives since the dawn of mankind. Through toys, children learn about themselves and the world around them. Toys are the tools of play, instruments that prompt the earliest curiosity, exercise physical skills, and open what Lewis Carroll has called "eyes of wonder." They make up a miniature world that never quite relinquishes its hold on the imagination.

It has been speculated that, in addition to the stick and the stone, one of the very first toys may have been a playful invention of Mother Nature, the maple seed. First *Homo sapiens* was no doubt amused, if not perplexed, by the winged fruits, which spin like helicopter blades as they fall from trees—when playfully tossed into the air. The rotary motion of the seed's descent, virtually unique in the plant kingdom, has been captured in a multitude of flying toys.

The More Things Change, the More They Stay the Same

Although only a few examples of prehistoric toys or games have been found it's a pretty good bet that some inventive Stone Ager drew pots, rings, and gullies in the dirt with his heels, pressed his knuckles to the ground, took aim with his favorite "game stone," and challenged his friends to the first known contest of Ringer. Marbles now are enjoying the resurgence of popularity as playthings and, for some of the more uniquely colored agates, as collectibles. Ray Frigard felt he was improving on the ageless classic when he conceived Squarbles, the square marbles introduced in 1988 by Hasbro. Unlike its predecessor, however, cubes did not roll very far with consumers and the item faded from retail shelves.

Another age-old toy can be traced back to primitive man's quest for food. The yo-yo originated when hunters would sit in trees and throw small rocks at animals below. With a vine wrapped around it, the stone could be retrieved instantly for another try. *Fact:* There are thirty-four manufacturers of yo-yos listed in the 1991–92 *Playthings Directory.*

In the third millennium B.C., archaeologists tell us, young boys played army with terra-cotta toy soldiers and girls cradled wooden dolls. Egyptian graves have yielded balls; crude pull toys; hollow whistles crafted from baked clay; rattles in the shapes of birds, fish, and animals; jointed puppets; whip tops; and dolls handpainted in vibrant hues. *Fact:* There are sixty-seven manufacturers of balls; forty-six of pull toys; thirty-one of whistles; thirty-four of rattles, seventy-one of puppets; fifty of tops; and several pages of doll makers listed in the 1991–92 *Playthings Directory*.

In the glitzy Caesar's Palaces of Las Vegas and Atlantic City, one instrument of gaming madness is a set of two small cubes called dice. At the original Caesar's palace, Romans tossed knucklebones (the ankle bones of sheep), thought to be the first dice. Today dice are a requisite part of many games of chance, be it Yahtzee or a path game where the dice determine how far you move your game piece. *Fact:* There are twenty-six manufacturers of dice listed in the 1991–92 *Playthings Directory*.

Greek pottery has lively examples of children playing with hoops, hobbyhorses, balls, and ceramic tops. One vase depicts a boy playing with a yo-yo, a toy that disappeared completely in Europe until it was reimported from the Far East in the late eighteenth century. The basic idea of today's classic flying toy, the Frisbee, can be traced back to Greece. *Fact:* There are nine manufacturers of hoops; twenty of hobbyhorses; and twenty-one of flying saucers listed in the 1991–1992 *Playthings Directory*.

At puberty, Roman and Greek children offered dolls at the altar of a god or goddess to symbolize a ceremonial relinquishment of childhood. Unlike today's high-fashion, coiffured, and anatomically sculpted dolls, these were mostly of wood or clay, although some were carved from bone or ivory. As for board games, their remains have been found in the ruins of Ur, one of the world's oldest known cities (circa 3500 B.C.), in the ancient region of Sumer. And handcarved wooden game boards, inlaid with gold and ivory, were found near the stone coffin of the Egyptian boy-king Tut, who died in 1339 B.C. These boards were for the ancient game Senat, an early form of backgammon. *Fact:* There are thirty manufacturers of backgammon games listed in the 1991–92 *Playthings Directory*.

The history of toy and game development is as rich in the East as in the West. The Far East is the birthplace of many popular modern games. Thirteenth-century Chinese paintings depict toy inventors as the figures holding satchels of proto-types in one hand and unsigned contracts in the other. Domi-noes, experts estimate, probably were invented in China and introduced in Europe in the 1300s. Playing cards are said to have originated in China, where paper was invented, about A.D. 800. It is unknown how they arrived in Europe, but they appeared in Italy by the late 1200s. Before the printing press, all cards were handpainted. *Fact:* There are thirty-six manu-facturers of dominoes listed in the 1991–92 *Playthings Directory.*

No one is positive about the origins of the tradition of carv-ing jointed wooden snakes, animals with nodding heads, and weighted tumbler dolls, but they too originated in China. Kites, perhaps the oldest form of aircraft, originated in China about 3,000 years ago. During the Han Dynasty (200 B.C.–A.D. 200), the inventive Chinese military lashed bamboo shoots to kites. As the kites soared above the enemy, the harsh whistling sound made by the wind passing through the shoots instilled fear and panic into the opponents, causing them to flee. *Fact:* There are twenty-nine manufacturers of kites listed in the 1991–92 *Play-things Directory.*

Wham-O's Hacky Sack footbag, acrobatically kicked around by today's youth, is based on a "football" kicking game in-vented in 2597 B.C. by the Chinese emperor Hwang Ti. Called Kemari, the game consisted of kicking a leather ball filled with hair.

Chess, historians believe, originated in India around A.D. 600. A war game, it is unique among the classic games in that each piece has a rank, paralleling India's caste system. The popularity of chess first spread to Persia, and then to neighboring countries, via warring Arabs. In the Middle Ages, chess became popular in Europe, brought to Spain by Muslim invaders, and was reportedly seen being played as far north as Scandinavia. Over the years many inventors have tried to im-prove on chess, but none has been able to break the enduring appeal of this strategy game. *Fact:* There are thirty-seven man-ufacturers of chess sets listed in the 1991–92 *Playthings Directory.*

During the Dark Ages and the Middle Ages, people contin-ued to play with clay marbles, rattles, hobbyhorses, toy sol-diers, weapons, stilts, bubble pipes, puppets, and dolls. But in contrast to the Far East, very little is known about European toys developed during this era. However, historians tell us that children of the poor, for example, played with simple folk toys made from scraps of wood and cloth. *Fact:* There are twenty-one of toy soldiers; sixty-seven of weapons; nine of stilts; and twenty-one of bubble pipes listed in the 1991–92 *Playthings Direc-tory.*

Children born to the purple, on the other hand, received dramatically costumed and detailed dolls with full wardrobes and miniature weapons, as well as replicas of men-at-arms in full battle armor. Only a few clay dolls and toy horses and knights have survived, so old pictorial sources and written rec-ords hold whatever evidence there is about toys popular in medieval Europe.

We do know that Nürnberg, a prosperous market and cul-tural center at the crossroads of many trade routes, became (and still is) the hub of Germany's toy industry. Near the high, rugged Black Forest region, scene of many German legends and fairy tales, Nürnberg was home in the fifteenth century to toymaker trade guilds, the first known professional associations of toy developers. Today this city hosts the annual Nürnberg Toy Fair, Europe's largest toy industry trade event, which ranks in importance with the American International Toy Fair in New York City. Toy professionals flock to Nürnberg in their unending pursuit of fresh ideas. It was at Nürnberg's 1959 fair, for example, that The Ohio Art Company found and licensed the rights to manufacture Etch-A-Sketch.

Europe was also the setting for perhaps the first toy craze. In 1747, French playwright and librettist Paul Jules Barbier wrote, "In Paris some toys have been devised called pup-

pets. . . . These little figures represent Harlequin and Scara-
mouch, or else bakers, shepherds, and shepherdesses. These
ridiculous things have taken the fancy of Parisian society to
such an extent that one cannot go into any house without finding them dangling from every mantelpiece. They are being
bought to give women and girls, and the craze has reached
such a pitch that this New Year all the shops are full of
them. . . .'' Perhaps it was Barbier who first observed that toys
can assume fad proportions and become ingrained in the culture, a thought certainly held by many toy executives today.

Explorer Discovers the American Toy Market

Back in the New World, long before Christopher Columbus
reached the North American continent in 1492, native Americans had made a wide assortment of toys and games. Among
the favorites were toy animals carved from wood and bone,
whip tops, bow-and-arrow target games, lacrosse, and cat's
cradle. The Pawnees invented an infant toy similar to today's
Fisher-Price Play-Gym. Squaws would hang rattle balls and
spinning wooden gripper hoops on a center axis over their babies' cribs to stimulate the infants' hand–eye coordination. Could
it be that Fisher-Price, long regarded as an innovator of infant
and preschool toys, was also a most astute observer of history?

As pioneers opened America's frontier from the Appalachian Mountains to the Pacific Ocean, few new toys or games
were developed, perhaps because children had little free time.
They worked alongside their parents to ensure the survival of
the community. Nevertheless, they improvised play and
adopted many native American toys and games. Dolls were
fashioned from corncobs, rawhide strips were rolled up to form
balls, whistles were carved from tree branches, and dried ker-
nels were used as game markers.

The first toy shops appeared in New England as Puritan prohibitions began to ease in the early eighteenth century, some 100 years after the Pilgrims came ashore at Plymouth Rock. The Industrial Revolution had begun in Great Britain during the 1700s and had spread to North America by the early 1800s. Industry began to overtake agriculture in the former British colonies and by the end of the century, the United States was the largest and most competitive industrial nation in the world.

The toy industry kept pace with mechanization, and in 1783, after the Revolutionary War, the first companies began to produce individual playthings in quantity. From being the creations of home tinkerers, with their handmade wooden outdoor wagons, sleds, kites, and other amusements, toys became the products of large-scale manufacturing firms.

On April 10, 1790, President George Washington signed the country's first patent bill. For the first time in history, the intrinsic right of an inventor to profit from his invention was recognized by law. Previously, privileges granted to an inventor were dependent upon the prerogative of a monarch or a special act of a legislature. As secretary of state, Thomas Jefferson, known to have invented a toy or two himself, was in effect the first administrator of the American patent system.

The Tower Shop, later renamed the Tower Toy Company, was perhaps the first American toy manufacturing business. Organized in the late 1830s by William S. Tower of South Hingham, Massachusetts, a carpenter who made wooden toys, the company was originally a cooperative guild of craftsmen representing different skills. By pooling their talents, they were able to create a wide range of items, including doll furniture, toy tools, and toy boats, mostly of wood. In 1878, the enterprise was successful enough to exhibit its toys at the Exposition Universelle Internationale in Paris.

At about this same time, the Crandall family, originally of Hopkinton, Massachusetts, began a toymaking business that was to last almost a century. At least eleven members from two branches of the family were involved in inventing and producing toys from about 1830 to 1929. They held several hundred patents, among them those for the spring rocking horse, velocipede, nesting blocks, and interlocking building blocks.

Children's Play
Becomes Adults' Work

In 1860, Milton Bradley, then twenty-four years old, established the Milton Bradley Publishing and Lithography Company in Springfield, Massachusetts. However, financial problems began to plague the printer before a year was up. Looking for innovative products to keep his presses rolling, Bradley decided to diversify by inventing and marketing a game entitled The Checkered Game of Life. This forerunner to the modern-day Game of Life (published in 1960, and still on the market) was one of the most popular and successful board games of all time.

Searching for another success, Bradley began to consider outside game submissions, thus initiating the company's long relationship with independent inventors. Today's game inventors can thank Bradley's early dependence on outside ideas for opening opportunities with major manufacturers.

In 1888, Jeanne P. Clarke sold Politics and the Race for the Presidency to Milton Bradley and became the first woman to license a game to the company. The firm then bought a board game called Eckha, a combination of chess and checkers, from a Harvard mathematics professor, and it became one of the most popular games of the late 1800s. Dr. Thomas Hill, a former Harvard president and pastor of a Unitarian church in Maine, licensed a board game called Kerion.

In 1883, in Salem, Massachusetts, George S. Parker, an enterprising sixteen-year-old, took $40 of his $50 life savings and started what would become one of America's largest game publishers. The entrepreneurial lad literally bet his last dollar on a roll of the dice when he opted to self-publish Banking, a game he had invented. Sales were brisk, and he not only got back his investment but also made a profit of almost $100. More important, The George S. Parker Company was in business. By 1888, the enterprise was going so well that young George was joined by his elder brother Charles, and they renamed the firm Parker Brothers. A third brother, Edwin, joined them a decade later.

The Parker Brothers line featured twenty-nine games in 1888, most of them invented by George Parker himself. Page after page of the 1892 mail-order catalogs from Marshall Field & Company, Butler Brothers, and Sears, Roebuck & Company show a plethora of Parker Brothers product. In the century since then, Parker Brothers has published more than 1,000 games, many of them world renowned. We have all grown up playing some of their classics, among them Monopoly, Sorry!, Risk, and Clue.

Milton Bradley and Parker Brothers games have always mirrored the era in which they were released. In the earliest days, their products were obviously influenced by Puritanism: New Game of Virtue Rewarded, Vice Punished, The Checkered Game of Life, and Happy Days in Old New England. In fact, the oldest known commercial American board game was Mansion of Happiness, a children's path game designed to challenge a player's moral fiber. Published by W. & S. B. Ives Company in 1843, it had a playing field boldly marked with such words as *justice*, *piety*, *immodesty*, and *ingratitude*.

Novel Materials for Novel Ideas

In the mid-1830s and 1840s, the new toy factories were equipped to use any and every kind of material that made toys better—and in more variety. Pull toys and miniature doll-house furnishings were die-cut from tin. Dolls' heads were made of ceramic in Philadelphia. The use of metal facilitated beautiful and complex shapes, and, of greater importance, improved the quality of toys with tougher wheels and more durable gears. Teething rings, dominoes, and bagatelle balls were produced from ivory; rubber from India and the region now known as Malaysia was used for balls, rattle boxes, and doll heads; and paper was used for playing cards and board games.

The toy industry had grown so much by the mid-1840s that nearly every town, no matter how remote, had an emporium in which to buy toys. In New York, Woolworth's Fancy Store advertised the arrival from Europe of popular playthings in time for Christmas of 1844. Locomotives and mechanical toys for children were being promoted in one of the first seasonal selling campaigns.

Although toy and game invention, patenting, and production did slow during the Civil War, manufacturers, as always, managed to benefit from the crisis. Toy guns, as might be expected, became very popular. In 1861, Milton Bradley designed a lightweight kit of popular games for the Union troops. Called Games for the Soldiers, it contained special, portable editions of chess, checkers, The Checkered Game of Life, backgammon, and five varieties of dominoes.

But Milton Bradley was not alone in capitalizing on wartime demand. Many years later, as the United States prepared to enter the Spanish-American War in 1898, Parker Brothers released such games as Hold the Fort, War in Cuba, The Siege of Havana, and Battle of Manila. Another company published Uncle Sam and the Don, depicting a fistfight in which Uncle Sam decked his foe with a blow to the solar plexus.

At the outbreak of the Civil War, twelve factories had reported combined annual sales of under $200,000. By 1900, volume had jumped to more than $4 million reported by 500 companies with a retail sales value of $20 million, a third from foreign imports.

In 1882, author James Lukin is reported to have observed, "Talk of the march of the intellect—the march of toydom beats it all hollow. I do not believe a modern body would look at such crude creations as delighted the babies 50 years ago . . . The really instructive and highly interesting toys of our time, the scientific and mechanical ones [were] a class utterly unknown in olden days." Lukin described the earliest "mechanical" toys of wood and cardboard, powered by fine sand running over a wheel that brought human figures to life, as "rude creations." On the other hand, in the 1880s, *Harper's Bazaar* described "The doll of today . . . endowed with an interior phonograph, and this enabled to reproduce the human voice." So the inventors of Teddy Ruxpin, the megahit "talking" plush bear of the 1980s, were not so original after all. Toys throw long shadows.

At this point, toward the end of the nineteenth century, toy and game inventors were still independent part-timers or in-house staffers. Except for those inventors who were entrepreneurial enough to establish their own manufacturing companies, no one was making enough money to survive without other income. Independent inventors needed to sustain themselves with alternate livelihoods. And in-house inventors often performed other tasks for the company, such as machine operator or sales clerk, occasionally providing a product idea that was considered worthy enough to bring to market.

Around the turn of the century, however, immigrant toymakers began to make their mark on America. What became known as the Golden Age of Toys saw the introduction of walking and talking dolls, toy pianos that plinked, wind-up clockwork, vehicles powered by friction motors, gravity gizmos, magnetics, and realistic steam toys, to name but a few. There was an electrified doll house with running water. Newly discovered scientific principles in optics were incorporated into toys. A.C. Gilbert developed the Erector Set. Entrepreneurs had arrived.

The First Megahits

Samuel Leeds Allen owned a successful farm equipment company in New Jersey. Farm equipment sales being seasonal, he sought to diversify his product line, and set out to develop a sled. Allen tested various designs on a slope at his Ivystone Farm near Westfield, and at nearby Westtown School, where his daughter Elizabeth and her classmates field-tested his designs. By combining features of each of his earlier models—called "Phantom," "Fleetwing," "Ariel," and "Fairy Coaster"—Allen perfected the first steerable sled with flexible T-shaped runners and a slatted wooden seat. On February 14, 1889, he applied for a patent for the Flexible Flyer. For more than 100 years now, that name has been synonymous with winter, snow, and kids.

Beatrice Alexander Behrman, who became known as Madame Alexander, was born above the first doll hospital in America, which her father, a Russian immigrant, started in 1885 in New York City. The recurrent scene of tearful little girls bringing their broken porcelain dolls to the "doctor" left an indelible impression on young Beatrice. When shipments of European dolls practically ceased during World War I, Behrman saw an opportunity to express her artistic talent, while also fulfilling a new need in the marketplace, by designing her own line of "made in America" dolls. Each requires an average of two to three weeks for completion, in contrast to Barbie, which has a gestation period of several minutes. To date, the Alexander Doll Company has introduced well over 5,000 different Madame Alexander dolls.

The Lionel Manufacturing Company opened for business in 1900. Its founder, Joshua Lionel Cowen, produced fuses, small low-voltage motors, and electrical novelties. He also invented the first dry-cell battery. In 1901 the imaginative Cowen put one of his electric motors in a model railroad car, and the best-loved name in trains then chugged its way into toy history.

Alice Stead Binney conceived the trade name Crayola for her husband Edwin's crayons in 1903. She derived it from the French word craie (stick of chalk) and the word oleaginous (oily). Research indicates that 65 percent of U.S. children between the ages of two and seven color or draw at least once a day for an average of twenty-seven minutes, mostly using Crayola crayons. More than two billion of them are manufactured each year.

Charles Pajeau, a stonemason by trade, invented Tinkertoy in 1913 and sold one million sets the first year. A display in a Grand Central Station window that year caused a massive traffic jam. Since then, more than 100 million Tinkertoy sets have been sold worldwide.

In 1916, John Lloyd Wright was with his father, architect Frank Lloyd Wright, in Tokyo, to observe construction techniques for an "earthquake-proof" hotel, the Imperial Palace. The twenty-four-year-old Wright returned home to Merrill, Wisconsin, and drew up the specifications for a new construction toy. Today, Lincoln Logs (Playskool) are manufactured in Walla Walla, Washington, from about four traincarloads per month of Ponderosa pine. Some 2.2 million board feet are used to produce 500,000 sets per year.

Fred A. Lundahl owned the Moline Pressed Steel Company in Illinois, where he made fenders and other heavy-gauge steel parts for International Harvester Company. As a birthday gift to his son, Buddy, he crafted a realistic, toy-sized, working replica of a dump truck from scraps of steel, thereby inventing the first heavy-gauge-steel toy vehicle. It proved so popular with Buddy and the neighborhood kids that, at the suggestion of a friend, Lundahl took it to F. A. O. Schwarz in New York. He was stunned to receive an order for a carload of his toys. When asked what he intended to call them, his choice was simple: "I'll call them Buddy L Toys."

With the Wright Brothers' first airplane flight in December 1903, the American love affair with speed and motion moved into the wild blue yonder. Toymakers began to foresee and outpace adult reality, as replicas of all sorts of flying machines would anticipate man's greatest adventure, the exploration of space.

One of the first examples of a manufacturer getting caught with its trends down was Kingsbury's introduction of a monoplane in 1924. It collected dust on the shelves because the World War I aces' kids adored biplanes. But Kingsbury learned. After Charles Lindbergh made his historic flight to Paris in 1927, the monoplane was redecorated to resemble the Spirit of St. Louis, and it sold. After the excitement over the Lone Eagle subsided, it was spray-painted green to resemble the plane used by Wrong Way Corrigan on his misadventure to Ireland, and sales soared again.

Rise of Modern Mass Marketing

The more innovative the toys and games, the more kids wanted them. Prolific inventors and manufacturers had a hard time keeping the ever-expanding market filled with fresh product. Even non–toy merchants saw the opportunities. Soon dry-goods stores and mail-order houses such as Sears, Roebuck and Montgomery Ward joined other retail outlets in devoting shelf space in their stores to playthings.

The first American Toy Fair took place in New York City in February 1902, when ten salesmen representing American factories set up exhibits at a lower Manhattan hotel for four weeks. They timed their trade show in hopes of catching buyers on their way to and from European buying trips. With the exception of 1945, when the Toy Fair was canceled in support of World War II priorities, it has been held annually in New York City since 1934—the same year that the Toy Center Building made its debut as an exhibition site. Since 1952, it has been a ten-day event. After the 1983 show, the TMA board of directors voted to change the name from the American Toy Fair to the American International Toy Fair to reflect its preeminence among the world's toy trade shows.

It was also in 1902 that America's love affair with the teddy bear began. The story goes that President Theodore Roosevelt, while on a hunting trip to Smedes, Mississippi, refused to kill a trapped bear cub that appeared in the cross hairs of his rifle sight. The shot not fired was heard from coast to coast. Newspapers reported the incident and political cartoonists had a heyday.

As legend has it, Morris Michtom, proprietor of a small Brooklyn, New York, toy shop—and no slouch when it came to marketing—wrote a letter to President Roosevelt asking for permission to name his plush bears Teddy's bears. Permission was granted on a royalty-free basis. "Never in the history of Wall Street was the country more at the mercy of bears than it is today," wrote the toy industry's trade magazine, *Playthings*, in 1906. It did not take long for word of the teddy bear to spread, and soon every toy company was making them. No matter to Michtom; he took his substantial earnings from the promotion and founded the Ideal Toy and Novelty Company. And for the cuddly critters, it's been a bear market ever since. Americans annually spend between $100 and $200 million on them.

Toy production in the United States doubled between 1900 and 1910. During the following decade, it soared to spectacular heights, experiencing a 500 percent increase—due in great part to an almost total disappearance of European imports during World War I. The war was not all bad for the American toy industry. Designers were creating war toys and war games. Milton Bradley, much as it did for Civil War soldiers, supplied game kits to General Pershing's American Expeditionary Forces on the battlefields of France.

When Germany got back on an even footing after World

War I, it launched an economic invasion of the American toy industry. Lower-priced, better-made German toys began to flood the U.S. market. Even the most powerful American manufacturers were affected, and many newer firms were forced out of business.

To stave off this economic scourge, A. C. Gilbert, inventor of the Erector Set and president of the Toy Manufacturers of the U.S.A., formed a delegation that went to Washington, DC, in 1921, and successfully lobbied the House Ways and Means Committee for a 75 percent protective tariff bill on imported toys and games. This helped smaller manufacturers survive and grow, and it protected the U.S. toy industry until it was strong enough to fight for itself, at which point the tariffs were reduced.

Perhaps the most significant business development of the 1920s, however, did not seem so at the time. This was the founding of Hasbro, Inc., in 1923 in Providence, Rhode Island. Originally called Hassenfeld Brothers (for Henry, Hillel, and Herman), the company began by selling textile remnants and then pencil boxes. In 1943, Henry's son Merrill was named president, and he expanded the product line to include toys. The company accepted ideas and suggestions from customers, family, and independent inventors. By the end of the 1940s, Hassenfeld Brothers had annual sales of $3 million. Mr. Potato Head was introduced in the 1950s, and the 1960s saw monumental growth with such items as Lite Brite and G.I. Joe.

The year 1929 brought the stock market crash, and the nation's economy toppled like a house of Bicycle playing cards. Curiously, however, what was to be the worst and longest business slump of modern times did not affect the toy and game industry as adversely as might be expected. It prospered through the 1930s and did not flatten out until World War II imposed severe material and manpower shortages.

At the height of the Great Depression in 1933, about thirteen million Americans were out of work, and many others had only part-time employment. With a lot of time on their hands, and little money to spend on entertainment, Americans stayed home and amused themselves with board games and toys. Others took advantage of the downtime to begin inventing.

The first millionaire game inventor was Charles B. Darrow, who was awarded U.S. Patent 2,026,082 for Monopoly, the most successful board game of all time. Introduced during the Great Depression, "Monopoly let people fantasize that they could win in the real estate market," said Robert Barton, George Parker's son-in-law. "It was a godsend. It rescued the business [Parker Brothers], which had come within an inch of disaster." Milton Bradley's Easy Money was another game that enabled players to cut deals and handle thousands of fantasy funds. What people found impossible to achieve in reality they could fantasize about in their parlors, with bundles of toy money and momentary fortunes.

In East Aurora, New York, on October 1, 1930, Herman G. Fisher and Irving R. Price established Fisher-Price Toys with a $100,000 investment. In 1937, Fisher-Price sold more than two million toys, and the company grew rapidly to keep up with consumer demand. Today F-P, the standard in the infant and preschool markets, has broadened its product base to become a billion-dollar producer of a highly respected brand of diverse playthings.

New Babies + New Companies = Burgeoning Business

After World War II, the United States entered a great era of economic growth. Notwithstanding periods of inflation and recession, more enterprises and people than ever before enjoyed prosperity. A new wave of materialism and self-indulgence struck the country. People had money and a compulsive drive to spend it. The baby boom brought a previously unknown commitment to family life and children. And the toy industry experienced unparalleled growth.

Marvin Glass opened his toy design studio in 1941 in a Chicago loft. By the time of his death in 1974, it had grown to become the finest and most successful industrial design organization in the business, and Glass himself had amassed a personal fortune. Known for his showmanship, Glass often would carry his toys in boxes handcuffed to his wrist. It was not uncommon for his items to arrive in an armored truck escorted by armed guards. Security at Marvin Glass & Associates was tighter than the controls at many of his customers' R&D departments.

In December 1984, in recognition of his outstanding contributions to the growth and development of the toy industry, Marvin Glass was inducted into the newly formed Toy Manufacturers of America (TMA) Toy Industry Hall of Fame, along with Herman G. Fisher, Louis Marx, A. C. Gilbert, Sr., and Merrill L. Hassenfeld.

Marvin Glass & Associates was a haven for young inventors such as A. Eddy Goldfarb (a partner of Glass's), Howard Morrison, Jeffrey Breslow, Gordon Barlow, Ed and Bonnie Fogarty, Bert Meyer, Mike Ferris, Bob McKay, Wayne Kuna, and many others still active in the toy business. Devoting full time to toy invention, they taxed technology with many innovative product designs. Goldfarb, in fact, was one of the first to use plastic, in such designs as the egg-laying hen Busy Biddy, the Merry Go straw, and Yakity-Yak Teeth. Goldfarb observes, "Toys change because of technology. Right after World War II, plastics became a boom industry and opened up whole new possibilities for toys. The companies that didn't get into plastics after the war went out of business."

When plastics hit the industry like a ton of Lego bricks, the process gave rise to a new family of toys. During World War II there had been severe shortages of elements such as brass and aluminum. Alternative materials were necessary, and the U.S. plastics manufacturers got together and unselfishly shared research and development information to fill the gap. New injection molding facilities were constructed all over the country. New materials, technologies, and techniques to increase production were developed.

Monogram Models, today one of the world's largest manufacturers of scale-model plastic hobby kits, got its start in 1945. Its first line consisted of only three balsa model ship kits. Today there are 250 Monogram plastic kits available, ranging from tactical fighter assortments to a nine-inch replica of Frederick Hart's "Three Fighting Men" Vietnam memorial statue. Lou Glazer of Revell, Inc., began to produce the first thermoplastic injection-molded aircraft hobby kits in 1951.

Today hardly anyone can remember when there were no plastic toys. "I can hardly imagine designing toys without plastics and the enhanced possibilities they offer," Maki Papavasilou, manager of materials R&D at Mattel, Inc., told *Modern Plastics* magazine.

Outside of the toy companies as well as inside, creative individuals powered new toys to the heights of success. Richard James, a marine engineer, watched a torsion spring fall off a table and bounce around the deck of his ship while on a tour at sea in 1943. When he arrived home, he said to his wife, Betty, "I think I can make a toy go down a flight of stairs." He did. And while the spring was flipping from step to step, Betty went to a dictionary and flipped from page to page to find a name that best fit their novelty. In the "S" section she found the perfect name: Slinky.

A similarly happy accident occurred to James Wright, an engineer at General Electric's research lab in New Haven, Connecticut. While trying to discover a viable synthetic rubber to aid the war effort in 1945, by mistake he let some boric acid drop into a test tube containing silicone oil. The chemical reaction that took place resulted in a compound that, to Wright's astonishment, had all the qualities of a rubber ball. Silly Putty thus came bouncing into the toy business. Today, about two million "eggs" of Silly Putty are sold yearly. About as close as anyone will ever get to the perfect toy, it has just one moving part.

In the late 1940s, Herb Schaper, a Minneapolis mailman, would whittle fishing lures while walking his route. He discovered that one in the shape of a flea captivated the interest of children. So, in 1948, with $75 in investment capital and one product, Cootie, he started Schaper Toys. In time, Schaper became a multimillionaire. Today the Milton Bradley Company produces the Cootie line.

Others were more consciously working on new playthings. Eleanor Abbott passed the long hours recuperating from polio by developing games for younger polio victims. One game, called Candy Land, eliminated the reading and counting needed for most board games by basing play on matching colors and objects. The game proved so popular with the youngest players that Abbott submitted it to Milton Bradley in 1949— and the rest, as they say, is history. Candy Land has sold more than twenty million copies.

While a manufacturing process (plastics) and a promotion strategy (TV commercials) drastically changed the business, so too did the practice of linking toys to other forms of entertainment. Manufacturers started slowly with radio tie-ins, but later they were much quicker to roll out items mirroring hot properties from TV and movies.

Radio offered the first major media tie-in for toys and games. Broadcast shows of the 1930s, such as Paul Wing's "Spelling Bee" and the question-and-answer favorite "Vox Pop," came to market in boxed versions, as did the first home-version adult party game based on the "Fibber McGee Show."

As television began its ascent in households across the country, millions of youngsters were able to emulate their small-screen heroes. The Hopalong Cassidy Game was one of the first board-game TV tie-ins. The Mickey Mouse Club, in its Disneyland Game, opened the door for in-home "mouseke-teering" in 1955. A steady stream of video personalities appearing on games followed, including Howdy Doody (1957), Mighty Mouse (1960), Looney Tunes (1961), Batman and Robin (1963), Yogi Bear (1964), Flintstones (1965), Man from U.N.C.L.E. (1966), Dastardly and Muttley (1969), Partridge Family (1971), and The Waltons (1974). Game companies used the same successful tie-in techniques with adult favorites such as Let's Make a Deal (1974), Family Feud (1978), and Wheel of Fortune (1979). As kids' programming increased in the 1970s and 1980s, toymakers kept scanning the ratings for crossover product ideas.

And paralleling the TV tie-ins was the equally strong influence of movie and book personalities on toys and games: Call Me Lucky: The Bing Crosby Game (1954); Mary Poppins (1964); Flip Your Wig: The Beatles Game (1964); Wizard of Oz (1974); King Kong (1976); Richard Scarry (1976); Star Wars (1977); and E.T. (1981). For under a dollar, kids in the early 1950s could play simple games featuring such cartoon characters as Nancy and Sluggo, Li'l Abner, and Captain and the Kids. As toy people began to recognize the power of licensed properties, they expanded the use of popular characters take any to all sorts of categories. Today the hottest characters appear in various toy forms from action figures to plush toys to puzzles to games.

Electronics: The Gold and the Dross

By 1970, three-dimensional action toy/games were emerging, with names such as Operation, Mouse Trap, and Hands Down. The infamous cautionary note, "Batteries required," now became common, as toys and games reached new levels of animation and mobility.

But the biggest technological change was yet to come. A search for the exotic and ever-increasing sophistication in playthings ultimately led toymakers into the world of computers and electronics. The endless capacity of microprocessors and microchips to generate beeps, boops, and blips, visual displays, programmable commands, synthesized sound, and variable play levels gave new forms to high-tech toy and game designs. In the late 1970s and early 1980s, many toy and game companies abandoned their known business charters and followed wherever the latest technology took them in a search for ''products of the future.''

It all started in 1962 with Steve Russell, an MIT graduate student, and a computer program for a game called Spacewar. The toy industry would never be the same. Nolan Bushnell, a creative force destined to play a major role in the electronics business, attempted a commercial version of Russell's game. In 1970, Bushnell soldered the final microcircuits into a game he trademarked as Computer Space. He licensed the manufacturing rights, but the game was unsuccessful in the marketplace. It was too complex. So Bushnell went back to the drawing board to design a simpler game. What he created was a mindless electronic table-tennis game he dubbed Pong. In 1972, he founded a company called Atari to manufacture and market it in coin-operated table units. The first Pong was installed at Andy Capp's bar in Sunnyvale, California, but after only a couple of days, Pong stopped working. After confirming that the integrated circuits were fine, Bushnell checked the coin box. It was stuffed beyond capacity—so much so that it had short-circuited the game. It was the beginning of the video arcade era.

The home version of video games, however, had been born in 1966, when Ralph Baer, a supervising engineer at Sanders Associates in Manchester, New Hampshire, assigned technicians to work on television games. By the first months of 1967, Baer and engineers Bill Harrison and Bill Rusch were playing table tennis and hockey on a seventeen-inch RCA color set. Sanders licensed its video-game technology to Magnavox, and by the summer of 1972, the Odyssey game system was in production. Odyssey used Mylar overlays taped to the television screen. Each overlay depicted a different game board, such as table tennis, hockey, or football. That first year, 100,000 Odyssey games were sold.

Atari moved beyond coin-operated arcade games into the home market with its model 2600 game console, Video Computer System (VCS), in the mid 1970s. The variety of games available for the VCS mushroomed. Activision, Epyx, and many other independent companies manufactured game cartridges for use with Atari equipment. The library of "carts" would swell to 1,500 titles in the early 1980s before the trade and the consumers signaled "overload."

The Glory Years of Great Expectations

When other established toy companies, such as Milton Bradley, Mattel, and Parker Brothers, saw the consumer's love affair with pricey video games, they too started hiring electronic engineers and ordering microprocessors. But instead of going up against the video games with more of the same, they produced handheld electronic games, dedicated tabletop games, and noncompatible software cartridges.

Milton Bradley brought out Comp IV, a tabletop brain baffler powered by a 9-volt battery (its packaging ran the headline, I AM PROGRAMMED TO BEAT YOU) and Electronic Battleship, a computerized version of its classic board game. To compete with Electronic Battleship, Parker Brothers produced Code Name: Sector, in which players command naval destroyers and match wits with submarines. Mattel came out concurrently with two pocket-size electronic games, Auto Race and Football. These five nonvideo electronic offerings brought in $21 million for their manufacturers.

1978: Total Toy Market $5 Billion, including 45 Electronic Items

Milton Bradley brought out Simon, a follow-the-leader game, and Star Bird, a realistic sounding toy aircraft that changed engine sounds depending upon its flight attitude. The company shipped close to a million Star Birds that year. Simon went on to capture a major share of the electronic game market and is one of the few original electronic games still marketed today.

Asked about Simon's longevity, Michael Langieri, vice president of creative development at Milton Bradley, says, "It was, and still is, a great product. It's a near-perfect blending of electronic technology and familiar game play. It seems so simple, yet it can quickly get complex. Best of all, it is not an intimidating product, and no one is really shut out of playing with some success. I don't think any other electronic product has had the range of usage that Simon does. From home to classroom, from preschoolers to adults, and from culture to culture—everyone can and probably has played Simon."

1979: Total Toy Market $5.5 Billion, including 125 Electronic Items

In 1979, consumers bought $800 million of electronic toys at retail. Handheld games represented a sizable proportion of that, with sales of $250 million. Some twenty million microprocessors were used in games and another ten million in toys.

Among the year's electronic toy and game highlights was Mattel's electronic Football, sales reaching one million units. Milton Bradley launched Microvision, a handheld, complete nonvideo cartridge game system that was one of the first electronic games to use a liquid crystal display (LCD).

1980: Total Toy Market $6.7 Billion, and Talking Toys, Too!

This was a pivotal year in the electronic toy wars. The first real shakeout took place as buyers were confronted with deciding among the many "me too" products. Shelves were beginning to bulge with undifferentiated electronics. Consumers seemed unable to absorb all the toy and game features, which were being introduced at a record pace. The electronic abracadabra included voice recognition and speech synthesis, features that never gained popularity with toy consumers.

1981: A Pause, a Breath, a Sigh

If 1980 was a year when the trade buckled under a flood of electronic SKUs, manufacturers in 1981 reacted with limited numbers of new products. Most notable on a sparse product menu were Atari's innovations: Cosmos, the first handheld electronic game that used holography, made a big splash at Toy Fair and then died; its new Video Computer System offered wireless remote controllers. Mattel entered the market with its Intellivision video game system.

1982: Total Toy Market $9 Billion and a Cartridge Avalanche

Video games sales skyrocketed to $3 billion. The industry sparked to Colecovision, Coleco's new expandable video game system. For the first time, a manufacturer had brought the superior visual excitement and challenge of coin-operated arcade games onto the home TV screen. With its "expansion module,'' Colecovision was able to accept game cartridges from the Atari 2600 VCS, its main competition. Soon Mattel's Intellivision and Atari were making Colecovision games for their own systems. Milton Bradley tried to keep pace with Voice Command video game cartridges tied to the Texas Instruments 99/4A home computer. But the attempt fizzled as the price of the 99/4A plunged and never reached a significant sales level.

1983: Cartridges Decline; Bring on Your Dolls and Trivia

After two years of shakeout in electronic toys, the record sales of video games in 1982 made for a decidedly mixed signal. The dumping and discounting of cartridges eroded the market by $1 billion in 1983, and by the end of 1984, it was a mere 25 percent of 1982 levels.

In a marketplace rife with rumors of the dawn of an immense home personal computer demand, Mattel (with its Aquarius and Intellivision II) and Coleco (with its Adam) were two toy companies that took the bait. Coleco's entry was heralded as the first $600 home computer complete with printer. If consumers were going to use computers to play games and expand into other "edutainment" activities, these two toymakers in the consumer electronics market would be well prepared. In addition, Coleco, whether as a strategic hedge on the Adam or merely as a stroke of luck, licensed for mass distribution Xavier Roberts's Cabbage Patch Kids—a property that reached $65 million in sales in the 1983 launch year. By 1984, sales from the dolls had soared to $540 million.

Another phenomenon introduced in 1983, during the electronics shakeout, was Trival Pursuit, a $40 question-and-answer game that eventually surpassed the $1 billion mark in worldwide sales, with some sixty million copies. Not only did it prove that the consumer would pay a rather high price for a game, it also broke the hold of video games. People began to return to the parlor and interact without a blipping, beeping video game in hand or on the television. Players spoke to each other again!

By 1984, companies that had missed the electronic bandwagon or at best had taken a short hitch were being praised for remaining neutral during the electronic wars. Many made a conscious decision to let the marketplace unclog from the electronic surplus as they prepared to emphasize the "basics." Non-electronic staples were given promotional bumps to rekindle trade interest and remind consumers of longstanding best-sellers. The year indeed was bleak: Mattel swiftly sold off its electronics division and Warner Communications sold Atari. And it became obvious that Coleco could not deliver what it promised with its Adam computer.

Although the industry in the second half of the 1980s stanched the unabated flow of electronic toys and games, it continued to use microchips as the heart of many lead Christmas items. Worlds of Wonder was incorporated in March 1985 to manufacture and market Teddy Ruxpin for Christmas that year. The figure may not have been new, but its mouth, nose, and eyes moved in sync to a voice played from an internal playback tape deck. It was an animated version of Mego's 1979 hit, 2-XL. Worlds of Wonder had one other hit before going bust with success. Lazer Tag, an interactive, infrared game of tag was high on hundreds of thousands of 1986 Christmas wish lists. In 1987, Mattel introduced a new generation of toys under the banner Captain Power that interacted electronically with special television programs. The line of twenty toys, which ranged in price from $30 to $40, was linked to a half-hour Captain Power TV program. Ohio Art's classic Etch-A-Sketch gave birth to the Etch-A-Sketch Animator and the Etch-A-Sketch Animator 2000, high-tech spinoffs that create moving pictures and store them in their memory banks. Fisher-Price developed PXL 2000, a camcorder for eight-year-olds that lets kids capture black-and-white video images. Hot Lixx and Hot Keyz, Tyco Toys' state-of-the-art electronic instruments, deliver perfect music—without a single lesson.

If electronics had an iron grip on the toy industry in the early 1980s, a strong parallel can be drawn to the $4 billion home video-game market today. First, traditional toy companies got caught up with investment in unfamiliar capabilities to gain a slice of the electronics market. Today toy-industry giants such as Milton Bradley, Acclaim, and Fisher-Price have invested in software development and marketing to garner a portion of the sales dollars from Nintendo cartridges. As was true in the early 1980s, dollars spent on cartridges detract from traditional toy purchases. Industry players chased a leader in the earlier market (Atari); today they chase—or participate with—the new leader, Nintendo. The giant commands an 80 percent market share of video games. It remains to be seen whether the parallels extend to a market shakeout.

Executives have been searching for the first signs of a video-game taper and a 20 percent sales drop in NES hardware in 1990 is just that signal. A sameness in software has resulted in price slashing of cartridges from $44.95 to $19.95 at retail. Unlike Atari at its peak, Nintendo carefully monitors the licensing of software producers and it can judge a cartridge's suitability as well as dictate market supply.

With this control of the market, Nintendo can more accurately read a changing retail demand and adjust product strategies accordingly. It gave some evidence of this uncanny market awareness with the 1989 introduction of Game Boy, its portable machine that requires dedicated game cartridges. Game Boy sold one million units in the last five months of 1989, going to 5 million in 1990 and projected to reach 12 million in 1991. In addition, Super Nintendo with 16-bit technology is now being launched to take game play on expanded cartridges to even higher levels.

The toy industry is in the midst of a technology explosion

unparalleled in its history. The pace of change is so dramatic and the economic stakes are so high that companies and independent inventors are increasingly focusing their attention on technology development. There are new pressures on technology in toys and games. Incremental improvements are not dramatic enough for sophisticated consumers.

The toy industry deals mostly with the inventor as artist, less with the inventor as scientist. The toy inventing community does not do basic research or make quantum discoveries. But, as history has shown, the inventors' skill is in capturing the technology of other basic industries and transferring it to toys and games. It was done with plastics, it was done with electronics, and it will be done with materials and processes yet unknown. Toy inventors tether themselves to other industries to adopt new technologies for the latest playthings.

It is impossible to predict just where the toy industry will be in another decade. Because of its entrepreneurial nature, there will always be startup companies seeking to dethrone the ruling manufacturers. Foreign corporate empires could come along with their strong financial bases and take control of U.S. toymakers, as they have done in sister entertainment industries. At the rate things are going, who knows? Maybe there will be just a few multibillion-dollar manufacturers and one zillion-dollar retailer.

Whatever happens, it is safe to say that no matter how technologically advanced toys become through microchips, the industry will always need the independent toy inventor and basic items that have the magic and the simplicity of a maple seed.

3 The World of Toys

AN INDUSTRY OVERVIEW

The toy industry is The Greatest Show on Earth. It is a high-wire act without a safety net in which manufacturers walk a financial tightrope that stretches from Christmas to Christmas. Corporate impresarios try their best to top one season's hits the next year, and they rely on the magic of toy-inventing gurus to make it happen. In few industries can one find such a blending of creative talents, disciplines, polytechnologies, media, theater, self-interest, circus, idealism, cynicism, masquerade, pomp, exaggeration, and ingenuity as prevails in the toy-and-game business.

It is a Barnum-and-Bailey, three-ring enterprise that, like the other entertainment industries of films, theater, and music, thrives on trends, ballyhoos, egos, advertising, originality . . . and smoke and mirrors.

David Leibowitz, senior vice president and seasoned toy-industry expert for American Securities Corporation, an investment banking firm, describes the toy industry as an art, not a science, and among the most competitive of all consumer-goods industries, a situation exacerbated by the fact that in any given year 60 to 75 percent of industry sales take place during an eight-week period. "It's manic-depressive . . . both a seasonal and a cyclical business that is probably a double whammy," he suggests. "The toy industry is the entertainment business with one season," offers Neal Kublan, independent developer and president of The Knack Group.

"Excitement sells toys and the manufacturers create excitement," says Paul Valentine, toy-industry analyst for Standard & Poor's. Much of that excitement is created by the annual avalanche of new products that come rolling, beeping, wobbling, spinning, oozing, talking, crying, and crawling out of toy factories from Maine to mainland China, many just in the Saint Nick of time to find a place beneath the Christmas tree. America's 800 toy companies—not to mention the hundreds of foreign producers—every year wage a campaign to try to keep their products under enough Douglas firs to get a larger chunk of retail toy sales.

At the 1990 American International Toy Fair, the largest toy trade show in the United States, more than 500 manufacturers exhibited in permanent showrooms in New York City: at 200 Fifth Avenue (Toy Center South) and at 1107 Broadway (Toy Center North). Another 600 satellite companies pushed their products at the Jacob K. Javits Convention Center. The 1990 Toy Fair registered more than 20,000 buyers from the United States and seventy-four foreign countries in search of everything from toy accordions to yo-yos, with 715 product categories in between.

The United States is the largest market in the world for toys and games, followed by Japan and western Europe. American retail toy sales totaled an estimated $13.4 billion in 1989, remained virtually flat in 1990, and are expected to increase only 5 percent in 1991 according to the TMA. According to *Advertising Age* magazine, toy manufacturers spend about $300 to $400 million on television commercials each year.

"The really interesting part about the toy business," says David Leibowitz, "is that this is an industry where the top management of the manufacturers tends to be in their forties, maybe early fifties; the buyer for the retailer tends to be in his thirties to early forties; the merchandise manager is in his forties, fifties, and sixties; and these are the people who are deciding what nine-year-olds like. If the incongruity is lost on the industry, it's not lost on the outside world.''

According to *The Atlantic Monthly*, numerous demographic trends in the nation have conspired to make today's children apt to receive more toys from more people who have more money to spend than ever before. Notably, the magazine cites the increase in the number of remarriages following divorce as the factor that has increased the ratio of grandparents to children, which has in turn increased the ratio of presents to birthdays. Whatever the factors, the toy companies are delighted with the extra business potential.

In the late 1970s, 70 percent of all retail toy sales occurred in the fourth quarter. Today, fourth-quarter sales account for 60 percent of the total dollars spent on toy purchases. This is due in part to the tremendous success of the so-called toy supermarkets such as Toys R Us (25–30 percent market share, $5.510 billion in sales) and its clones, Child World, Kiddie City, and Children's Palace. These one-stop retail toy bazaars look more like warehouses than traditional toy stores. Through excellent pricing and promotional programs, these retail discount chains have helped extend traditional Christmas toy purchases to year-round consumer buying. Now toys are given for Mother's, Father's, and Valentine's Days; Chanukah; graduations, birthdays, and housewarmings; get-well gifts; Easter treats; and for "being good" days.

According to Toy Manufacturers of America, other contributors to the reproportioning of retail toy and game sales were the inflation levels and fuel shortages of the late 1970s, which caused people to stay at home. During those years there was an increase in the demand for toys and games by teens and adults. These "older kids" have not lost their enthusiasm for the industry, not only swelling the consumer age base but also causing a year-round search for toy and game entertainment.

Manufacturers were quick to take advantage of the consumer's appetite for products by expanding channels of distribution to include nontraditional outlets such as supermarkets, bookstores, hardware stores, and other magnet shopping places. Bookshops and larger drugstores often run ads for the most popular toys and games. Video games appear at video rental stores alongside feature motion pictures, and in record stores too. Toys are for sale at every turn in the road.

You're Only as Good as Your Latest Hit

The toy industry is like a target game. It is a business of hits and misses, booms and busts. When a company hits a bull's-eye with a major product, it can mean tremendous earnings that often translate into mass hirings, diversification through acquisition, category expansion, larger corporate showrooms at 200 Fifth Avenue, and exotic sports cars in the company's executive parking lot. When a company misses the mark with a major product, it can mean tremendous losses that translate into large-scale layoffs, sales of acquired assets to stave off financial ruin, reduction in product, smaller corporate showrooms in New York City, and great deals on used exotic sports cars.

A hit item can take a company from relative obscurity to stardom overnight. Fortunes and careers rise and fall on products with names like Teenage Mutant Ninja Turtles, Gnip Gnop, Ring Raiders, Barnyard Commandos, Cabbage Patch Kids, and Slime. Successful items mean a boom for jobbers and retailers, as well as for manufacturers and inventors. And just as quickly, the lack of strong product can reverse fortunes. "The industry is ever-changing, faddish, transitory, sometimes whimsical, sometimes volatile," states George R. Ditomassi, president of Milton Bradley. He compares it to the fashion industry, adding that "if you don't stay current in either you're dead in the water." George B. Volanakis, president and CEO of The Ertl Company, agrees with this assessment, saying that the toy industry is a fashion business whose well-being is subject to the whims of five-to-twelve-year-olds around the world.

"I think he gave a pretty accurate summation," says Matchbox Toys (USA) president Andy Gatto of Volanakis's statement. "But there is another aspect to the business, the huge number of dollars that are being spent by parents for preschool [five-year-olds and under] products, family games, and for categories where there is a great deal of parental influence."

Hasbro's Steve D'Aguanno, senior vice president of R&D, says that his group is mandated to "get up to the plate and try to hit the ball over the fence. We're not supposed to bunt to get on. We're not supposed to hit singles. We're supposed to hit home runs. We hope if we miss hitting a home run we'll get at least a double." He adds, however, "If this were the philosophy of your entire company, you would eventually go out of business, as we've seen in our industry. In this company there is a balance of divisions, which allows us to go for the long shots that have had the greatest potential for returning the profits we need to make the acquisitions and develop."

Lee Gelber, national sales manager for The Games Gang and former head of Invicta USA, says the toy industry is "small, incestuous, and at its best when it's entrepreneurial."

One of the most dramatic illustrations of the industry's volatility is the recent history of video games. In 1982 the retail sales of video games soared to $3 billion; within three years it was only $100 million. During this roller-coaster ride, Atari and Mattel were almost bankrupt and many other players were hurt just as much.

In the ashes of the first video wave, an aggressive Kyoto,

Japan, company, Nintendo, decided to develop a new generation of video games with superior controllers, play, and graphics. Founded a century ago as a manufacturer of playing cards, Nintendo rose rapidly to a prime position in 30 million American households (and 37 percent of all Japanese households). Not only did it capture an 80 percent share of the American video-game market, it also siphoned off so many consumer dollars that it ultimately accounted for 20 percent of the total toy industry's business. A look at the best-selling lists in the trade publication *Playthings* shows cartridges for the Nintendo Entertainment System dominating the top ten.

Thomas J. Kalinske, president of Universal Matchbox Group and a former Toy Manufacturers of America board chairman, says that it is always healthier for the industry when there is a balance of strong product lines among the companies. He likes to see ten or twelve product lines in the $20 million to $50 million range each year. In this way, everyone gets a piece of the action.

But blockbusters do not always translate into success in the toy industry. Many hit products have been so successful that they damaged a company beyond repair. The latex-faced Cabbage Patch Kids made independent Georgia artist Xavier Roberts a multimillionaire after he licensed the rights to Coleco. And what a masterful job Coleco did at selling them. We all saw the headlines about shortages of the dolls back in 1984. Remember the lady in Wilkes-Barre, Pennsylvania, who suffered a broken leg, and the other four who were injured, when some thousand or so people rushed a Zayre's store looking for the then-hard-to-get dolls? There were the five thousand shoppers who nearly rioted at a Hills Department Store in Charleston, West Virginia. And who can forget the mailman from Kansas City who flew to London to purchase one?

Coleco Industries, in spite of more than $1.5 billion in sales of Cabbage Patch Kids alone from 1983 to 1985, filed for protection from creditors under Chapter 11 of the federal Bankruptcy Act in July 1988. The company showed $384 million in assets, $540 million in liabilities. A few weeks after an attempted comeback at Toy Fair, in February 1989, the company ceased operations, writing the last page in its fifty-seven-year history. The remnants of Coleco can now be found adding to the revenues of industry giant Hasbro.

Experts agree that Coleco basically invested all its cabbage in one patch, and it could not overcome past bad debt that contributed to its downfall. In simple terms, there was no powerful new product in its line to pick up the slack when the doll sales fell off. Everything it attempted failed. Costly introductions such as Furskins, designed by Xavier Roberts, and a Rambo action figure line were quietly received by unimpressed consumers.

Selchow & Righter, in the midst of success with Trivial Pursuit, was put on the block and purchased by Coleco for $75 million in cash and notes in mid-1986. Trivial Pursuit's sales neared $400 million in the item's second year (1984); in 1983, sales of all board games in this category totaled only $142 million. The company's management did not know how to handle such success and overproduced the game. As sales slowed, there was a glut of games, which sat in S&R warehouses and on retail shelves. Today this past industry phenomenon is marketed by Parker Brothers.

Worlds of Wonder presents another case in point. The manufacturer of Teddy Ruxpin (invented by Neil Simmons of Alchemy II) earned $93 million in revenues and $8 million in profits in 1985, its first year, and more than $300 million by the end of its second year. Its public stock offering in June 1986 opened at $18 a share and within a few days shot up to $29 a share. Overnight, the company started by Donald Kingsborough, an ex-Atari executive, was worth $550 million, or sixty-five times earnings and almost six times sales. But alas, it turned out to be an Icarian flight.

Worlds of Wonder was "the hottest new company around,"

according to *Fortune* in March 1987. But by the end of that year, the "unbearable" had happened. The company was carrying a creditors' debt of more than $200 million and a tremendous inventory, and declared bankruptcy (Chapter 11) on December 21. "Worlds of Wonder has been in a world all its own," toy analyst Paul Valentine told *Toy & Hobby World* magazine.

Fortunately for Worlds of Wonder, a private investment group took over the company and installed savvy industry pro Josh Denham, former president of Mattel Electronics, at its helm as president and CEO. "We're going to manage the company financially," he said. "That means inventory and some risk management. The old company never tested anything and did no market research."

In the toy-and-game industry, the valued chief executives are those who can unhitch the horses when the wagon is thundering downhill. Riders may find high G-force ascents more enjoyable, but top executives agree that they must know all the angles to orchestrate a soft landing when the orders turn to vapor. Hasbro's late chairman and CEO, Stephen D. Hassenfeld, liked to remind people, "Product is king, but even the king must be managed."

Ertl president George B. Volanakis notes, "Those companies who survive this unstable consumer environment are those who masterfully manage its increases and decreases." Adds Worlds of Wonder CEO Josh Denham, "The difference between 50,000 over and 50,000 under in inventory can mean life or death."

As Dick Grey, president of Tyco Toys, puts it, "It's not difficult to take advantage of a trend when it's hot. What requires skill is to manage it down when the trade wants to walk away from it."

By Book or by Instinct

In 1989, according to *The New York Times*, 68,000 new MBAs graduated from American universities, and the toy industry gained its share. Some toy people feel that the case-study approach used in business schools is having a pernicious effect on the industry. One outspoken critic is former Kenner president Bernard Loomis. "Management must work to overcome the MBAs," he states. "The industry has had a sickness that American industry has, and it's managing earnings and working for Wall Street. At the root of it is this inability to run a company where the company wants to go in a natural way."

Loomis, now president of Bernard Loomis, Inc., a product development and management consulting company, continues, "The assumption that if the stack of paper is high enough an answer will come out of it is one of the most negative things that has ever happened. We've taken the best minds and we've talked them into going to business schools and they're coming out as automatons believing that research is the answer. There is a place for research, but it is not the guiding tool. You're not going to do research and identify what's new and different. You're going to get a good look at yesterday."

"Part of the way the MBA looks at it, I look at it," says Saul Jodel, executive vice president of marketing and R&D at Lewis Galoob Toys, who does strategic analysis in terms of market size, pricing, merchandising, and financial planning. "I think the split between the MBA and a guy like me is that the MBA operates out of a handbook and I'm still a toy person. I'm a toy person first. I look for good toy products and *then* I make sure that I figure out how those good toy products fit into the niche and how I can market them. And I also make sure—which is the MBA part of it—whether or not I'm going to make money at it."

Neal Kublan, a former senior vice president for R&D at Mego Toys, feels that because today there are a lot of "bean counters'' in control, ''the corporate guys take the easiest possible road. They don't want to be hassled. They want to get into budget, make a profit, and sleep nights. There are very few gutsy guys left in the business.''

Professional inventor Gary Piaget, once a vice president of R&D at Mego Toys, agrees with his former colleague and says that with the advent of the MBA into the industry, the traditional creative approach to product selection has all but disappeared, except for those few companies still run by visionaries. ''The change to the 'MBA approach' has limited creativity in an industry whose heart and soul is creative,'' he laments.

''We are no longer a product-oriented business,'' says Howard Wexler, inventor of Touche (Gabriel) and Wilson Stuffs (Lewco). ''We're more like give-me-a-good-package, give-me-a-hot-license . . . Batman or Care Bears . . . anything that already is in the public's eye.''

Inventor Eddy Goldfarb subscribes to the belief that picking a winner takes a certain intuition. Says Goldfarb, ''To get the gut feel, I think it takes a lot of experience. It takes working experience. If you're dealing with someone who has been an independent inventor, a buyer, or in sales and marketing—I think these people have a good feel and a lot of experience. But you just don't graduate with an MBA and then say you're going to choose product.''

Corporate R&D and marketing executives in the toy industry are called upon to make more new-product decisions in any one year than most of their counterparts in other businesses do in ten. Their minds and eyes are required to adjust to more new arrangements of colors, shapes, textures, dimensions, and proportions in any one year than most of their counterparts in other businesses do in twenty. It takes a special breed of executive to operate in this atmosphere of constant change, embellishment, and adornment. The most successful seem to project—mentally, physically, and vocally. They are guided more by instinct than by reason. They have that proverbial "golden gut." And, above all, they are people who see not only the promotable features of an item but also the magic that is innate in the most special products.

In what other industry would an executive approve the selling of empty boxes? "It certainly worked," beams Bernie Loomis, as he reflects with pride on his decision to ship empty boxes to toy stores in 1978 upon realizing that Kenner would not have its Star Wars product ready for Christmas. "I said to myself, hey, the kid is going to get a lot of things Christmas Day. I am going to give him the prettiest picture of Star Wars and I am going to make a deal with his parents, not with the child: Pay me for the figures and we will deliver them before the end of May; and I limited the sale to 500,000 units. The parents read it and understood it." Loomis's scheme worked, the empty boxes blew off the shelves, and one of the most gutsy marketing gambles of any industry went into the history books. "If there is any genius involved, it is the genius of being able to function alone and make a decision," suggests Loomis.

Another example of marketing finesse was exhibited when Tyco Toys introduced a new multimillion-dollar line of toys called Dino Riders the day after Christmas! That's right: after Santa had gone home. That was 1987, and, according to Neil Werde, marketing director for the product, the company felt that it was worth the risk because after Christmas there would be less advertising clutter to cut through on the tube, and the cost of media would be a fraction of what it would have been the week before Christmas. Tyco Toys was able to do a two-minute animated TV spot and air it for the price of a sixty-second commercial. In addition, kids have lots of buying choices the day after Christmas. There are gifts to be returned and exchanged and gifts of money they can go out and spend. Werde says the innovative scheme moved $3 million worth of product in the first quarter of 1988. The first full year, the company did $48 million worth of Dino Riders.

So, even in recent years, with the industry in turmoil, daring ideas have been known to pay off handsomely. Yet in the past, single new-product concepts launched entire companies. There are dozens of inspiring inventor stories that show how timely ideas were used to establish businesses or expand lines dramatically through creativity and imagination. It is very unlikely, however, that in the 1990s, an industry so bound to million-dollar promotional budgets, expensive tooling, complicated financial statements, convoluted distribution, and aggressive offshore competition will allow the most creative and entrepreneurial inventors to match these birthing stories of the past.

Queen of Fashion

Why not a plastic fashion doll for girls? Ruth Handler asked herself. And what if we gave it breasts? Ruth was president of the Mattel Toy Company, which she cofounded with her husband, Elliot, in 1945. She answered her own question with a five-ounce, eleven-and-a-half-inch-tall, epitome-of-fashion doll that she named after their daughter, Barbie.

Ruth Handler observed that out of all her daughter's dolls, Barbie most enjoyed playing with shapely paper dolls, those that she could gussy up in different fashions. In the mid-1950s, the only doll available in the U.S. market was a baby doll, to whom little girls pretended to be mommy. But Barbie Handler was doing something quite different. She was pretending to be a hip teenager who got "all dolled up" and went to high school proms and sock hops. Ruth felt that proverbial light bulb go on.

Barbie has been "in the pink" since she made her debut back in 1959, and so have all the toy stores that display shelf upon shelf of her distinctive packaging. But anyone who was solely responsible for generating $700 million, or over half of Mat-

tel's annual earnings, also would share that success glow. A
Barbie doll is sold every two seconds. As Tom Castle, a toy
buyer for the Broadway Department Store in Los Angeles, told
Toys, Hobbies & Crafts magazine, "Barbie is more than just a
doll, it's a system. The others are just dolls; they simply can't
beat the system."

Pretty good for a gal who can't even stand on her own two
feet—they are permanently shaped for high-heeled shoes. And
speaking of shoes, Barbie's feet have slipped in and out of more
than 1,200,000 pairs of them in her fashionable career.

Today Mattel sells more than twenty million Barbie fashions annually, making the manufacturer the largest producer
of women's wear in the world. More than 250 million Barbie
fashions have been sold since the doll's introduction to the
trade. According to Mattel, this adds up to more than seventy-
five million yards of fabric. No surprise: More than 500 million
Barbies and her playmate dolls have been sold worldwide in
the past thirty years. Placed head to toe, they would circle the
earth three and a half times. Ninety percent of the girls aged
three to eleven in the United States own at least one Barbie
doll.

The world's second-largest toy company, Mattel employs
five full-time fashion designers to keep Barbie, the undisputed
queen of glamour dolls, dressed in the *dernier cri*. Her apparel
is enough to turn any clotheshorse green and includes unique
fashions custom-made for her petite frame by some of the
world's best-known haute-couture designers.

There is the rub, for Mattel's fortune was made not in doll
sales. It entered the gates of heaven (pink gates, no doubt) by
selling Barbie's fashion and nonfashion accessories. Hemlines
up. Hemlines down. The total look. Pizzazz. Mystique. Working zippers. Tiny buttons. Real fabrics. Satin linings. That's
what generated the money. After all, what stylish and attractive teenager in a consumer-oriented, prosperous, and up-
wardly mobile society can get along with just one outfit?

Girls role-played and fantasized with Barbie as a stand-in for themselves. Every little girl wanted to have the "Barbie look." Moms got caught up in it all and eagerly paid $3 or $4 for outfits for their daughters' $3 dolls. Imagine the Handlers' glee. If a kid could persuade Mom to buy ten Barbie dresses, that amounted to about twelve times the cost of one Barbie doll.

The fashion accessory that sells best is a wedding gown for the ever-single Barbie—more than five million gowns since 1959. Barbie's endless array of nonfashion accessories includes the Dream House, MovieTime Prop Shop, Ferrari, Beach Blast, Pool and Patio, Step 'n Style Boutique, '57 Chevy, Surf 'n Shop, Soda Shoppe, Beauty Bath, and thousands of others that have come and gone over the years. In 1989, Mattel offered more than 250 individual Barbie packages, including fifty-nine different dolls, 153 new fashions, and forty-three accessories.

The world of Barbie also includes such specialized dolls as Day-to-Night Barbie, Dreamtime Barbie, Peaches 'n Cream Barbie, Great Shape Barbie, Sun Gold Malibu Barbie, Super Hair Barbie, Horse Lovin' Barbie, Ice Capades Barbie, and Barbie and the Rockers—to name but a few. Of course, there is also Ken (introduced in 1961 and named after the Handlers' son), as well as other companion dolls. While Barbie's first sidekicks—Skipper, Midge, and so on—are still around, newer friends have names that the next generation can relate to more easily, such as Nikki, Kayla, Courtney, Steven, Christie, and even Miko and Nia. Barbie always moves with the times.

In March 1989, the best-known fashion doll ever created, and one of the most popular toys of all time, turned thirty. And she has never looked prettier. Barbie's not getting older, she's getting better. Sales have never slowed. Time and again, other toy manufacturers have attempted to grab some of Barbie's precious market share. Most recently, Hasbro launched Jem and the Holograms, a fashion doll designed around the MTV look. Mattel hit back with Barbie and the Rockers. Bye-bye, Jem. "Barbie can move over with flankers and counter anyone's move," says Bill Dohrmann of Tiger Games.

Barbie was not always universally embraced by the trade. In fact, when the first non–flat-chested doll with rooted Saran hair, earrings, and individually painted red fingernails was introduced, Sears, Roebuck, then the nation's largest toy retailer, didn't order a single one. But after the initial 35,000 dolls that hit the market sold instantly, the love affair with the Barbie doll never flagged.

Barbie products have sold more than $1 billion at retail. Even when Cabbage Patch Kid fever was at its height, the stylish and attractive Barbie outsold it. At one time, the leading lady of fashion dolls, through her fan club, reportedly received more than 10,000 letters a week from children around the world. Only Shirley Temple received more!

In 1986, Mattel started producing limited porcelain editions of Barbie, and each year 25,000 of the dolls are offered to collectors at a pricey $200.

Blown up proportionately to human dimensions, Barbie would chart 33-18-31½ and stand five feet nine inches tall, more than half of that in shapely legs. At thirty-two she is still a perfect size 10. But this is no surprise. It's all by design.

The All-American Hero

Inspired by Barbie's tremendous success, executives at Hasbro 3,000 miles away in Rhode Island thought that if girls liked such a highly accessorized fashion doll, maybe boys would like the submission from Stan Weston, then president of Weston Merchandising Corporation. Weston was representing the concept of a friend, independent inventor Larry Reiner: a line of military dolls, designed to scale, including wearing apparel and vehicles.

At 1964's Toy Fair, in a bold leadership move, Hasbro president Merrill Hassenfeld introduced the line of boy dolls under the trademark G.I. Joe. There were four characters: Action Soldier; Action Sailor; Action Marine; and Action Pilot. Almost a foot tall and carrying authentic equipment from head to toe, the item had twenty-one movable parts and was hyped as "America's Movable Fighting Man."

Just as the trade initially was slow to warm up to Mattel's Barbie, toy-store owners were hesitant to join the ranks of G.I. Joe's retail forces. The item contradicted the popular concept of boys' toys—it was widely held that parents would not purchase dolls for their sons—and the trade did not want to invest in such an iffy product. But Hassenfeld stuck to his howitzers, and the first year Hasbro sold more than $30 million worth of G.I. Joes (two million dolls) and accessories. Today, two out of three American boys own a G.I. Joe.

Hasbro, which unseated Mattel several years ago to become the world's largest toy company, has to date sold nearly 200 million G.I. Joes—including more than 230 different G.I. Joe action figures and 100 million of his tanks, trucks, and planes—for an estimated $1.2 billion, or, according to the *Wall Street Journal*, the equivalent of Austria's annual defense budget. If you take into account all of the G.I. Joe ancillary products, such as videos, shoes, games, puzzles, clothes, and comic books, Hasbro says the retail sales are closer to $2 billion. In 1989 alone, the Pawtucket, Rhode Island, toy firm racked up sales of Joe and his line extensions totaling over $180 million—putting it among the year's top five best-selling toys and ranking Hasbro as the world's largest manufacturer of military equipment.

But things were not always so green. Joe sales fell off in the late 1960s, with the growing unpopularity of the Vietnam War. In fact, he was almost removed from the line. Hasbro moved with the times, however, and kept him alive by quietly converting the World War II groundpounder into a rugged adventurer. Instead of making reconnaissance patrols, he began to go on missions to encounter lost treasure. The strategy worked, and G.I. Joe was back in action.

In 1978, America's defender met an enemy he could not handle. Boys turned to new, space-age heroes such as Luke Skywalker, R2D2, C-3PO, and the menacing Darth Vader in Kenner's Star Wars line. Combined with the higher price of plastics brought on by the oil crisis, Hasbro was forced to furlough its original G.I. Joe.

Then in 1982, as the Reagan administration built up America's military strength and Rambo dominated the silver screen, G.I. Joe burst back onto the retail battlefield a lot shorter (3¾ inches) and a lot market-wiser. Hasbro introduced two Joe assortments consisting of eleven figures, including nine different Joes and two figures from the enemy camp, COBRA Command. This 1980s Joe could fly high over danger by means of a twin-rocket Jet Pak, race into battle on his Rapid-Fire motorcycle, and defend his troops with Attack Cannons. By 1985, "The Adventures of GI Joe" was a half-hour animated television series, and his fan club boasted more than 130,000 members. The line was expanded with such enemies as the Crimson Twins, Zartan the Enemy, and vehicles such as his COBRA F.A.N.G. (Fully Armed Negator Gyrocopter). Each year Hasbro introduces to the line over twenty different action figures and over twenty different vehicles, plus an abundance of G.I. Joe complementary items.

Almost five years to the day younger than Barbie, G.I. Joe celebrated his twenty-fifth birthday in February 1989. Together these two items account for more than 700 million dolls, or nearly three times the number of people in the United States.

Realistic Replicas

Until World War II, most American farmers used horses to plow and harvest their fields; tractors were expensive. But during the war, the United States required increased grain production and farmers needed tractors. The importance of this second revolution in American agriculture did not go unnoticed by at least one highly talented and imaginative individual. His artful touch and the end of World War II brought another new line of products to toy stores. This one came from America's heartland.

It was a frigid winter when the first Ertl tractor replicas were created in 1945 by an immigrant German journeyman molder named Fred Ertl, Sr. A ten-week labor dispute in the Mississippi River town of Dubuque, Iowa, had cost him his livelihood, and he decided that he no longer wanted to work for someone else. He and his family decided to go it alone in the true American way. Since then, The Ertl Company has grown from literally a mom-and-pop operation to become the world's largest manufacturer of farm equipment and trucks. It produces more farm tractors than every tractor company combined, and more trucks than the largest truck manufacturer. The Ertl Company is recognized as the only manufacturer that makes miniature replicas of farm equipment based upon original blueprints from such giants as John Deere, Allis-Chalmers, Ford, International Harvester, and Massey Ferguson.

Fred Ertl began by assessing his skills and the way they could be utilized best. Over the years he had made toys for his five children—partly for economic reasons but also because he liked doing it—so he thought that might be a rewarding and enjoyable undertaking for the entire family. With the John Deere farm-equipment company opening a plant on the outskirts of town, and understanding the increasing importance of "tractorpower," Ertl decided to launch his business by making toy farm equipment. He intuitively felt certain that children would want toy replicas of farm tractors.

Fred and Gertrude Ertl and their children began manufacturing the replicas from war-surplus aluminum aircraft pistons in the basement of their home. He melted the metal in a furnace and poured it into sand molds, the sons assembled the tractors, and Gertrude Ertl painted them by hand. Today, approximately 250 sets of hands are required to produce a one-sixteenth-scale tractor from start to finish.

Within four years of going into business for himself, Ertl had secured a contract with John Deere to make replicas, relocated to a building in town, incorporated, and was producing about 5,000 toys a day. At full capacity, The Ertl Company now can make 1,200 toy tractors in one hour, 9,600 in one day, and almost 50,000 in a week. Each year it uses 1.75 million pounds of steel, 100,000 pounds of wire for axles and shafts, and 26,000 gallons of paint.

For forty-five years, The Ertl Company has been producing the world's finest exact-replica tractor toys. Thousands of its farm toy models are on display today at the National Farm Toy Museum, which opened in April 1986 in Dyersville, Iowa. There is lots of money not only in making the tractors but also in collecting and trading them among the tens of thousands of tractor replica collectors. At an auction in Dyersville, for example, more than $50,000 changed hands among several hundred collectors. One gold-plated Ertl John Deere 630LP replica sold for $2,500.

Unreal Real Estate

Billions of dollars, pesos, schillings, cruzeiros, drachmas, guilders, francs, lire, rupees, rands, kroners, and escudos have been made and lost over it in a few short hours. It has landed people in jail from Argentina to Finland to India to the People's Republic of China and forced them into bankruptcy, with no choice but to turn over all of their assets to a hardhearted landlord. People have met, fallen in love, and married over it—and who knows how many arguments it has caused?

It, of course, is Parker Brothers' "Real Estate Trading Game," Monopoly, perhaps the most famous board game the world has ever seen. Who could fail to recognize the origin of that familiar imperative, "Pass Go, Collect $200"? An estimated 250 million players have "passed Go." And where else but in Monopoly would going to jail be a welcome respite from an exorbitant rent bill?

Since it began publishing the game, Parker Brothers has "constructed" more than 3.2 billion little green houses, making the Beverly, Massachusetts, manufacturer the largest housing developer in the world.

Monopoly is marketed in eighty countries and has been translated into twenty-two languages. In most cases, the property locations take the name of local real estate—Boardwalk becomes Mayfair in the British edition, Rue de la Paix in French, Paseo del Prado in Spanish, and Schlossallee in German. Once banned in the Soviet Union as being "too capitalist," Monopoly is now played by Russians "building" little hotels and trying to "get out of jail" quickly. Their comrades in the Caribbean, the Cubans, however, have not been introduced to the joys of Monopoly; all known sets were ordered seized and destroyed by Fidel Castro, who denounced the game as "symbolic of an imperialistic and capitalistic system."

Monopoly, which has sold well over 100 million copies worldwide, is attributed to the genius of Charles B. Darrow, an unemployed heating engineer from Germantown, Pennsylvania. In 1933, during the Great Depression, Darrow came up with the game as a substitute for the entertainment he could not afford while on a visit to nearby Atlantic City, New Jersey. We say "attributed to" Darrow because game historians have pointed to a woman named Lizzie Magie, who created and patented something called The Landlord's Game. Magie's board is even reported to have featured a "Go to Jail" space. Parker Brothers executive Phil Orbanes, author of "The Monopoly Companion," writes, "Strictly speaking, Monopoly got its start the day Elizabeth Magie began to sell her Landlord's Game in 1904." Although her game was not a commercial success, Orbanes points out that it did find its way into the economics departments of colleges and that "at one—or all—of these schools arose the improvements that transformed The Landlord's Game into Monopoly."

It is, however, Darrow who created the game as we know it today. In hopes of licensing the game, he took it to Parker Brothers in 1934, but they passed. It took too long to play, the rules were too complicated, and players kept going around and around the board instead of ending up at a final goal. It was rejected as having "fifty-two fundamental playing errors." Undeterred, Darrow proceeded on his own to publish and market the product. When reports of the game's success began to reach Parker Brothers, the company reconsidered, and licensed the rights early in 1935. Subsequently, Charles B. Darrow retired a millionaire at the age of forty-six. The first inventor to make a million dollars from a game, he became a world traveler and a collector of exotic orchid species.

Monopoly was the biggest thing that had ever hit Parker Brothers. Sales of the game skyrocketed, and by mid-February 1935, the plant was producing 20,000 sets a week, a great number even by today's standards. Before Christmas that first year, so many telegraphed orders had poured in that they were filed in oversized laundry baskets and stacked in the hallways. With an ever-increasing backlog of requests, a bookkeeping firm in Boston was summoned to help keep things in order. As Parker Brothers tells the story, the firm's representatives took one look and refused the job, no matter what the price.

Despite the public's initial reaction, the company viewed Monopoly as an adult fad game that would sell for about three years. Certainly it was too complicated for children. And just as expected, sales soon began to level off. On December 19, 1936, instructions came from George Parker himself to "cease absolutely to make any more boards or utensil boxes. . . . We will stop making Monopoly against the possibility of a very early slump." But, then, as is often the case in the fickle game business, sales went up again, and the upward spiral has never stopped. Three million games were sold in 1989!

Unmatched Miniatures

Detroit, Michigan, is indisputably one of the world's greatest industrial centers. But its self-proclaimed title as Automobile Capital of the World is questionable. Moonachie, New Jersey, a borough of 2,706 strong with no national ranking worth mentioning, easily overshadows the so-called Motor City and every other global industrial city when it comes to motor-vehicle production.

A multinational enterprise with its own indoor test track, located in a two-story warehouse a short walk from the Teterboro Airport, assembles more motor vehicles than Ford, Honda, BMW, Mercedes-Benz, Jaguar, Volvo, Volkswagen, Subaru, or any other manufacturer. It even outproduces the powerful General Motors.

Richard Maddocks, then a senior designer at Matchbox in England, says that in the late '60s and early '70s the East London facility was producing one million vehicles per day to fill a worldwide market. But the vehicles caused no overcrowding of highways or city streets, no gridlock. They released not a single molecule of harmful pollution. And not a single vehicle was engaged in an accident. Because none is more than three inches long.

Now amusing its third generation of consumers, Matchbox Toys (USA) originated from a British partnership originally

known as Lesney Products, a brand name forged from a combination of the owners' names. World War II veterans Leslie
Smith and Rodney Smith (not related) started with an investment of £600, or about $1,000. It was all they had left of their
service pay.

During the summer of 1947, the two mates, who had served
together in the Royal Navy, bought an old bombed-out pub
called The Rifleman, near London. But they never poured a
single tankard of Guinness. They equipped the place with surplus government die-casting machines and poured molten metal
to produce industrial zinc castings.

Like many involved in the die-casting business at that time,
the Smiths needed a proprietary product to pick up the slack
during slow periods. When Queen Elizabeth II ascended to the
throne in 1952, they crafted a one-sixteenth-inch replica of her
gilded processional coach and its team of horses. Faster than
you could say Buckingham Palace, the toy sold a million pieces.
Soon die-cast miniatures of cement mixers, quarry trucks, die-
sel road rollers, dumpers, and double-decker buses were selling
to the likes of Woolworth. In 1953, the celebrated I-75 series
was established, and one year later, the company began using
Matchbox as its trademark and packaging its micro-machines
in distinctive yellow cartons the size of a matchbox.

Just about every vehicle you can imagine has now been
immortalized in the Matchbox line—from the Model A and
the Lamborghini Countach to the Blue Bird school bus and
the Kenworth big rig. Yes. Even your father's Oldsmobile.
Thanks to Matchbox, everyone can own a piece of driving
history. Kids and adults are equally attracted to cars, and
Matchbox keeps the price within everyone's reach. The company believes dreams should never be expensive.

Building Blockbusters

People who enjoy crunching numbers have estimated that between 200 and 300 million children and adults play or have played with Lego building blocks. Sold in more than 60,000 stores in about 115 countries, the Lego idea is universal: The company estimates that kids around the world spend about five billion hours a year playing with Lego blocks.

Founded in 1932 in Billund, a Danish hamlet on the Jutland moors, by Ole Kirk Christiansen, a carpenter and joiner who was forced out of work by the Depression, Lego Systems now comprises twenty-one sales companies, five manufacturing companies, and three tooling shops throughout the world. Christiansen named his toys Lego as a contraction of *leg godt*, which in Danish means "play well." He later discovered that Lego also has a Latin meaning—"I assemble."

When Beijing's gray eminence, Deng Xiaoping, visited the United States in 1979, one of the few things he took home was sets of Lego building blocks for his grandchildren. The toy was also high on Raisa Gorbachev's shopping list when she visited New York City in 1988.

In a $45 million building housing the Massachusetts Institute of Technology's Media Laboratory in Cambridge, Lego modules built in the form of robots, vehicles, and merry-go-rounds are connected directly to Apple II computers via special sensors and actuators. Using Logo, the popular computer language for children devised by MIT mathematician Seymour A. Papert, youngsters learn to bring Lego creations to life, causing gears to move, wheels to rotate, and lights to illuminate. The American Institute of Architects uses Lego bricks in design competitions. Author Norman Mailer reportedly has a 15,000-brick "city of the future" in the living room of his Brooklyn apartment. Mailer has even been known to drive to the company's Enfield, Connecticut, facility to pick up elements he wanted.

When presented with piles of the colorful blocks for the first time, primitive tribesmen from the deepest rain forests of the Brazilian Amazon to the Australian outback knew instinctively how to build with them.

It's not very difficult to understand why the plastic bricks are so loved by both parents and children. They fulfill even the most exacting parent's standard for a toy: Kids cannot break them, they're nontoxic, and they have multiple incidental learning values. Above all, Legos satisfy three fundamental juvenile proclivities—to construct, to play, and to demolish.

The world's largest manufacturer of bricks and building elements, Lego Systems, Inc., has no equal. Approximately eleven billion are produced each year—or enough bricks to circle the globe fourteen times and ring up about half a billion dollars in sales. Nearly 100 million homes worldwide have Lego toys. In the United States, Lego products can be seen in 50 percent of all households; in Europe, the number is closer to 80 percent.

In 1958, the stud-and-tube clutching principle that we know today was patented by Ole's son, Godtfred Kirk Christiansen. As a result, a brick manufactured back in 1958 will fit any element made in 1990. More than 1,200 pieces and elements are fully compatible with each other. The creative possibilities boggle the mind. For example, you can take six eight-stud bricks of the same color and put them together in almost 103 million different ways (102,981,500, to be exact!).

"Give a child permission to create and it will build a world far richer and more imaginative than anyone would dream of," said Lego founder Ole Christiansen. He did just that, and children prove him right every day.

Back to the Future

Such stories of megahits sustaining entire toy companies are part of industry lore. Our snippets of toy legends—the lithesome teenage queen, the muscular all-American hero, the buy/build/bank-a-fortune game, miniature vehicles, and multifaceted blocks—provide a flavor of the industry's past. But what does the future have in store for the toy industry?

"It will always be bright," suggests toy analyst David Leibowitz. "There will always be a Christmas and there are always going to be children. The children of America aren't going to be denied and children around the world aren't going to be denied."

From this bullish forecast, one might conclude that there will always be a Barbie, a G.I. Joe, a real estate game, diecast wheeled miniatures, and creative blocks. Indeed, inventing pros regularly use their special talents to reinterpret the best of such classic playthings with contemporary flair. With a tweak here, a living hinge there, variants of classic playthings are redesigned to accommodate the tastes of future kiddie consumers.

For the toy executives responsible for choosing future hit products, there may be comfort and confidence tying selections to past successes. They know that in the toy market of the 1990s, a fizzle could lead to the financial tremors that shut down powers such as CBS, Coleco, Gabriel, Knickerbocker, Kusan, Lakeside, Mego, Schaper, Selchow & Righter, Skilcraft, LJN, and Ideal.

They know, too, that some of the marketplace fizzles stem from a whole gamut of distractions unknown when the first Barbies, G.I. Joes, and Legos reached toyland. Video, CDs, game cartridges, audiocassettes, fashionware, and other non-toy fads are competing for many of the same disposable dollars previously earmarked for toys and games. To maintain and expand their share of those purchase dollars, toy people are looking for all the innovations that technology and inventiveness can deliver in new playthings.

The manufacturing and marketing of toys and games has long been a fast-track business. It is an industry that is contagious, one with a glamour that attracts and holds a core group of "toy people." Key among this group are the independent developers, who know that their best products are yet to come. Once they've been bitten by the bug, few opt to leave the industry. Jack Morrissey, vice president of sales at TSR, sums up the affliction: "It's like the roach motel: Once you check in, you don't check out."

4 Santa, Take My Idea . . . Please

HOW A CONCEPT IS SOLD

Professional inventors have paid their dues and established track records and thus can get the attention of R&D and marketing executives. Experience and success have given them the savvy and leverage to open the right doors. Many were "insiders" themselves, before opting to take their shows on the road.

But even professional inventors, with the strongest product concepts, represented by the most attractive, functional prototypes, still find numerous barriers to selling their latest ideas. As inventors, they speculate with time and money to bring an item to the sales stage. Then the challenge is to get a manufacturer sufficiently enthused to make the investment and commitment to take a product into the marketplace.

Knowing how to sell original concepts to the toy industry is almost as important a skill as inventing itself. Luck can go just so far. The most successful inventors know how to sell their ideas; they have to show a vision and sell expectation. Selling is not an easy or polished art for most inventors; they have been trained as designers, artists, engineers, or marketers, not as experts in the art of hard sell or sales dynamics. But they become the consummate commission representatives. If they don't make their sales goals or reach their quotas, they simply do not remain independent inventors. Perhaps these creative people couldn't sell real estate, used cars, or term insurance. But the winners find ways to weave paths around the barriers to place product year after year.

D. H. Lawrence once observed, "A picture lives with the life you put into it. If you put no life into it—no thrill, no concentration of delight or exaltation of visual discovery—then the picture is dead, no matter how much thorough and scientific work is put into it." And so it is in selling a new toy or game concept. The idea often moves in direct proportion to the depth to which it is felt by the inventor, and to his ability to instill that feeling in the "lookers."

Professional Inventors

Professional inventors must get a manufacturer to commit to their ideas in a timely manner. If an inventor is unable to close the deal, the idea remains only that—an unfulfilled dream destined to remain pinned to the drawing board, stored on the shelf, or locked in the closet. However strong the concept, whatever the investment of time and resources, the payback only comes with advance check, signed contract, and production shot all in hand.

Pros understand that it takes so much more than a good concept to make the sale. This is a business of taste, personalities, and dramatic market fluctuations. All kinds of factors go into whether or not a manufacturer will accept or reject a concept. How many? "A zillion," responds Elliot Rudell. "Is it a good toy? Can it be made at a profit? What else is out there? Is the category hot? Does the manufacturer want to do something unique or just follow the herd?"

Bob Fuhrer cites originality, play value, timing, extendability, and the track record of the inventor as important factors. Eddy Goldfarb believes that an inventor has to get the manufacturer to focus on the current market. "The biggest obstacle I find when I show a product is that someone will say, 'We had an item something like that or in that category twenty-two years ago that didn't sell,' " he notes.

"There are too many committee members in-house eager to fault any outside submission," says fifty-six-year industry veteran Ray Lohr, holder of more than a hundred patents and a major contributor to the Big Wheel bicycle (while working for Marx Toys).

Tony Miller, senior vice president of R&D at Tonka, says, "There is no good reason for things turning out the way they do. A totally stupid idea may successfully run the gauntlet and make it into production, while really good product ideas may be seen and rejected by twenty-five companies."

"The parameters for product are really broad. For every great concept that has ever been done, there have been legitimate reasons why not to do it,"says Steve D'Aguanno, senior vice president of R&D at Hasbro. "Cabbage Patch Kids were ugly dolls and research told us they were ugly dolls and therefore they shouldn't sell. I am not going to give you rules. You can be made a fool of too easily by following them," he confesses. "On the most simplistic level, I first ask myself if the product excites me," he continues. "Do I have to overintellectualize something—to say, hey, that's a good idea? I want it to hit me. It has to be an emotional response."

Asked what makes a great product, Playskool president Steven Schwartz answers, "It depends what kind of product you are talking about, a great basic product or a great promotional product. On Transformers or a phenomenon like Cabbage Patch Kids, you've got to catch the wave. You just have to be at the right place at the right time. I would like to say as a marketing person that you make the wave, but I think there has to be something there before you get to market. Then great marketing people push the envelop all the way on it.''

Of Hasbro's megasuccess Transformers, Schwartz said he had picked up information that an imported toy from Japan called Diachron was selling very well in a couple of small stores in New York City. When he saw it, he thought it just had magic. ''I think we forecasted $20 million the first year and ended up doing $100 million. There was no testing of the concept whatsoever. We put that program together in three months,'' recalls Schwartz.

Fit the Puzzle

There are differing views among independent inventors about ''product fit.'' When an inventor invents, does he invent for a specific manufacturer? According to inventor Paul Gruen, this is the primary factor. He will study a company's product line and try to design a concept that is a fit and/or an extension of its current product line. ''However,'' Gruen says, ''because the 'outside' inventor is just that—outside—it is often difficult to accurately determine the current needs and future plans of the manufacturer.''

On the other hand, Vic Reiling prefers to design in a black hole. He doesn't want to stifle his creativity or second-guess manufacturers' marketing plans. If a concept is good, it will sell. If it isn't a fit with a particular company, that company may see its potential and make it fit, or he will take it elsewhere.

Judy Blau feels that some companies are so tied into conservative marketing plans that they are afraid to try something new. She states, ''Some of the most successful products were rejected for years before they were accepted. They just didn't fit the thinking of management at the time of initial showing and they needed to make a comeback when directions/plans were different.''

Marty Abrams, former president of Mego Toys and now head of Abram/Gentile Entertainment, the product development company responsible for the Power Glove (Mattel), cautions against looking at a manufacturer's product line for inspiration. Says Abrams, ''You cannot go into a toy store to see what they're doing because if you do, you'll wind up knocking what's already there. The only way to be a success in this business is to design away from what exists in the business.''

Other pros are advocates of a strong market awareness before taking time to refine and push a latest creation at a manufacturer.

''One thing that used to bother the hell out of me was to have an inventor come in and waste a lot of my time showing me something I felt he never should have spent time on in the first place,'' says Mel Taft of his days as senior vice president for R&D at Milton Bradley. He tells attendees at a Toy Fair seminar, ''I tried to be courteous, but I would have loved to have said, 'For God's sake, would you go out and do a little homework, and then you wouldn't come in and try to sell me this. . . .' ''

Staple lines provide the foundation for most companies and clear targets of opportunity for outside inventors. For example, Mattel will always be looking to accessorize and refresh Barbie; Ohio Art wants to continue extending its Etch-A-Sketch line; Hasbro's G.I. Joe requires new and innovative battle vehicles and accessories; and there can't be too many Nerf sports for Parker Brothers.

The ''hit'' mentality makes the industry one of dramatic new directions. Some companies turn on a dime; others turn like the *Queen Mary*. But sooner or later, they all turn. Change and new products are as inevitable in this business as the coming Christmas season. It may have been planned as part of a long-range goal or it could have been caused by seeing the right product at the right time. All it takes is support of a "hot button" opportunity and the right set of circumstances to make a company react.

"I think if you can anticipate where the market is in terms of clutter and you can be innovational and not in the pack, you've got a lot better chance than fighting to split up the pie," exclaims Galoob's Saul Jodel. "I constantly look for niche businesses," Jodel continues. "If somebody's doing boys' transformers, I don't look for another way to do boys' transformers. I look for a category that was a success at one time or if I have the right idea I can make a success. And I look to be in places where the other guys aren't."

There is a very fine line when it comes to the new directions a company will take, as opposed to remaining on a conservative course. The most surprising moves usually seem very logical in retrospect. Take Milton Bradley's entry into the toy market with electronic Star Bird, Simon, Battleship, and others, in the late 1970s and early 1980s. It surprised a lot of people. After all, Milton Bradley up to then was exclusively a manufacturer of board games.

In fact, the company had accumulated in-house expertise in microelectronics that few other companies had at that time. It made perfect sense for Milton Bradley to decide to put its electronic capabilities to work building a strong category where no other toy company had such expansive plans.

The most successful inventors develop an innate sense about whom to approach with what product, and where the fit is most appropriate from a market and trade position. And if they stray from a company's "wish list" or obvious marketing strategy, they must be prepared with very convincing arguments to get a manufacturer to make a midcourse change.

Hitch Up with a Champ

Every product needs one or more champions inside a company, people who have the dedication to ensure its survival, give it the care and feeding it requires, and see it through to becoming a viable commercial force.

"The more senior the champion, the more likely the product is to be successful," advises Matchbox president Andy Gatto. When asked in which department the independent inventor is likely to find the best champion for a product, Gatto responds that it depends on whether the company is marketing-driven or R&D-driven. "The industry as a whole, I would say, is marketing-driven."

Woody Browne, vice president of marketing at Tyco Toys, says, "The champion could be in R&D, but it's very much more difficult. If you don't have a champion in marketing, the toy is going to have a rough road." He explains that two weeks after a product first has been seen by management, "in the cold light of day, it's the marketing champion who says, 'Hey, this is still terrific!' "

The pros know the importance of champions. According to Marc Segan, developer of Kawasaki musical instruments (Remco), "Without one, the concept can wither even after a deal is done. If you have someone in R&D or marketing who really believes in the concept, you have someone more likely to shepherd it every step along the way."

"In the last five or six years, most companies have put people into an area called inventor relations," says Larry Jones, president of Cal R&D. "They collect material from different inventors and present it all at once to top executives. The president or the VP of marketing walks around the room and looks at thirty items on the table in ten minutes. The guy says, 'OK, this is pretty good. What's this thing?' The inventor-relations guy says, 'I don't know, it's from so and so.' That's a hell of a way to risk your livelihood." Jones says he still has contacts with inventor-relations people, but he'd rather talk to the very top people. Many pros share his attitude.

Derek Gable, creator of Masters of the Universe while at Mattel and now an independent inventor, claims that there are screeners within some of the major manufacturers who do not have sensitivity to product at a concept or early idea stage: "If you have a screener who doesn't fully understand your concept, there is little chance that your concept will be represented properly to the other decision-makers within the company."

According to Julie Cooper, a former product development and marketing executive at Ideal Toy and now an independent inventor, "Sometimes R&D loves an item when we present it, but when it is presented to marketing internally, they may not like it. This can be very frustrating. When presenting from the outside of an organization, it would be helpful to have internal representation from across the decision-making departments."

The Right Time

Timing is another crucial factor in successful product placement. The casual inventor or those unfamiliar with the toy industry often approach a manufacturer at midyear with the expectation that the item will be ready by Christmas. This belief shows naivete about the business. The new-product process runs a full year ahead of a Yule season. Ideas presented in mid-April will not make it to stores until Christmas a year later. Toys and games promoted to consumers in December have been bought by the retailers at the February Toy Fair months earlier.

The industry operates on a sales cycle built around showing new product at the American International Toy Fair in New York each February. Although there are occasional exceptions, manufacturers gear their product development primarily to this keystone event and have timing requirements for outside idea submissions.

The closer it is to Toy Fair, the shorter the lead time to design, engineer, and plan a new concept. Whenever the "go" decision is made, the goal usually is to ship the finished product as soon as possible after Toy Fair. The less time a manufacturer has before the Toy Fair, the later the post–Toy Fair shipments. Paper and cardboard products normally have shorter development and production cycles than complex plastic-intensive toys or sophisticated electronic items. Manufacturers often "close their lines"—i.e., cease seeking and selecting new ideas for the coming year—in early summer, and they focus on execution in order to meet shipping dates for new products in the year ahead.

On the whole, inventors who come through the door in the last quarter of any year are not carrying introductions for the coming February Toy Fair. Rather, they are fueling the Toy Fair fourteen months away.

Parker Brothers likes to finalize product twelve to eighteen months before its introduction. Chris Campbell, director of acquisition, says that his 1991 spring/summer items will ship by October or November of 1990 and that Christmas 1991 product will be delivered by May of that year. "Product that is received and bought early stands a much greater chance of staying in the line if a stronger item comes along later, only because we have the investment in it—both emotional and financial."

"We've got to have our product decisions made for the next year's line no later than the first of June to really plan correctly," says Lowell Wilson, vice president for product development at The Ohio Art Company. "Right now, for any kind of a major tool it takes from sixteen to twenty weeks. So if you want to have shots off the mold at Toy Fair you are going to have to get your product done before the first of June. You need your shots off the mold to get corrections made, to make your television commercials, and guys like to know that you're committed.''

But if there are rules, there are always exceptions. Although inventors respect companies' timing rules for when to sell, there are always special products that bend the rules. The ''perfect'' time to sell a concept to a toy manufacturer appears to be whenever it is possible. ''Don't let a company tell you they're closed, because they are open for new ideas until the day before Toy Fair starts and back in the search the day after Toy Fair begins,'' says Bill Dohrmann of Tiger Games. One of his company's most successful games, Super Mario Bros., was shown to him two days before Christmas, and it made the Toy Fair less than six weeks away.

When asked for his ideas on the ''perfect'' time, Roger Lehmann exclaims, ''Anytime! You never know when an opening exists in a company's market plan because of changes in the market, items that were dropped, or plans for new expansion in new categories. In addition, the development lead times vary tremendously from company to company depending on their internal workload and the complexity of the program.''

No one agrees more than inventor Bob McKay, who says, ''I think the best time to sell a toy is anytime it's ready. When you talk about timing, it's not necessarily only the date on the calendar. Obviously, certain times of the year are easier to sell a product than others. But timing really is having a product ready at just the time that a company is looking for it, and that takes luck. I have never figured out how to do that skillfully.''

Inventor Jeffrey Breslow also sees ''timing'' from two vantage points. ''There's timing in terms of the yearly cycle and then there's timing in terms of what's out there competitively. I would not want to come out within a high-priced electronic toy in the middle of this Nintendo craze. We did it and we got killed. We did Mr. Game Show for Galoob. It was expensive and it was at the height of Nintendo. Given the choice—Nintendo or Mr. Game Show—the kids bought Nintendo.''

Since the toy industry is a business of fad and phenomenon, some companies keep product lines open for the longest possible time, waiting for a ''winner.'' As with Tiger's Super Mario Bros. game, items arriving as late as November and December still emerge at Toy Fair just two short months later.

The prototype for Blirds was presented to LJN Toys on December 8, 1989, and the line of plush toys was licensed by senior executives the same day. Over the next two months (minus time out for Christmas and New Year), nine months' worth of work was completed. Blirds was fully engineered; two different-size assortments were designed, matched with a manufacturer, and packaged; 54 camera-ready samples were ordered and photographed for brochures and packaging; a TV spot was produced (on February 5); and two LJN showrooms at 200 Fifth Avenue were dressed for the February 12, 1990, Toy Fair bow.

Greg Hyman took Major Morgan to Playskool in December and it showed up at the next Toy Fair. ''These things happen,'' he says. ''Why? Maybe because something fell out of the line,'' he speculates. ''If you're too early, a product sits around, and very often if a product sits around too long, they lose interest. It's there, it becomes familiar.''

''It is always worth an inquiry call or two later in a manufacturer's new-product cycle for an update,'' observes Norman Fabricant. ''If the company can flag a hole in the product plans, it may well be that you have the right patch for their needs. There may be that coincidental situation where you might have received back from one manufacturer a concept that you thought was a sure sale and it seems to fit nicely the late-developing need in the line of another company.'' If he's lucky, muses Fabricant, ''I can use the same packaging material to ship off the concept to the new manufacturer that was just used to return my idea. If the fortunes are really with me, the 'drop' from one line becomes the 'add' to another.''

Companies constantly juggle and purge the new product lineup. Add one and, most likely, another inventor's item will be canceled or postponed. At some point in every inventor's career, a product falls victim to what is called ''product displacement.'' The amount of new product ''in'' is proportionate to the amount of product ''out.''

Too Big/Too Small/Just Right

An inventor, like a good sales rep, must know the territory. If there is ''no sale'' at the first call, you must always have a fallback position. A commitment from a major manufacturer is the number-one choice, for many reasons. The majors, for instance, will spend more dollars in new-product execution. There will be larger promotion budgets to reach sales expectations. There will be greater product reception to the brand name by both retailers and consumers. Also, the inventor stands a good chance of placing more than one concept with a broad-line manufacturer. From a single presentation it may be possible to gain commitment to a novelty item, an action-figure accessory, and a sports-related toy. Inventors know that the ''biggies'' need more product ideas just to stay big.

''We'll go to Tucumcari if needed to sell one of our toy or game concepts,'' says Maria Girsch of Girsch Design Associates. ''But if it is a nonsale and it was a one-product presentation, we have a long, lonely ride home. To do a good job of presenting a concept, you have to prime yourself and be really prepared. Once you are prepared for that presentation, you might as well show ten items as opposed to one or two,'' advises Girsch. ''In a meeting with a major manufacturer who markets an extensive and varied line, you may be showing to product managers and R&D people for action figures, girls' toys, wheel goods, preschool, and games all in one day.''

When asked what criteria he uses to select a company for his product, Greg Hyman quips, ''Who's still open?'' He always starts at the top because, ''Number one, I would rather sell 400,000 of a product than 40,000 of a product. It's economics. Number two, my best relationships that have developed over the years are with major companies.''

But big is not always better. Says agent George Delaney, president of Delaney Development, ''There may be a tendency to go to only the largest manufacturers, but if they don't have a foothold in a market segment, it probably will take too much time to convince them to go into it in spite of the opportunity for the unique idea. In the toy business a lot of goods get moved by specialty suppliers. To some inventors, it doesn't matter whether you are placed with Company A or Company B, just as long as some marketer is going with the idea. Of course, you would like to have the idea be with the industry leaders, but sometimes a small company with few products will give more attention to an idea than a large company with a long product line. With the giants, a good idea can get lost in the sheer volume of products they have to sell.''

When it comes to failure, however, better it should happen with a major manufacturer. More often than not, the royalty earned from the amount of product required to fill a large company's distribution pipeline is more than a successful product might earn at a smaller company. Whereas a small manufacturer is lucky to sell more than 50,000 pieces of a game in a year, the major marketers may ship 500,000 pieces in the same period.

Eighty percent of the sales volume is done by 20 percent of the companies. The best placement for an inventor is with companies that are the biggest and most financially sound. They do not necessarily have greater imagination or product sensitivity than some smaller companies. What they do have is the money for marketing and advertising; strong lines of distribution; large sales forces; and deep market penetration. The odds are simply better that an item will reach the desired altitude and distance in the hands of a major manufacturer.

There is a place for emotion in product development, but not in product placement. The bottom line is that on average it takes as much time and effort to sell to a major company as it does to sell to a smaller one. In fact, experience dictates that often the smaller company is more costly to deal with because so much more is required of the outside inventor's own resources.

No one need remind Eddy Goldfarb, a leading product source for more than forty years, of the advantages of major companies. But he takes a benevolent posture toward small, startup companies, saying, "If someone makes the effort to come out and see me, I will certainly show them concepts. A new company, one born in enthusiasm and having a real will to make it, is exciting."

Since a product may not always be taken by the manufacturer of choice, inventors must be ready to pack up their passed-over prototypes and move on to another maker, and then, if unsuccessful, move to a third, and to a fourth, and so on. It is sometimes only the inventor's perseverance and tenacity that lead to the sale of an idea. What one manufacturer rejects may be just what the next company is seeking. Rather than dwell on rejection after one stop, the inventor must have the energy and faith in the idea to shop it around until it hits a responsive chord. After making the complete circuit, all that may be left is to place the idea on the shelf to be dusted off for another year.

Too Innovative

As Hank Atkins laments, "The two main reasons toy and game companies turn down a game are that it's similar to something that has been done before, and that *nothing* like it has ever been done before.'' What a double-edged sword for inventors! Not wanting to repeat oneself is understandable, but why wouldn't manufacturers want to produce something that's never been done before? Bob Fuhrer, developer of the games Backwords and Locomotion, feels that since mistakes are very expensive, many manufacturers are reluctant to take risks and pioneer a category.

Betty Morris, inventor of Shrinky Dinks, states, ''A really, really new idea is almost impossible to sell. Not because it isn't any good, not because the industry isn't looking for it, but because when you come right down to it, it costs the manufacturer too much money to get it marketed. They have to educate the consumer. This means a lot of advertising dollars. A new concept,'' continues Morris, ''may also be impossible for the manufacturer to get past the retail buyers.'' Most major toy and game manufacturers now host special product previews for the major retail chains, such as Toys R Us, Child World, and Sears. If a buyer doesn't show enough interest, an item can actually be dropped or undergo major pre–Toy Fair changes.

Developer Ron Dubren agrees that negative buyer reaction is a threat to ideas. ''While it is understandable that manufacturers would like to think they have a guaranteed sale,'' says Dubren, ''they have allowed the retail buyers to become too important in affecting decisions to go forward with a product.'' Inventors chafe at the influence of major retailers. Shouldn't the end users, they feel, ultimately judge the merits or demerits of a product? In the reality of two-tier toy and game selling, however, the trade comes first. ''If I had a dollar for every good game or every good toy that didn't make it because a buyer didn't buy, I wouldn't be in the industry anymore. I'd be retired,'' says Mike Cook, vice president of new product development at TSR.

Control of the high-volume retail shelf space is strongly

characterized by the emergence of Toys R Us (TRU). In 1980, the chain operated 85 stores. As of February 1991, TRU had 451 toy stores in the U.S., 97 stores internationally, and 164 Kids R Us children's apparel outlets. Retail sales for the chain have rocketed from half a billion dollars in 1980 to over $5.5 billion in 1990. It accounts for 25 to 30 percent of the total industry sales volume at retail. Hasbro (13 percent of annual sales from TRU), Tonka (18 percent of annual sales from TRU), and other leading manufacturers rely heavily on Toys R Us to get their products to consumers, who are indeed the final judges. It is just as disappointing to these retailers as it is to inventors and manufacturers when consumers ignore their enthusiastic plans and forecasts.

Not Invented Here

In Bethesda, Maryland, NIH stands for National Institutes of Health. In the toy industry, it is corporate jargon for "not invented here." It describes a negative attitude to outside submissions, seen in manufacturers with strong in-house development departments. "In the past, Mattel didn't talk to outside inventors. Fisher-Price didn't use anything from the outside for a long time, now they do; but Little Tikes doesn't and there are other guys who are difficult, inaccessible to inventors," says Tony Miller of Tonka, former Mattel employee. Phil Orbanes at Parker Brothers says that his in-house people "react well to outside submissions because of the common objective to gain in sales volume each year. We're just looking for the best ideas to do that."

Companies may not outwardly post signs of the NIH syndrome but may suffer from it internally. The simple fact is that many marketing executives and staff designers at toy companies would rather be on the outside working independently. They see profits go to an inventor for a product they actually made happen, including, frequently, features that make a concept far more commercial than when it arrived.

"There are inequities," admits Mike Meyers, senior vice president of R&D at Milton Bradley. "I don't know of any company that has really worked out the problem." Meyers feels one of the major industry problems is that creative people aspire to management in order to get better compensation and the perks that go with the territory. "So you take brilliant developers and turn them into mediocre managers—not in every case, generally—and you do that because the system drives them that way."

"All of my management is on a bonus program based upon their grade level, salary, and performance," says Steve D'Aguanno of Hasbro. "The only problem inside a company is that there is generally not one inventor; you always have five or six people contributing."

At Fisher-Price, Peter Pook says that all of the designers are required to spend three months a year developing original concepts. "We're entirely unique in that respect, and they do it very well," he feels. A lot of them have come from other toy companies, according to Pook, where, "frankly, many of them have been beaten down so badly that they find, even without getting the inventor check, sheer joy in seeing something they have initiated in the line."

Darwin P. Bromley, president of Mayfair Games, has one way to recognize and compensate in-house innovation. If Mayfair decides to go with a product based upon a staff designer's original concept, the work will essentially be freelanced back to the employee on a nonroyalty, flat-fee basis, to be done on his or her overtime. "Then one of the other editors has to apply the same standards to the in-house work as they would if it were an outside submission," he explains. "It is treated as a normal product. We do one or two of those a year."

Throughout the lengthy review process, in-house designers may put the kibosh on a concept without an inventor's having a chance to defend it. Negative vibes and jealousy can easily thwart much-needed development effort.

"I think that it's always there," says Greg Hyman, referring to the NIH syndrome. "It may not be apparent to you when you're making your presentation—people are very nice to you, especially if you are known—but I think it still exists," not with the most senior executives, but at the product management level.

Inventor Mike Satten confirms that as an internal designer he operated with an adversarial attitude early in his career. He says, "NIH definitely does exist in some companies. I know from my own experience. When I worked as a designer internally, I felt compelled to get as many of my ideas into the line each year as I could. It was disheartening when outside people were sometimes given more credibility than the internal staff. . . ." As Satten took on greater corporate responsibility, he arrived at the realization that the whole was greater than any of the parts. "The most important part of the picture was to have the most exciting product line, and whether it was conceived internally or externally did not matter," he remarks.

David R. Berko, vice president for marketing at Buddy L Corporation, says, "The thing you have to admire about the inventing community is that they're taking some risks. Sitting inside, you resent guys who are getting their 5 percent off the millions that we're making, but, at the same time, if a product fails they don't get that paycheck coming in."

"I suppose there are those people who resent seeing somebody become a millionaire off your so-called hard work, but I suppose those same people don't see the guys who are starving out there and having hard times," Berko adds.

Larry Jones, head of the creative group at Cal R&D, says, "It depends on the level. The higher you get, the less it [NIH] is. If you're talking to the president, there's absolutely no problem. NIH doesn't exist. All he wants is product that will generate money for the company and increase profits. The lower you get, the more the NIH, because their main concern is protecting their jobs, not making money for the company.''

"My biggest frustration is trying to sell manufacturers,'' says Arthur Albert. "They keep coming out with concepts that are inferior because they are generated internally. We have a very difficult time overcoming the inertia of the internal creative staffs.'' A former Ideal Toy executive, Albert feels that top management is not so interested in saving the royalty, but that the problem is at lower levels. "It's the level of competence in the internal staff. It's a threat to them if the products keep coming in from the outside,'' he adds.

"Yes, definitely, I've run into NIH,'' says Eddy Goldfarb, who has seen just about everything during a career in which he has inked 500 toy contracts. "There was one instance where I talked to someone in-house, at a later date, who told me that he didn't want me to get more than one item in. . . . But it's never at the top,'' says Goldfarb. "No, it's your own peers. And it's too bad because these same people at your level are tremendously talented people. Once they take your item, there is a tremendous amount of effort and ingenuity that has to go into it to manufacture it. They deserve all the credit in the world.''

"It [NIH] exists in some companies,'' says George Dunsay, an independent consultant to toy manufacturers. "I tend to think it exists less than it used to. I think companies are far more open to buying product from the outside, which is really a function of their desire to keep down their internal costs. On the other hand, some companies tend to be very protective of their ongoing product lines and you have a greater difficulty in selling extensions of products than in coming in with brand-new products.''

"I've heard a great deal about NIH mostly from external people who may be grasping for a reason an item was returned or for why in retrospect a design execution proved anemic,'' says an R&D executive speaking on background. The twenty-five-year veteran says that no single R&D designer is able to sabotage or undermine an external selection; the process is too diffuse and expansive. "External submissions are always subject to critical scrutiny by internal staff, since evaluation and selection are so much a part of the job. But since the goal is to create the strongest possible line, no one is going to stand in the way of a new product just because it came from an external inventing source versus in-house inventing," he concludes.

Other than an entrepreneurial bent, there is often not all that much more difference between the talents represented on staff and outside. "An in-house developer could have the same attributes as an independent but for personal reasons may enjoy the comfort of an organization as opposed to the years of sacrifice required to be a successful inventor," says George B. Volanakis of The Ertl Company. "Many in-house personnel have tried independence, but through failure return to the safe 'cocoon' of an organization," he notes.

Hurry Up . . . and Wait

Selling ideas to a manufacturer almost always is a protracted affair. Rarely does the inventor walk away at the close of a presentation with check in hand. A particularly fortunate one may come away with only the first step to the sale—namely, retention of the prototype by the company for further examination.

An inventor may have a valued idea rejected or passed over for a variety of reasons: duplication of internal R&D work; it has been done before; it is perceived as too expensive for what it delivers; or there is just no interest in the idea. On occasion, a manufacturer may ask an inventor to do more work before bringing in the concept for further consideration.

The product review process involves many steps. There are play sessions with the internal decision-makers and with players from the target audience. There are consumer focus groups to measure the idea's market strength. And there is a thorough cost analysis to determine whether the product makes sense as a business undertaking. The process may take the manufacturer months, and inventors need to be optimistic throughout it. An item kept by a manufacturer for review is not bankable: It's a long way from a presentation to an agreement to purchase.

Independent inventors are people who have learned to accept the fact that waiting is *de rigueur* in any sales exercise. They wait by the phone to learn the status of the next blockbuster idea they flew across the country to present. They wait to hear if the item Fed-Exed the week before has been opened yet. They wait to see if an item has been accepted for line review. They wait for manufacturers to cost their products. They wait disappointedly for prototypes to be returned. They wait to learn whether the overdue advance check will arrive by the time they leave on a rare holiday. They wait for contracts to be negotiated and finally signed.

"In the earlier days, you would see Elliot Handler at Mattel and he would tell you, 'That's a great item and we're going to take it. We're just going to make certain that historically it's OK.' He could tell you on the spot or tell you three days later, it's a deal," recalls Eddy Goldfarb. Today Eddy says such quick deals only happen at small companies: "There's too much involved for a big company."

"I am trying to come to a yes/no decision within thirty days," says George Propsom at Western Publishing. But he notes that it's not easy to get quick decisions. There is lots to be done before his company will make a total commitment. For example, when Propsom decides to retain an outside submission, it first goes into his design group to be play-tested, but "they're swamped. I have three designers and I think each one is working on three projects," he regrets. If it plays well, he may bring in some kids for play-testing. "If we still feel the product is a strong enough concept, then it is presented to marketing as a viable game. Marketing may then say, 'Let's test at a central location like Chicago, or Los Angeles.' All of this takes time. However, if we want to keep a product for testing, the inventor is paid a holding fee, usually $10,000. Western's standard advance against royalties is $20,000, so if the product is ultimately contracted, the inventor receives another $10,000 at that point.''

While items are held in the review process, they are in a highly competitive arena. More ideas come in daily to compete for the same development resources and marketing commitment. Neil Werde, director of marketing at Tyco Toys, says that his company's attitude toward a new product is, "How do we kill it? Even if you really like it, you have to play devil's advocate: 'Let's try to step on this and see if it comes back to the surface.' You have to ask yourself if a product is worth taking a $3 or $4 million flyer on.'' The toy business is not fun and games.

"Every inventor that I've talked to has the same complaint," says Eddy Goldfarb. "Every manufacturer says, 'We're going to try and get you answers quicker.' '' Even an advance or option is not a solution. Goldfarb does not like to option his product because for not much money, manufacturers have the right to hang onto an idea indefinitely.

In fact, according to Elliot Rudell, "Lengthy evaluation time frames, because of in-house bureaucracy, have tied up some of my concepts so long that it diluted the concepts' timeliness to subsequent manufacturers. You have to know when to pull an item and take it to another manufacturer.''

Create a Little, Sell a Lot

One of the most innovative selling schemes was the 1987 "toy fair" organized by some clever Minnesotans as a way of getting the manufacturers to visit their area. Calling themselves the Uneasy Alliance of Northern Toy Inventors, the current members include Charlie Girsch, Marie Girsch, and Tim Moodie at Girsch Design; Frank Young at Trixie Toys; Tony Morley at Red Racer Studio; Rick Polk at Leisure Design; Steve Taylor at Taylor Design; Mike Marra and Andrew Burton at Excel; Clem Hedeen at Fun Maker; and Steve Kiwus. Their event is called Elvenbasch.

"Maybe you've heard of ELVENBASCH, the traditional Nordic festival of the Toy Elves, up here near the North Pole," read the original letter of invitation. "Every year, after cleaning up the mess that Santa has left, all the Toy Elves celebrate the thaw, the end of hibernation, the taking down of the igloos. As the first leaves appear and bird calls are in the air, they invite their friends, the toy company executives, to come and join in the celebration of Spring and New Toy Ideas." Now R&D representatives religiously trek to the Land of 10,000 Lakes twice a year in search of winners.

Most inventors would rather devote 100 percent of their time pondering "what if?" questions, creating new ideas for toys, or just daydreaming, instead of pitching the fruits of their labors to manufacturers. But sell they must, and, according to our survey, most inventors spend an average of 20 percent of their time selling their creations. Though selling ideas is very tough, the income potential is what keeps many inventors in the business. Once his or her product gets into a line, the inventor can expect a contract with a sizable advance against future royalties. Up until that point, it has all been a one-way street: the company's way. The manufacturers do not pay just to poke, play, and ponder a concept.

Not many companies pay for an option, until after lengthy

evaluation. "Normally we don't give money out to an inventor until we've had an opportunity to test the item. Maybe three or four years ago, there may have been a situation where the company would have paid an option to hold onto a product, but frankly, in today's marketplace, there are fewer promotionally oriented toy companies that have the resources to make a product happen. At this point, I feel we're in a buyers' market for inventions," says Andy Gatto of Matchbox Toys (USA).

Normally, the toy industry's standard royalty is 5 percent of the manufacturer's selling price to the trade. If an item sells 400,000 pieces at $10, the inventor's share of the sales receipts will be $200,000. If the annual sales pace of the plaything escalates to a million units and gains longevity, so too will the royalty income to the inventor. When such a level of sales is reached or surpassed, the inventor is very well rewarded for the patience, perseverance, and creative brilliance that helps make it happen.

Rumors constantly fly around the industry about the size of advances that new toys and games are getting. Certainly one of the highest was paid by Coleco when it came time to extend the license for the Cabbage Patch Kids. Coleco agreed to pay Xavier Roberts's original Appalachian Artworks a nonrefundable license fee of $7.5 million, as well as guaranteed minimum royalty payments through the term of the agreement—July 20, 1988, to December 31, 1994. With the demise of Coleco, it is now up to Hasbro to push the dolls into the market at a pace to justify the seven-digit advance.

Despite the best plans and highest expectations, the entire new-product process in the end is a gamble for all parties: speculative for the inventor in creation; speculative for the manufacturer in execution. And each year, independent inventors and manufacturers/marketers change partners in the merger of creative product ideas with creative merchandising.

But to survive as a product source, inventors must prevail,

despite the pitfalls of the business—a selection process too slow, advances too low, buyers too few, creations seen as not new, corporate directions uncharted, key contacts departed, and rejection . . . rejection . . . rejection.

Nonetheless, one can sense, in talking with toy and game inventors, that they genuinely love what they do. Helping Santa fill the toy chest each year can be fun. And the prospect of getting a royalty on every piece of a hot-selling product delivered to market is highly motivating. Toy and game invention for love and fun—yes; for high financial profits—definitely!

5 From Mind to Merchandise

HOW TOYS AND GAMES ARE DEVELOPED

Ideas for new toys and games are not made. They are born. And, like all living organisms, there is tremendous variety among them. Their common denominator is that their origin is in curiosity and their growth is nurtured by a combination of intelligence, imagination, originality, motivation, persistence, and wonder.

Ideas won't keep. They go stale quickly, so something must be done with them. They are plans of action. Ideas are the stock and trade of a toy inventor, his or her prime assets. It is vital not only to know how to generate them, but also to know what to do with them afterward.

American's independent toy inventors are the most prolific and entrepreneurial in the world. It should come as no surprise that people in this country have more individual freedom and more encouragement to innovate and be different than anywhere else on earth. The nation's marketplace is restless and ever-changing, with a constant demand for new products. We are, after all, a ''throwaway'' society.

Just as mere shape determines whether iron shall float or

124

sink, so it is that ideas must be well-formed in order to survive. As the inventor's idea develops from its conceptual stage to "looks like, works like" prototypes, it will be touched by many people and go through many hands and many creative—and not so creative—minds. It has been said that an idea can turn to dust or magic, depending on the talent it rubs up against. A new idea is a fragile thing, and it doesn't take much to kill even the best one. It can be knocked out of consideration by a yawn; it can be butchered by a quip; it can be nitpicked to death by a scowl on the right executive's face.

The longer an outside submission is inside under review, the greater the company's investment of time and personnel. But there is a saying in the industry: "No comes fast; yes takes a long time."

There are a few instances where an inventor may walk in with an item and out with a check, but these are the exceptions. Typically, a concept must pass the hurdle of both R&D and marketing people to continue on in the new-product selection process. Then it can be 120 to 140 days before the product is defined to everyone's satisfaction and is on track to Toy Fair. If an item falls out of favor after several months, it is a major disappointment to everyone who worked to design and plan the product. Most disappointed of all, however, is the inventor, who came close but must now try to sell the concept to another manufacturer. In such cases, many of the larger companies will give their model work to the inventor to help the sales effort at the next stop.

Roger Lehmann, inventor of Bathing Beauties (Tonka), every year sees several of his products dropped by manufacturers before Toy Fair. "It is a loss to all parties involved because of all the efforts, energy, and dedication to develop the product by the internal staff and us. To lose a program is very painful and disheartening."

Of all the factors brought to bear on a new idea, "certainly the first one is our own impression of the product," says Andy

Gatto of Matchbox Toys (USA). "The second is the consumer's impression of the product, and that order doesn't necessarily indicate the level of significance. I think the consumer impression is to us the most important thing we deal with. If kids in testing ultimately like the product a lot, that makes it easier for us to invest the necessary human and financial resources to make the product go. If we have any reservations whatsoever about the consumer reaction to a product, then it's going to make the risk more intensive, and in today's economy you try and eliminate as much of the risk as possible."

Like the manufacturer, toy and game inventors have a single goal: an idea that might become the next Hula Hoop or Trivial Pursuit. A megahit. Creating for the sake of creating is not the task. Creating a plaything that reaches retail and sells in quantity is the true payoff. In reality, however, of the 5,000 to 6,000 new products launched every year, only 25 percent have the glide rate required to carry them into a second year.

There is no one way, no single procedure for firing the human imagination and sparking new ideas. It is always a challenge. The methods are as varied as the inventors behind them. Successful inventors are those who have learned how to detect and follow what Emerson referred to as a "gleam of light that flashes across the mind from within."

"If there was a formula, an exacting process to germinate ideas, it would have been plotted and charted long ago," says Gordon Barlow, inventor of such classic games as Mouse Trap, Stay Alive, Pivot Pool, and Gnip Gnop and holder of close to 400 patents.

"Everything I do and see feeds into the creative process," says Judy Blau, who annually records between 100 and 200 new product ideas. The inventor of Sweetie Pops, a preschool doll line by Playskool, she particularly likes to watch children play and to keep up with their current interests.

"You never know exactly what will trigger an idea. It could be an object, a conversation, anything," says Randice-Lisa

Altschul, inventor of the Miami Vice game (Colorforms) and Clay to Win (Coleco). "But one thing is for sure, when the idea hits my conscious level, it takes precedence over everything."

Greg Hyman, inventor of Alphie (Playskool), says he sparks ideas while lying on the nude beach on the island of St. Martin. He also keeps a lighted pen near his bedside, so "when an idea jolts me awake, I can write it down."

And after the inspiration strikes, what then? "This is an industry of delayed gratification," says Maria Girsch. "Even if you sell your very first concept, it will be about one and a half to two years before you will be bringing royalty checks to the bank on a regular basis."

"It takes a lot of luck and connections. Tenth on a list is product originality," says Ron Milner, inventor of Hot Lixx (Tyco Toys). "I think marketing forces are really the key to the whole thing. Ideas don't sell themselves. Ideas are sold." Whereas the pros may originate new concepts, it is up to the producer/marketer to transform the basic idea into a successful mass-market plaything. And, again, that takes time. The play value and sales appeal of each idea put into the development cycle have to be ensured. All of the carefully orchestrated steps by a toy manufacturer are intended to get an idea to market in an appealing form and at a price that may make it an annual best-seller. Today's mass-market producers need a minimum of 200,000 to 300,000 units in annual sales to justify the investment; 500,000 to 600,000 shows stronger market acceptance. The dream of any manufacturer is to produce a million-seller in the first year . . . and for many years to come.

Every toy and game company is ecstatic when a new entry provides it with solid sales for three or four years. Though all toy people, from idea to fulfillment, plan on longevity, too often the idea that was spawned in enthusiasm and launched with high expectations and a multimillion-dollar media campaign disappears unceremoniously from toy shelves after a year or two (or less). Does anyone remember such recent examples as Battle Brawlers (Kenner), Put'ns (Mattel), Spiral Zone action figures (Tonka), and Life of the Party games (Milton Bradley)?

On the other hand, some strong sellers remain on Christmas wish lists after four or more seasons. They take on "classic" status, like Play-Doh (Kenner), Boggle, Monopoly, Clue, Risk, and Nerf (Parker Brothers), Barbie and Hot Wheels (Mattel), Mr. Potato Head, My Little Pony, and G.I. Joe (Hasbro), and Frisbee and Hula Hoop (Wham-O). These products are representative of a core of strong toys and games— or *staples*—that except for periodic cosmetic updates are much the same as when they appeared at their first Toy Fair. They can be counted on for virtually guaranteed sales each year. The "classic" seller is every inventor's dream, every manufacturer's expectation.

The most successful companies are those with the most classics. As George R. Ditomassi of Milton Bradley says, "We have a solid, well-rounded line of staple merchandise that forms our sales and marketing base. This fact alone establishes our leadership in the game business."

Inventors dream of having staple products that continue to generate royalty income year in and year out. There are inventors who receive many hundreds of thousands of dollars, if not millions, each year from just one solid hit the likes of Operation (Milton Bradley), or Micro Machines (Galoob), and Super Dough (Tyco Toys). Advances against royalties are nice for annual cash flow, but the true foundation of any inventor's continuing business is the solid royalty base provided by a staple.

"There is no doubt that as we start our product cycle each year, we are looking for winners," says Mike Meyers of Milton Bradley. "We look at thousands of ideas in search of the best new entries to our line. Sometimes the potential hits are obvious. Most times we are looking at the germ of an idea that will transform during our internal-development cycle into something our people feel will be a sales success. Anywhere during that cycle, if our confidence level does not remain very high, we will discontinue work on an idea regardless of our investment of time, design efforts, and dollars.''

Independent developers can only hope that their ideas will be picked up by a manufacturer captained by the likes of a Hassenfeld, Grey, Ditomassi, Galoob, or Kalinske, and entered into the company's structured design, engineering, packaging, and promotional development cycle. They know that the idea must have definition, a physical presence that takes it from the "what if/imagine this" vision into an appealing, playable form.

The most successful products have what many in the industry call a "wow factor." This is often some promotable feature that, combined with a product's natural magic, delivers excitement. Hasbro's Cabbage Patch Kids come with adoption papers and one-of-a-kind looks, names, and birth certificates; its Flying Fighters have patented microelectronics that permit the aircraft to accelerate and decelerate without the aid of buttons. Tyco Toys' electronic instruments Hot Lixx and Hot Keyz let kids make great-sounding music without a single lesson. Games such as Trouble and Headache (Milton Bradley) incorporate a unique Pop-o-matic dice roller. Purr-tenders (Fisher-Price) are plush felines in masks pretending to be other animals. Ya gotta have a gimmick.

And your gimmick has to be in working order when you make your presentation. The easiest ideas to sell are those that have already taken on concrete form.

"The more I can do on the front end to develop the toy or game," says Barlow, "the faster the internal staff at the manufacturer can get into an understanding and familiarity with my concepts. I want them to feel that I am bringing something very unique, something very special."

"When I meet with a manufacturer to present product possibilities, I make certain that every concept is in workable, functional form,'' says Jeffrey Breslow, president of Breslow, Morrison, Terzian. "Each item has a limited time to make an impression, and I try to leave very little to chance, to the viewer's imagination. I don't want the manufacturer to guess at the new idea. I want the viewer to see the idea, feel the idea, hear the idea, and play with the idea.''

The saying "necessity is the mother of invention" came to life for Mike Satten, who, along with Roger Lehmann, created Sports Starters Baseball Glove (Playskool). Satten was teaching his son, Brett, to catch a baseball. Noodling the problem, the partners realized that many gloves have no flexibility and are inappropriate for younger kids. To solve this, they made numerous gloves in different sizes, pocket configurations, and bumpers before settling on a tricot model with a removable "catch guard" that prevents the ball from popping out.

Tongue-in-cheek, Chris Campbell, director of product acquisition for Parker Brothers, tells inventors that to be successful with him at a presentation, the idea has to say NO TRUMP. The more they say NO TRUMP, the more successful they're apt to be. NO TRUMP is his acronym for:

No: *Know* your client, because tailoring a product is better than throwing something against the wall. **T** = Theme; **R** = Rationale, **U** = Uniqueness; **M** = Mass Marketability; **P** = Promotability.

The Development Cycle: Milestones and Deadlines

Inventors who specialize in toys and games have to understand the manufacturers' product cycles—and every manufacturer has a same slightly different variation of the development process.

Hasbro, as the world's largest toy and game manufacturer,

has three different product cycles occurring simultaneously. A specific cycle depends on the complexity of product or products to be launched. Soft goods or plush toys may be developed in a short development cycle of three to four months. During this time, designs are finalized, specifications established, sewing patterns created, materials selected, and prototypes safety-tested. This relatively short cycle is possible since most cute, cuddly, soft goods are simply a matter of style and design. There is no complex engineering, intricate tooling, or ongoing tweaking to maximize play value.

Board games and single toy concepts are usually developed within a cycle of eight to ten months. The rules for play for each game must be exhaustively thought out so that all predictable situations and outcomes are covered for every level of player. Once the idea is boxed and in the market, there can be no unanswered questions about how to assemble it, play it, and get maximum fun from it. In the case of some games, all that may remain of the initial idea is the basic play pattern or the special hook that captures the important ingredient of repeat play. As the game evolves, it is possible for the theme or content to be altered entirely. Final colorful artwork changes the look or aesthetics of the game dramatically from the inventor's prototype. Or early designs may be dropped in favor of using popular licensed characters such as the Sesame Street or Disney gang.

Finally, complete lines of many related playthings require fifteen to eighteen months in the development process and represent a truly major investment. Such line ideas can include both horizontal and vertical development. Horizontal development brings out variations on the same theme at similar price points, as in Micro Machines (Galoob). Vertical development will produce items that vary in magnitude of execution and price, as in Dino Riders (Tyco Toys).

Whatever the company, the critical events in transforming

an idea to packaged product are the same. Omitting any stage or neglecting any detail will merely increase the gamble for ultimate success.

Hasbro, with more than $1 billion in sales, offers a basic model of how an idea moves through the development process to get to the retail shelves (see Fig. 1).

Market Research and Product Testing

Companies are very different when it comes to how much they rely on market research techniques, but most consider some research and testing valuable to check reaction to product. Most important, the product must hit the executives right in the stomach.

"I think the value of market research is overrated. Truly great toys still come from the gut," says Playskool president Steven Schwartz. "I've tested products that have done very well, and when they got to the marketplace, they were decimated by some product I never even knew was coming out. Research can never predict who your competition is going to be, and that's where you get blindsided all the time. I think if the toy is right and you feel it's right, you go with it." He offers some examples of the limits on research: "You're testing against what's known. So when we tested My Little Pony, we tested it against Strawberry Shortcake. Strawberry Shortcake was very powerful in the market. My Little Pony was an unknown with no advertising or anything, and we got destroyed in the research. The truth of the matter is that My Little Pony blew away Strawberry Shortcake once it got to the marketplace. We tested Cabbage Patch Kids and what the mothers said was, 'My daughter has no idea what adoption means and, boy, is this doll ugly!' So what did that tell us? And Mattel tested it also, and I believe Kenner tested it, too. I think Coleco probably didn't. That's why it was such a success."

Standard & Poor's toys analyst Paul Valentine says, "I think what is extraordinary is the rejection rate on what became highly successful toys. Cabbage Patch Kids were rejected by five major toy companies, including Mattel and Hasbro, before Coleco accepted them. Teddy Ruxpin was personally rejected by Stephen Hassenfeld of Hasbro, who was a legend in picking product in the industry. It was also rejected by Mattel. Coleco only made a nominal offer. Hasbro gave up the technology that became Lazer Tag. You look around the industry and it's amazing to see the product rejected. You like to think there's some science and skill to it, but after a while you think all these guys might as well be using darts."

"I don't do research to validate my position to management," says Saul Jodel of Galoob. "I do market research for information. If I want to find out what my best themes are for Micro Machines cars, so I can weight my assortments, I do that kind of research. . . . Net, net, I'm not a big researcher. I use it where applicable and where it makes sense. And I do not use it just to cover my bases."

Loren Taylor, senior vice president for marketing at Nasta International, says that any market research he does is more qualitative research. "Eighty, well, 90 percent will still be gut," he says. Woody Browne, vice president for marketing at Tyco Toys and the person responsible for the development and management of such lines as Dino Riders, Super Dough, and Super Blocks, says that Tyco tends to do market research to measure kids' interest, but that the results of such testing comprise only 40 percent of the decision-making process. "Sixty percent of our decision is gut," he notes.

"Hasbro depends on market research," says Neil Friedman, senior vice president of marketing for Hasbro, "but a product will live or die of its own volition." He uses market research for support, or to give preferences if a product is on

Figure 1. Product Development Milestones: Time Line of Key Events

Phase 1

NOVEMBER

Product Concept Approval

MARKET RESEARCH
Preliminary Costing
PTO Model From Shop

MARKET RESEARCH: The marketing, design and engineering team links together to assess consumer reaction to new concepts by interviewing consumers about a product's attributes or observing children field-testing a product. Consumers' input is valuable in evaluating the potential of a new concept or in fine-tuning a product prior to its launch in the market.

DECEMBER

PTO (PRELIM. TAKE OVER)
Marketing Line Review

PTO (PRELIMINARY TAKE OVER): The PTO conference is a critical stage in a product's transformation from concept to reality. At this phase of development a product passes from the hands of designers to engineers with close scrutiny given to such issues as design, cost, reliability, packaging and manufacturing plans.

R&D MODEL FINISHED

R&D MODEL: The R&D model shop constructs product prototypes early in the development process. Later, model makers may fine-tune product mechanisms and build models for use during the ongoing product review process. They also construct the hand-samples displayed at Toy Fair since full production of many new products only begins later in the year.

Phase 2

JANUARY

PTO Package Approved
Appropriation Approval Requested
FTO (Final Take Over)
Marketing Line Review

Phase 3

FEBRUARY

FINAL SCULPTURE

SCULPTURE: Product sculptors work in consultation with design engineers and marketing managers to transform a product idea into reality. The sculpting studio plays an important part in the complex process of creating a new toy by preparing a variety of studies for new product components and producing an array of new shapes, forms and functional pieces for use in the design process.

MARCH

Preliminary Drawing Release
EDM Review (Engineering, Design and Marketing)
Final Drawing Release

APRIL

Pattern Release
Cost Verification

JULY
Final Engineering Changes
MTO Costing (Manufacturing Take Over)
Final Packaging Specs.
Final Product Specs.

AUGUST
MTO
Marketing Line Review

Phase 5
SEPTEMBER
PACKAGE AND ART RELEASE
Preliminary Instructions

PACKAGING: Designing a product's packaging is an important part of the overall product development and marketing process. An effective package brings together various elements of art, copy and package construction, calling out the key features of the toy or game it contains. Package design also must be responsive to retailers' display and shelving requirements.

OCTOBER
Art Release
First Shots (Samples of Molded Parts)

NOVEMBER
MARKETING LINE REVIEW

MARKETING LINE REVIEW: All the functions involved in the creation of a product including R&D and engineering come together for the marketing line review. Features such as design, packaging and advertising are evaluated and the overall design and production schedule is monitored.

Phase 6
VSP (VENDOR SAMPLE PILOT)
VSP Domestic

VSP (VENDOR SAMPLE PILOT): Some of Hasbro's products are manufactured by outside vendors. Before full production is begun, a sample product is produced by the vendor. Hasbro's marketing, design engineering and R&D team evaluates all aspects of the pilot product to determine that it conforms to design and engineering specifications prior to authorizing the start of manufacturing.

DECEMBER
Final Packaging
Final Instructions Release
Marketing Line Review
FEP (Final Engineering Pilot)
RTP (Release to Production)

Phase 7
JANUARY

FEBRUARY
TOY FAIR

TOY FAIR: Months of design, development, engineering and marketing effort culminate in the unveiling of the year's new product line at Toy Fair each February. The Hasbro, Milton Bradley and Playskool sales forces show the line to representatives of the trade at this important industry event. Toy fairs also are held at the beginning of the year in other leading international markets.

MARCH
Production Start

the fence or controversial. Friedman may also use market research to help sway an issue one way or the other or to obtain
a better definition. "You have to get issues while they're hot
and topical into the marketplace," Friedman says. His feeling
is that too much market research can bog down a manufacturer.

"We see hundreds of toys a month, and it's gut that initially
would give you a feel as to whether or not the product has
some level of appeal; gut along with historical reference," says
Andy Gatto of Matchbox Toys (USA). But no matter how
innovative an item is, he still believes in market research, especially quantitative research, which measures consumers' specific likes and dislikes. "Initially we do focus groups, but
depending upon the nature of the product and the risk intensity
of the investment involved, we'll often do quantitative research
behind that to establish whether or not our findings in focus
sessions were, in fact, accurate," he adds. Focus sessions, in
which children are exposed to new product, can be misleading,
according to Gatto. There are many variables that may skew
the results, including the number of them, the socioeconomic
backgrounds of the kids, the locations at which they're conducted, the composition of the group, the quality of the mod-
erator, and so forth.

"We did extensive market research quite a few years ago
on girls' products, back when the phenomenon was D&D
[Dungeons & Dragons], role-playing for boys," relates George
Propsom of Western Publishing. "We said, 'There has to be
something for girls.' We did extensive testing and we met with
psychologists. After a year and a half of testing, we couldn't
come up with anything. And when Kathy Rondeau came in
with Girl Talk (submitted as Pillow Talk), we opened the game
and said, 'This is what we've been looking for.' She was at the
right place at the right time."

This is a prime example of how difficult it is to determine
what people want. Consumers—or parents of targeted consum-

ers—are not likely to be able to articulate their basic play needs starting from scratch, a blank slate. But if they see something they like, they will let you know. Rather than to try to describe the perfect product, they will react to what's good—or bad— about the product in their hands. Therefore, the industry commonly gains insights into products through "negative testing," focusing on what is not liked about a concept; or by soliciting opinions about what nuances or features are missing from selected products currently on the market. In an effective product test environment, consumers can be brutally frank about their likes and dislikes, especially if there is an opportunity to see, feel, and play the new toy or game.

Another complication, however, is that usually the potential user and the potential purchaser are not one and the same. "We can never forget that we are dealing with two tiers of consumers," says Kate Stanuch, associate director of market research at Hasbro. "On one hand we have the kids who will use the toy, and on the other hand is the parent who makes the purchase decision. When we talk toys and games with kids, it's all performance, fantasy, excitement, play patterns, and peer acceptance. With parents, toys and games are defined in relation to durability, repeat play, entertainment, and pricing issues."

But parents don't always have the last word. "Ultimately," Stanuch says, "we have found that if a parent expresses neutral or a slightly negative response to a product and the children are highly motivated to want it, the parents can be swayed."

One way to increase the likelihood of succeeding with your target audience is to pay attention to their interests outside of toys and games. Elliot Rudell of Rudell Design says that his designers take into account the broadest umbrella of interest for potential users when executing a new idea. "Of course, we must know if there is anything like our idea already in the toy or game market; that is a given. But when we are doing our theme, our design, our *raison d'être* for the idea, we look at what else the target audience is into, where they are with TV, books, magazines, music, clothes, general interests. Our toy or game has to appeal to the same senses that are diverted toward other things in the environment. When it becomes playtime, we are looking for the same energy and appeal that is coming at our users from everything else around them.''

Few inventors have access to large groups of players for extensive play-testing of new ideas. Most, however, do varying degrees of ''kitchen research,'' and more and more inventors are videotaping these sessions, studying the players' reactions for ideas on changes and improvements. Play-testing is the only way to be certain of the appropriate age range for a product; it is the only way kinks and quirks can be identified and ironed out. Inventors have to put their idea for a toy or game into a usable form and play . . . play . . . play.

Product testing begins early in market research and continues throughout the entire development process. It can be no other way. Adults decide on the selection, function, and structure of new toys and games, but for most product, it is children who will determine whether this adult wisdom was accurate. Rather than rule in presumptuous isolation of kiddie consumers, management is inclined to involve children in all the key stages of product development. It is far better to get reactions early than to wait until there is a warehouse full of miscalculations. Despite industry enthusiasm for a toy or game, in the end, it is very possible that little Tyler or Bettie—or their mothers—just won't like it. Early testing and accurate interpretation of consumer data help prevent later market rejection.

Product Development

Former independent inventor Peter Pook, now at Fisher-Price, calls product development the reworking of a simple idea to the point where it needs $2 million in advertising to explain and sell it. Actually, product development takes an idea with appeal to both executives and children and considers it from a business angle. "When new game concepts come to us, it is not just that they must be clever, cute, unique, appealing, innovative, and interesting to the target audience," says Mike Langieri, vice president of creative development at Milton Bradley. "We must also be confident that we can make the game and sell it at a price that allows us to earn a reasonable profit. We must first determine if our marketing people see a spot in our line for the concept and a dynamic way to promote it. They give us the go-ahead with a target sell price attached. We can then put all the development disciplines to work to determine if we can make a solid, highly playable game for that target price while yielding a profit at a forecasted sales volume."

Those development disciplines are indeed numerous, for to get a sense of the true cost of an item, you must take into account much more than parts and labor, particularly the expense for art and design, capital investments for tooling and equipment, and the costs of advertising and promotion.

It is impossible to do these projections for every new product concept, so the number of products under consideration is constantly being winnowed out. "This is a very judgmental time," notes Langieri. "Often a real good game or two falls from further work and is returned to the inventor—not because a concept isn't good, but because we feel we have an alternative that ultimately will be more salable and more promotable."

During the selection process, new toys and games are played and played and played. They are stretched and enlarged to convey greater price–value relationship, greater presence at retail. Or they may be reduced in size to have a portable travel feature, possible collectibility, or a lower price point. In-house people will be involved in product naming sessions. Countless catchy names will be considered, favorites will be researched for prior use, and the final choice will be trademarked. These

Figure 2. Steps to Product Selection

Step	Responsibility	Objective
1. General survey of opportunities (may be 2,500 possibilities)	R&D and marketing	Separate product wheat from chaff, dross from gold
2. Focus on manageable number of product developments (may be 200 possibilities)	R&D and marketing	Build a line with strongest candidates throughout
3. Define final product form and function, establish packaging	Designers, artists, engineers, modelmakers	Establish design and functional specifications at target sell prices
4. Review playability, consumer features, and point-of-sale appeal	R&D and marketing	Build in all game features and make sure product and package convey features and benefits to consumer
5. Coordinate product, packaging, promotion, and advertising	R&D, marketing, advertising, and sales	Position product to yield expected sales volume and pace
6. Sign off of line introductions for Toy Fair (may be 25 selections)	Senior divisional and corporate management	Approve investments in new product that will contribute to overall corporate growth

same products will be safety-tested for puncture points, ingestion, toxicity, durability under misuse and abuse. They will be sculpted and modeled into a three-dimensional shape. Parts will be engineered and made functional; parts will be added or taken away. Plastics will be weighed and thicknesses specified. Factory assembly will be costed if done by the manufacturer. Instructions will be diagrammed when assembly by the customer is required. The new items will be decorated with appealing colors and lively graphics and anchored in protective, appealing packaging. Every possible factor that has an impact on cost is examined for its effect on the bottom line. From an inventor's first prototype, a commercially viable product now exists: a plaything for kids but a true business opportunity for senior management.

Warren Bosch, director of product development at Tyco Toys, says, "It's one thing to make a piece of something and another to make two and a half million of them. That kind of development work is often just as creative as coming up with the idea itself."

"As an independent developer, it is an exciting time when your product is in the R&D process," says Charlie Phillips, inventor of Advance to Boardwalk, Roller Coaster, Clue Jr, Detective, Vegas Nites: Casino Card Games, and other popular board and card games. "You know what you brought to the manufacturer and you have their commitment to bring the idea to market. What you don't know is exactly what the product will look like when it comes through the transformation from original idea to manufactured product. After eight to ten months, when you see your fully executed idea, you recognize it as your offspring even though you may be unfamiliar with its final form."

Mike Satten, nineteen years in the business, is so familiar with all the stages along the long road that he can recite them with staccato emphasis. "Things have to pass through so many people. Imagine. You have to show it to a guy who has to like it; he has to take it back and show it to a group that has to like it; the engineering has to work; it has to work at a cost; it has to be tested with kids and tested with parents; the trade has to see it, the trade has to like it; the agency has to see it, the agency has to like it; the agency has to do the commercials; the commercials have to be tested with kids and parents who have to like what they see; then the trade has to see the product again and like the commercial. And after all that, there is a problem in China. It's mind-boggling.''

Manufacturing Takeover

When senior management makes the decision that a product is a "go," months of creation now dovetail into months of production. It is up to the engineers, toolmakers, procurement people, and production staff to bring the toy or game through manufacturing according to schedule. Estimates become actuals; plans become reality.

"Once we know that management is committed to a new game and we have all the final specifications for the product, we turn on all the capabilities of a fully integrated manufacturing facility," says Joe Gullini, senior vice president of operations at Milton Bradley. "What we don't make or convert in our own plant we procure from external suppliers, whether domestic or offshore. We become dedicated to producing the best possible product within the time frame and within projected costs."

"The development process and the manufacturing takeover can be likened to a relay race in a track meet," says Michael Langieri. "Every part of the event takes an all-out effort to progress through some very clear objectives. You meet those objectives and keep moving farther along until you pass the challenge onto someone else. Although you move the product on to the next development stage, you remain interested and involved so that the item stands a better chance of finishing as a winner.

"In the toy business, we may not be passing a baton," he adds, "but rather an engineering blueprint, a batch of specifications, a finely tuned mold. As the idea moves through progressive stages of development, it will cross the final milestone in a schedule through the involvement of many skilled and specialized people. If they all do their jobs well, the idea—not the baton—will be passed along through key steps toward initial production. Manufacturing will then be called upon to make reruns as needed. The 'new' will become the familiar, the standard.''

Marketing Line Reviews

While the daily details of product development and manufacturing move the toy or game idea toward final form, periodic reviews check that the product is on course as far as marketing expectations are concerned. All the stops are out to create a marketable, salable product, but a slight pause on a regular basis allows for assessment of progress and direction. The review brings package design and advertising into focus. "Our commercial for a new game is intended to capture a strong point of difference between our product and everything else that is out there," says Dale Siswick, vice president of marketing at Milton Bradley. "The message has to be hard-hitting and memorable. If targeted at the child, we want the commercial to create reasons for the child to ask for the game. If targeted at parents, we want the commercial to be memorable so that they remember the product when making a buying decision. "If the commercial is our sales message in a TV spot, our commercial at the store level is our package," continues Siswick. "We want that package to have as much energy, as much appeal as our most animated thirty-second spot. In the stacks of boxes, in the aisles of choices, we want our package to stand out.''

A marketing line review is a time of assessment and a time to update R&D marketing, sales, manufacturing, and senior management issues. Each review, at any point along the development cycle, may turn up important information. If all does not fit into place, if later information refutes previous conclusions, a product candidate may fall from favor. The farther along a product may be in a cycle, the more costly it is to abort its development. However, the financial gamble is never greater than when a product has gone to full term, with hundreds of thousands of units in inventory. With that in mind, a new plaything can be changed—or scrapped—right up to its Toy Fair debut.

''I've seen products fall at every step of the way during my years in the business,'' says inventor Jeffrey Breslow. ''At first we want to know if the idea will be selected to go into the development cycle. But even after that happens, and I have a contract as a firm commitment from a manufacturer, I know a product may be dropped unless it has strong buyer support at pre-Toy Fair. At the fair, without significant buyer interest and orders, an item may be dropped. It is a tremendous disappointment to us all and a major financial setback as well. In this business, you learn that it is never out until it is out . . . on retail shelves.''

Toy Fair: The End of the Cycle

The stakes are high. For the thousands of hours of creative effort and dollar investment to pay off, sales must begin at the rollout of each new item, so little about that rollout is left to chance. At the Toy Fair in New York, products are displayed on pedestals for peak visual impression. Enthusiastic, well-coached demonstrators extol product features and invite visitors to play. Nearby TV monitors flash soon-to-be-aired commercials that are just one part of the major-market media campaigns in support of the new product.

The most common question asked at the American International Toy Fair? Without doubt, that question is, "What's new?" Buyers know the past winners that continue to sell. Salespeople prefer not to talk about what hasn't met expectations. The starting place for the coming year's business is with innovative new products, slick new packages, and hard-sell commercials.

The inventor, of course, takes pride in seeing his or her product on display and takes interest in its sale at Toy Fair and beyond. More than ever, he or she is now inextricably tied to the manufacturer. "When Toy Fair comes around, you either have items in the marketplace or you don't," explains Mike Satten. "If I don't, I feel I have wasted a year. The way I look at it, you've beaten the odds, sold a few items, and you're a winner. If they happen to be well received, then you're a bigger winner." "I come to Toy Fair to get a reading on what's new in general, but more specifically to see how our new placements are accepted by the trade," says George Delaney of Delaney Development. "I try to get to all the showrooms for a look at what we will be up against the coming year and to see where the holes may be in any line. But I particularly delight in visiting those showrooms where our items are being unveiled."

"Toy Fair is a highly charged and frenzied event. You go to keep up with the latest ideas and see old friends," says inventor Charlie Phillips. "There is a special twinge of pride when you see your products in a manufacturer's showroom." But as Phillips explains, the end of the cycle is also the beginning of the next cycle: "Those displayed products are history to you now. Your main focus is on your latest creations, products that you hope to see displayed at a future Toy Fair. In the inventing business, you force yourself to think of the future and not pause too long in the glory of the present.''

As intensive as the ten-day Toy Fair may be, some major manufacturers host special receptions to recognize the inventing community and privately showcase product lines to the idea people. Companies such as Kenner, Mattel, Ohio Art, Parker Brothers, Nasta, Hasbro, Tonka, and Western Publishing invite the pros to their showrooms or hotel suites. At such affairs, grateful senior executives get a chance to express thanks to the inventors, in the company of their peers, for their contributions.

This is perhaps the only time in the year that Fred ("Hungry Hungry Hippos") Kroll, Marty ("Omni") Blumenthal, and Ray ("Big Wheels") Lohr will get to see fellow inventors Howard ("Ready, Set, Spaghetti") Tarnoff, Ted ("Thunder Cats") Wolf, Larry ("Little Maestro") Greenberg, Larry ("Cricket") Jones, and Gary ("The Star") Piaget. The inventors have the opportunity to see what their creative colleagues have been doing, to assess possible future product placement opportunities, to build new relationships, and to kibitz with each other about their latest introductions.

All companies use some form of internal development process to constantly churn emerging lines with even newer candidates, comparing the features of one new toy with the benefits of another and playing the new forms against the old classics. Where there are doubts about direction, market tests search out consumer reactions and preferences. Throughout the process, new ideas are being revised, recast, and, if necessary, replaced. Inventors may be impatient with such processes, but quarter-million-dollar tooling costs, hundred-thousand-dollar art expenses, and million-dollar promotion programs for a single item make product selection very high-stakes decision-making. Inventors focus only on their own items and always are confident that their concepts will not be multimillion-dollar mistakes. But company executives selecting ten to fifteen promotable items for the coming Toy Fair are thinking about the $20 to $30 million gamble across an entire line of new playthings. They cannot help but be influenced as well by thoughts of the recent industry bankruptcies of Worlds of Wonder and Coleco and the financial woes of Tonka, Galoob, and Matchbox Toys (USA). And then there are the companies that simply disappeared. The lessons learned by others do teach caution.

Product development is a protracted and careful exercise. Just as in aviation, there are preflight checklists to be followed. And each manufacturer has some sort of centralized warning system that puts on the FASTEN SEAT BELTS sign as soon as there is an indication of any failure of the item being developed and/or in the marketplace for which it is destined. Unlike aviation, however, there are no flight simulators in which executives can learn how to handle dramas and catastrophes out of harm's way. In the toy industry, every product launch is for real, so it must be taken *very* seriously.

6 Batteries Not Included

HOW A PRODUCT IS POWERED

Is selling the sizzle every bit as important, maybe more important, than the steak?'' CBS News correspondent Dan Rather asks Milton Bradley president George Ditomassi during the taping of *Toy Money*, the ''48 Hours'' behind-the-scenes look at the toy industry. ''Yes, I think that we're in show business,'' responds the man who oversees the 130-year-old game giant.

A look at the way some manufacturers describe their products in slick catalogs, ubiquitous press clippings, and promotional activities illustrates how much show business there is in the toy business.

Hasbro's COPS, a line of action figures for younger boys, licensed from Marvin Glass & Associates, was launched with a multimillion-dollar advertising campaign and its own syndicated animated television series. ''Fightin' Crime in a Future Time!'' ZAP . . . BANG! All the good guys and their vehicles have unique cap-firing weaponry that creates a big-bang effect for what the manufacturer calls ''crossfire fun.'' Hasbro wrote an action-packed backstory against which to sell the assortment of characters. It includes Big Boss, the crime lord; Sgt. Mace, a SWAT officer; Buttons McBoomboom, a machine gunner; and Dr. Badvibes, a mad scientist. It's the twenty-first century, and organized crime has gained the upper hand in its struggle with the law. Under the evil influence of CROOKS, crime has spread across the country like wildfire. Everywhere there is fear that a total collapse of law and order could happen at any time!

Dino Riders from Tyco Toys challenges kids to "Harness the Power of Dinosaurs!" It's 50,000 B.C.—The Ice Age! In a world of endless winter, cavemen struggle for survival against giant prehistoric mammals. There the Dino Riders find powerful allies to join them in their battle against the Rulons.

In addition to a multimillion-dollar advertising budget, Tyco Toys wrote and produced a fully animated Dino Rider Ice Age adventure that was offered to kids on videocassette in toy stores for under $5 in 1990.

Mattel went to even greater lengths during its run with the Masters of the Universe action-figure line: The California toymaker backed a feature-length motion picture starring its characters. The brainchild of independent pro Derek Gable while he was working for Mattel, Masters of the Universe took children to the fantasy world of Eternia, a place beyond all time. Characters such as He-Man ("the most powerful man in the universe," and Skeletor ("the lord of destruction") played out their story line around Castle Grayskull, the centerpiece of the toy collection.

But in the final analysis, it is consumer demand that makes one product more successful than another, not designs and backstories. "Toys are not sold. Toys are bought," points out David Leibowitz, at American Securities Corporation. "As each child on the block gets a new product, he invites other friends to play with it. If the peer group enjoys it, they're going to tell whomever the toy-buying member of their family is to get it for them. You replicate that experience in enough parts of the country and you have a winner.

"You can fool a parent, you can fool a retailer, and," Leibowitz admits, "Lord knows you can fool an analyst, but you can't fool a child. If the child expects that a product can stand on its head and spit wooden nickels while whistling Dixie, it doesn't matter what other attributes it has; if it doesn't meet those first three requirements, the product won't sell."

"I agree with David," says Steve Schwartz of Playskool. "In the collectible category, getting the first sale is real easy, which is why whenever you come out with a new boys' toy, you see what's called 'the bubble.' The first two or three weeks, the category just takes off, and if you make it into the fifth week, you're almost home free. But I've seen more products drop dead after the third week. Why's that? Because the kid gets it home and it doesn't live up to the promise. . . . They tell their friends, nobody buys the second one, and you're done."

Toys and games must appeal as products. But the transition of a good idea into a mass-marketable plaything is only the beginning. The five most important elements for cutting through the clutter of choices facing a buyer are packaging, pricing, personality, promotion, and public relations.

It's not enough that the inventor's neighborhood kids like a new plaything, or even that it tests well in formal focus groups. "We see hundreds of good playing games each year as we put a new line together," says Larry Bernstein of Parker Brothers, "but the game's playability is only one part of the success formula." He continues: "We have to answer questions about other elements in the formula before we can feel good about a product's chances in the market, questions like:

Does the package merchandise well and promise high product expectations while displayed on the retail shelf?

Can the product be positioned at a price to overcome any consumer resistance and avoid a buying choice with competitive items?

Can we tie in the product with some hot consumer fantasy or identifiable personality?

Is there a memorable point of difference about the product that will pop in our TV promotion?

Is there some element of the product that makes it newsworthy and allows a strong public relations campaign?

"The more elements the product has working for it, the more energy it will have at retail. The stronger the integration of product with package and promotion, the more likely there will be a consumer purchase and after-purchase satisfaction."

The sheer mass of product offerings is an indicator of the volatility of the toy-and-game industry. According to the Toy Manufacturers of America, 150,000 playthings are available from various companies. Each year producers "churn" their lines, dropping mediocre sellers and adding new products in hopes of catching greater sales. In such a product-intensive environment, the independent toy inventor exists to answer the manufacturer's call for something better, something cheaper, something never done before. The function of the inventing community is to provide a great product year after year, each year topping the sales of the previous year's outpouring.

Product

Inventors concentrate on toy and game creations because they know there is a high demand. When asked why Girsch Design Associates concentrates its inventing skills on toys and games, Maria Girsch says, "If you mention royalty in some industries, they think you are talking about British aristocracy. Other businesses are very slow to infuse new products. We are where we are because we know there is a premium placed on new ideas each year. There's a lot of room to churn and earn.''

Paul Lapidus agrees. ''Toy and game inventing can be more lucrative than most other areas of product design,'' he asserts. ''Manufacturers in this business actively seek out new ideas from the inventing community-at-large. Unfortunately, many other industries seem uncomfortable working with outside inventors and do not regularly invest the dollars on new products at the levels you find in the toy-and-game business.''

If the toy business has an insatiable appetite for new ideas, it also provides the professional inventor huge targets for creativity. The *Playthings Directory* differentiates more than 700 categories of toys and games that manufacturers bring to market. In the doll category alone, there are twenty-seven different types, from baby to fashion to walking. Or you could direct your efforts at some of the twenty-five recognized doll accessory categories, ranging from fashion to furniture. Is your specialty game development? The industry recognizes forty-six different categories of games from A to W: action games to word games. The inventor not only has a choice of the category and type of toy or game but also must focus on who will use it and in what type of environment (i.e., preschool or adult, boy or girl, artistic or athletic, outdoor or indoor).

Although the industry thrives on product ideas, the demand is not always for totally innovative approaches in new designs. There is something to be said for new products that bear a similarity to something that has been done in the past. Truly innovative products offer no experiential reference. They are unknown and unproven. Both the toy trade and the consumer are sometimes less than willing to try unfamiliar products.

This security from ideas born in the past and rehashed in the present does not trigger innovation. The ''creative'' activity is more reinvention. As long as there is no infringement on patents or trademarks, new play on a borrowed concept is a time-honored tradition among inventors and manufacturers. It is quite common to hear such comments as, "It plays a lot like a yo-yo, but it has a new twist." Or "It doesn't look like a Frisbee, but it seems like Frisbee revisited." Though he has created many unique concepts in his thirty-five-year career, Ted Wolf sees part of his role as "adapting previously known devices to previously unknown products." Inventors do not speak only of "original," "innovative," "never before," and "unique" in describing their creations. "Recombining" is an acknowledged skill of the toy pro.

The history of toy inventing is filled with stories of successful products that came about through a new interpretation of long-established playthings. Examples would certainly include Eddy Goldfarb's toy line, Stompers, and Jeffrey Breslow's Trump, The Game.

Invent a new toy truck? Nothing exceptional about the specs—two axles and a chassis. But what Eddy Goldfarb and his partner, Del Everitt, brought to an eager market of young boys was the off-road craze in toy scale. Goldfarb recalls, "Here in southern California we started noticing a lot of 4-wheel-drive, off-the-road vehicles and thought they would make a nice toy item. But what we wanted to do more than anything was to make it very, very small, very powerful, and small enough that you wouldn't be able to tell how you got the battery in. And we used known trucks; but changed them to make them more macho."

Goldfarb first took his 4 x 4 concept to Kenner. The manufacturer bought it immediately and made plans to introduce eight to ten items. Then, after Kenner worked for three months, Goldfarb was surprised to learn that the company's design department had changed his original concept and showed Kenner president Bernie Loomis a big vehicle—not what Goldfarb had submitted. Loomis reportedly complained, "I didn't want big ones, I wanted small ones." After three or four more months, Loomis told his people to give the concept back to Goldfarb. "And he's still ruing the day," adds Goldfarb.

Goldfarb then took the concept to Schaper Toys and sold it on the spot. Schaper made the vehicles according to the inventor's concept and named them Stompers. Now there are more than 200 models, and many millions—Goldfarb isn't sure how many—have been sold worldwide.

Invent a new wealth-accumulation real estate game? Certainly done before with the all-time favorite, Monopoly, and a host of clones over the years. But what Jeffrey Breslow did was weave the charisma of billionaire developer Donald Trump into a wheeling/dealing investment game—his 1989 Milton Bradley entry, Trump, The Game.

It took Breslow three or four months to put the deal together. He claims to have read Trump's best-selling book three times to get a feel for what the man was all about. "We told him that if he gave us the rights, we would spend our money to develop it. If he liked what we did, then we would sell it to the right company. Then he flipped over what we showed him," says Breslow. "It happens to be a great game. We had many toymakers who wanted to make the game even without his name, so we were very satisfied with the product. The tie-in with him just made it even better."

The magic of the Trump name attracted toy and game buyers to the new game with an old and tried theme. They bought hundreds of thousands in 1989 in hopes that consumers would want to play the role of the freewheeling real estate developer. Only time will tell if the marketplace supports the crossover from Boardwalk to Breslow's claim to game fame.

Package

Most consumer products reach the end-user in some form of
package, from giant reinforced appliance cartons to stylish jew-
elry cases. Some packages contain inner linings of protective
packing materials, others have contoured inserts to anchor
pieces securely. All packages perform the function of carrying
the product from point of manufacture to place of consumer
use. They protect products from the bumps, bounces, and
tosses from dock to door.

Manufacturers know that packages must be dropped,
torqued, crushed, punctured, and baked during tests to measure how well they protect their valued contents. Underpacking
a product can have disastrous effects at retail. Consumers seeing damaged packages on the shelf will assume concealed damage to the product and will instead select a crisp, unscuffed
container. Left behind will be crushed and abraded packages—
a very poor reflection on the product, the manufacturer, and
the retailer.

Packages for toys and games are expected to go beyond
merely carrying product to the consumer. They are also intended to provide after-purchase storage. Even if kids seldom
use the function, reusable boxes keep a game board and play
pieces safely together.

But packages have an even more important purpose than
protecting the contents before and after purchase; in addition
to transporting and storing products, they must merchandise
them as well. Whether hung from hooks, stacked on shelves,
or aligned in point-of-sale displays, packages must draw attention to the products. In a high-traffic, impulse-buying arena,
the package should be an appealing, attention-grabbing bill-
board that stops the consumer in the aisle and invites handling
and examination in a matter of seconds. It must influence the
decision to buy on the spot.

Says Milton Bradley's Dale Siswick, "Packaging is so terribly important in the competitive retail environment. Consumers are making buying choices in a matter of minutes, seconds even. You want your package to convey a price–value relationship that makes consumers feel they got a value for the price. A large package in good structural condition, showing and promoting an attractive product, goes a long way toward helping your product move off the shelf. Packaging must close the sale at shelf level.''

Many toys are displayed at retail in open-faced or see-through packages. The charm and aesthetics of the plaything come through the polystyrene film or thermal-formed blister. The consumer sees exactly what is inside. Other packages use photography or illustration to capture the essence of the product. Vivid, high-energy graphics promise endless hours of entertainment from the toy or game inside.

In a traditional box package, every square inch of the six panels offers valuable space for sales messages. Even a box bottom is used to carry the story of features and benefits. Two side panels and two end panels usually shout the product name and a miniature reproduction of it. Not surprisingly, the face of the box is the most important side. No package is successful without a powerful face panel. All the product life and personality must come through on this facing. Consumers should be brought into the promise of fun through a dynamic product presentation with age-appropriate kids happy in their play. Features and benefits are either shown or listed. If the brand is a trusted name, that name is carried prominently on all panels.

Ron Magers of Magers Products for Children knows from experience the importance of packaging: ''As a toy inventor, I have always concentrated on product design. When a manufacturer contracts to produce one of my concepts, I try to follow progress on development as closely as I can as an external partner. But I'll never forget the packaging issue on one of my toddler toys. Clik-Claks had a whimsical animal design with sound and visual movement. In depressing two big buttons, however, the toddler could get a flapping movement and a cute clickety-click sound. The execution of the two versions was just delightful; everything worked just as I planned and designed.

"But," he recalls, "when the product was packaged, even though you could see the toy through a window, only half of the play possibilities came across to the consumer. There was no way to activate the buttons at point of sale. Since the package was quite small, there was no way to tell the story of the full play potential. Here was a great product in a less-than-great package. No one will ever know the amount of lost sales; I will never know the lost royalties! This product would have been a perfect candidate for a 'try me' box."

Pricing

On the matter of pricing, veteran inventor Gordon Barlow says, "For more than thirty years I've had too many ideas turned down by manufacturers for costing reasons not to take production issues into mind as I design a new toy. At the outset, I just let the concept flow. When I know I'm really on to something, I try to step back and formulate some engineering and production parameters in my design as suggestions to the manufacturer.

"But in the end," he laments, "my thoughts as an inventor won't matter. What I think may be a retail bargain at $14.99 may be targeted for $9.99 by the manufacturer. When there is such a wide differential, unfortunately, I know my product will not be accepted into the line. You reach a point where nothing more can be taken from a toy or game to reduce costs."

Everyone involved with new toys and games must ask the question, "At what price product?" To the inventor, a pet idea is extremely valuable. The more pieces sold, the higher the rewards. Every inventor feels that all kids should have his or her creation, maybe even two or possibly a whole collection.

It is not surprising for the inventor to be deeply emotional about the creation; how else could a manufacturer or consumer be expected to be interested? However, it is the marketer/manufacturer's job to place a "price–value" on an idea. Both marketing and manufacturing analyses are done to determine a sufficient profit margin, a level at which the whole exercise becomes worthwhile. In the end, it is the profit dollars generated from sales that measure true success.

Staff designers and engineers establish the product's dimensions and component specifications. Amount of decoration, number of parts, how things work, how things get made, and choice of materials—all influence the cost, as do labor rates on product assembly and packaging. Then there are the molds, tooling, product and package artwork, and production costs. Manufacturers best able to plan all product details will have the best preproduction estimates and more accurate postproduction costs. Every toy and game carries the burden of these startup costs for molds, fixtures, and other tooling; product and package artwork; and promotion until a sufficient number of units is sold to pay back the investment. Startup costs are a major reason why it is hard for many new products to capture market share from well-established products, even though the new products may be more innovative. The old standbys have already paid back their investment dollars and can, therefore, be sold for much less than the new entries.

The toy manufacturer establishes a "sell price" to the retail trade that includes a fair profit above all production costs. Then the retail outlets determine a markup from the price they pay the manufacturer, and that is the price customers pay. Some stores choose a full 40 percent markup; others take a short markup and offer discounted pricing. It is up to the sharp-eyed consumer to find the best price on a favorite toy or game. Price variations splashed in the Sunday circulars reflect retailer differences in their pricing strategies to move merchandise off their shelves. Retailers with the best selection and the sharpest prices usually attract the largest consumer traffic and move the most products.

Considering the high stakes involved in launching a new toy or game, manufacturers obviously must rely on more than just gut-level intuition when choosing new product. The more orchestrated and controlled the whole rollout process, the more likely it is that toy people will be on target with new introductions that meet consumer expectations. When applying the hard realities of product cost and investment to a new toy or game, it becomes clear why only one idea in 100 is marketed.

Personality

"Kids like to play with friends. So when you make products for kids, it's nice to have help from a friend they know." This is the opening in a trade ad taken out by Licensing Corporation of America promoting to U.S. toymakers some of its famous character licenses, such as Batman, Bugs Bunny, Frosty the Snowman, Superman, Wonder Woman, Gumby, Alf, and Police Academy. "If you want to build new excitement in staple or generic products," the ad continues, "our classic . . . characters can add terrific fun."

Licensing is the business of leasing the right to use a legally protected name, graphic, logo, saying, or likeness in conjunction with a product, promotion, or service, according to the Licensing Industry Merchandisers' Association. *Playthings* magazine lists more than 1,500 licensed properties in its 1989–90 resource issue, and inventors and manufacturers make wide use of these opportunities in each year's new toy lineup. In 1980, sales of licensed products worldwide were $10 billion. In 1990, sales of all types of licensed products worldwide hit an all-time high of $66.5 billion (up from $64.6 billion in 1989), according to *The Licensing Letter*, a newsletter. Sesame Street Wrist Jingles (Playskool), Mike Tyson's Punch Out (Nintendo), Babar plush toys (Gund), Alf and Muppet Babies jigsaw puzzles

(Milton Bradley), Looney Tunes vehicles (Ertl), and thousands of other items are license-loaded products.

"Modern licensing was started by the Walt Disney Company," explains Stanley A. Weston, chairman and founder of Leisure Concepts, Inc., one of the nation's leading licensing organizations. "The Howdy Doody property in the early 1950s started what I consider modern TV licensing. Then you go into a much more expanded list of properties, ranging from a classic like Snoopy to current ones such as Cabbage Patch Kids and Batmania." Such industry favorites as Sesame Street and Disney move millions of dollars of product each year. Batman spin-offs have sold more than $500 million. According to Weston, the average royalty paid by a toy company for a license is in the range of 6 to 10 percent of net wholesale dollars.

Licensing is a sophisticated way of marketing and merchandising products that cross many industries. Toy manufacturers and retailers are always seeking new methods of attracting and holding customers, and licensing represents a cooperative attempt to reach that consumer. Knowledgeable toy and game inventors have been aware for many years that having the right license on their products can mean lots of extra income, in spite of the reduced royalty that it typically requires. Many professional inventors, therefore, clothe their designs in an existing license or develop and license their own properties.

"Adding a licensed character to a toy or game has the obvious benefit of bringing an identity to the product," says James Walsh, vice president of licensing and premium sales at The Ertl Company. "It should have a positive impact on sales. However, just putting a personality onto the artwork or into the molded pieces will not make a bad product good. Though many people are comfortable seeing familiar faces on toys and games, it can be a tricky business for the manufacturers. If the personality weakens in the marketplace, ratings drop, or some unforeseen event casts badly on your personality, that kind of news can take the product down with it. A superhero is a help in this business; on the other hand, nobody wants to play with a fallen hero.''

Another attraction of licensing from a manufacturer's viewpoint is the all-important bottom-line profit. Says Walsh, ''When you market a licensed line of product, it requires less advertising expense than for a similar line of goods without a license attached to it. The cost savings on advertising, even when you consider the royalty fee, can provide added profit dollars versus the nonlicensed line.''

''Certainly Sesame Street and Disney have shown that licensing is tremendously important, but they're not panaceas either. You put them on a bad product and you get a bad result,'' warns Steve Schwartz of Playskool. ''I think in terms of some of the hot licenses, like a Batman, an E.T.; it's all timing.''

Richard Sollis, senior vice president at Playmates, the company that launched Teenage Mutant Ninja Turtles, agrees. ''The marketplace is constantly changing and timeliness is an important element. A license that would work at one particular time may not necessarily work at another time.''

Much of the appeal of a licensed property comes from the design and graphics that can be built in by the unique personality. A strong, recognizable figure catches the eye of the consumer and rivets interest on the product at point of sale and throughout repeat play. The popularity of personalities, celebrities, and events current in the culture flavor the tone and form of playthings stacked on the toy shelves. This is evident on any walk through a favorite toy-and-game store.

But not all licensed properties meet with success. After a strong launch of Evel Knievel in the early 1970s, the abrupt demise of his popularity nearly sank the Ideal Toy Company. Toyland's Boot Hill is jammed with ''former favorites.''

Vic Reiling, a ten-year independent inventor, has learned to live with licensed properties in his creative world. Notes Reiling, ''When I come up with a new concept, I don't necessarily plan it for any specific celebrity or personality. I make my concept relevant to what is going on with kids and wherever possible weave a contemporary feeling into my design. The more 'now,' the better. When it comes to a specific personality being applied to one of my concepts, what they add is entirely the call of the manufacturer. Usually I'm asked to take a reduced royalty when some cartoon character or superhero is added to the product plan. If a mouse or bird can double the sales of one of my concepts, I am very interested in a partnership. I want to see my ideas sell." Stanley Weston says that to a toy company licensing means "presold." A good product that's properly priced and manufactured can be given an added presold advantage over its competitor when identified in a logical way with a well-known license or property.

Promotion

The 1989 toy industry advertising budgets read like Third World bank loans: Hasbro, $115.5 million; Kenner/Parker/Tonka, $60 million; Mattel, $48 million; Tyco Toys; $32 million; Fisher-Price, $30 million. By way of comparison, the nation's largest national advertiser, Philip Morris Companies, spent $2.06 billion. The entire toy industry spent over $400 million in all forms of advertising in 1989, according to BAR/LNA Multi-Media Service.

"One of the major changes I've seen in the industry through the years is the extensive use of TV commercials to promote toys and games to consumers," says Eddy Goldfarb. "I recall bringing product concepts to top executives and if they had a favorable gut reaction, we had a deal. Now the decision-making process has been strung out, much of the reason being the tremendous expense associated with promotional campaigns."

"Ad agencies are extremely important," says Neil Werde, vice president of marketing at Tyco Toys. "They create the image that the child sees. They do the commercials and those are what sell the product. It's an advertising-driven business. We must have a commercial to hit the big numbers."

"I feel I am making a major investment of time and effort to come up with a new concept. I prefer to get that concept placed with a manufacturer who is also making a major investment," says Eddy Goldfarb. "Although I have no control over the decision, that means making my item a promoted new entry. With TV support, the product will have a running start on the thousands of other new products introduced each year at Toy Fair."

Goldfarb's impression of the importance of TV promotion is held by many of his colleagues in the inventing community. Of a hundred leading inventors, more than seventy feel a TV commercial is very, very important to the success of a toy or game. More than half of these seventy inventors attach greater importance to the TV effort than they do to play value or product design.

"Let's face it," says Paul Lapidus, former design manager at Playskool before becoming an independent inventor. "With all of the options parents have when shopping for toys and games, a memorable commercial is a real boost for a product in this business. No toy or game is a certain, guaranteed success until both the trade and the consumers make it happen."

"We only do TV items," says Larry Jones, head of Cal R&D and inventor of many products, including Tyco Toys' Data Race 500 and Sounds of Service by Matchbox. "I guess a lot of little guys will do non-TV toys, but I'll tell you from this standpoint—and I've been in the business since 1969—the only way you have staying power in this industry is to generate royalty income, and a solid TV-promoted item will help you survive."

Manufacturers of course know that they cannot silently introduce a significant new toy or game into the market and expect a hit. Consumers are not looking for playthings as necessities. Before they enter a toy store, they must receive a message about what to buy. In fact, that message from a TV spot often sends them shopping.

Some TV spots are targeted toward parents, others toward children. Messages for parents create an impression that children will benefit from and enjoy the promoted plaything. This is certainly the approach of all preschool commercials. Messages for children aim to create excitement and a lasting impression so that they will ask their parents for the plaything by name. Parents will make the decision to buy, but they are strongly influenced by the demands of their children.

Manufacturers know that if there is no presell through hard-hitting TV spots, the product will be lost among the thousands of toys and games stocked by today's high-volume retailers. Promotion must get the purchaser through the doors of a local toy store looking for a specific product. Once he or she gets there, product design, interesting packaging, appealing personality, and the right price may close the sale. But the whole motivation for the consumer to buy many playthings starts with the television commercial.

It is not uncommon for a major manufacturer to create a million-dollar media campaign. Between production costs of the commercial and buying the media placement, a seven-figure campaign is minimal to get the attention of the trade buyer and ultimately the consumer. In many cases, the promotion budget exceeds all the other costs of developing and bringing a product to market.

According to the Toy Manufacturers of America, studies have shown that toys with heavy advertising budgets generally result in lower consumer prices than those backed by smaller ad budgets. As a result, the average retail profit margin for television-advertised toys is now 15 to 25 percent, while the average for nonadvertised items is between 35 and 40 percent. Several factors contribute to this phenomenon. At the store level, retailers use TV-promoted toys in their local advertising to create competitive prices with other retailers. In addition, these toys, at reduced prices, are used as "loss leaders" to build general store traffic and more rapid inventory turnover. At the manufacturing level, the high demand created by TV and other advertising allows for economy scale and the purchase of raw materials in volume, thus further lowering the toy's price.

Retailers expect the manufacturers to support their toys and games with TV commercials. Ten years ago, it was common to find four or five items in a given line with TV support. Now many manufacturers have plans for new major introductions to be promoted on television. Retailers place such great value on their shelf space that they will not commit to a product with no commercials to help pull it from their stores.

"At one time I was concerned about the play value of every item I bought for my stores," says one major mass-market buyer who asked not to be identified. "But today, I am more interested in how much money the manufacturer is planning to spend on promotion than in what's in the box."

Public Relations

"We are in the most unique position of any toy company in the business from a PR point of view," says Jeanne Hopkins, public relations manager of Lego Systems. "How many companies have a whole theme park devoted to their products? Our Legoland in Billund, Denmark, has a million visitors during the short, half-year season and more than half of them are non-Danish. It is hard to visit the facility and not come away with a desire to get into building with Lego bricks. That park experience is worth a lot of hard-sell TV commercials. Such commercials are usually fifteen- or thirty-second 'buy me' messages. Public relations efforts such as the park and other programs at

Lego build the popularity of our products through real-life experiences."

Public relations people know that bringing attention and interest to a toy or game before a broad audience can only help sales. Consumers have a natural tendency to "join in the fun" or "share the experience" when they become aware of a hot, topical product. Tournaments, play-offs, challenges, and high-visibility celebrity endorsements get the media coverage that builds demand for products in the marketplace. Such events are also economical and effective. Not only do they build sales, but they also focus favorable public attention on brand names.

Picture, if you will, a toy disk being hurled almost a quarter-mile through the southern California skies. The 1,126-foot toss becomes a world record for an Aerobie, a disk-shaped toy invented by Alan Adler. The challenge is set for all ages to match. The news brings sales of this performance flying disk not only from those who want to play but from those who seek the competitive test of breaking a world record.

A lovely eight-year-old girl proudly displays her collection of My Little Pony toy friends to members of the local press at the invitation of the manufacturer. Billed as the world's largest private collection of My Little Pony, it consists of 364 well-manicured, colorfully maned pastel ponies. The subsequent news story of one little girl's hobby leads others to a fixation with large numbers of the collectible toy.

The high school gymnasium is filled with tables containing setups for the popular word game Scrabble. In this arena of intense, concentrated play, word-game buffs are battling for supremacy in a regional contest sponsored by the game's manufacturer. The winner will move on to the national championships. Only a game, yes, but the activity has passed beyond play and is now a serious competition.

"Event publicity can create a great deal of excitement and capture the attention of the media if done correctly," says George H. Merritt, vice president of public relations at Milton

Bradley and an experienced advertising and PR professional. "Of course, the 'newness' of some games gives you an advantage, and we select a handful of new games every year and create special publicity programs for them. The media like anything new, or at least they'll take the time to review it. But how do you promote the old favorites—Candy Land, Chutes and Ladders, Battleship, Operation?"

He gives as another example the twenty-five-year-old game Twister. In Twister, players stand on a plastic mat printed with different-colored circles. As the game director spins a spinner, the players must place their hands and feet on those colored circles without losing their balance. They twist, turn, and contort until the one left standing wins.

"I remember the tremendous boost that was given to Twister when Johnny Carson got into the game on his show with shapely Eva Gabor. Everything was so spontaneous and frolicsome that for weeks after, we had people calling and writing to find out where they could buy the game," recalls Merritt.

Now picture many hundreds of the 54-inch-by-69-inch vinyl mats strewn around the football field of the University of Massachusetts. It is May 2, 1987, and thousands of people are simultaneously playing Twister, the largest organized group of contortionists ever brought to the game at one time. News of the mass play session motivated a lot of others to try the game—and, in fact, for many years it has been a fad among college students. This for a game originally targeted for kids ages six and up.

"Whenever we see that a game has real PR possibilities, we exploit all channels of exposure," says Merritt. "Some games that may be perfectly good playing games may not have PR opportunities."

Toy-and-game companies know the vital elements needed to support their commitment to a strong product. What starts with product excitement takes heavy investment in packaging and promotion, licensing support, energetic PR, and sharp pricing to feed the new idea into the trade and consumer arenas. Mission Control for such a launch is in the sales and marketing offices of major manufacturers. The power for launching toys and games into the marketplace is time, people, and dollars—all invested to get the product into sales orbit.

Professional inventors, the very sources of the magic and excitement of new toys and games, have little or no input into the marketing and merchandising needed to make an industry hit. An inventor delivers basic ideas and then relies on the licensee to execute new products effectively using all the available skills and resources of the company. The product may be play; the business is sales and profits.

The key decisions affecting product form and function, market presence, and salability are beyond the control of a product's creator. Phenomena like Trivial Pursuit and Nintendo could be delivered to consumers in plain brown boxes. But there are few such phenomena in the business; playthings need attractive packages. Classic or fad toys and games may sell on nostalgia and word-of-mouth, but new items need strong TV support in major markets if they are to reach high-volume sales levels. Without million-dollar ad campaigns, the trade is noncommittal and consumers are left to search out potentially popular playthings in spotty distribution.

In an industry where product is recognized as king, the inventing sources of new product ideas are certainly part of the royal court, but in today's mass market filled with endless choices, kings are made through excitement and hype. They are not born quietly into brand pedigree.

7 Advance to Boardwalk

HOW TO SELL
YOUR IDEAS

Ring! Ring!

Operator: Good morning. Total Play Toy and Game Company, the world's largest producer of quality playthings. How may I help you?

Caller: Hello. I've invented a great new game that is better than any other I have ever seen. My family and I play and enjoy it all the time. The kids on the block like it. I would like to talk with someone at Total Play about buying my idea and producing the game.

Operator: Thank you. Let me switch you to the appropriate department. Have a good day!

TPCSD: Good morning. Total Play Customer Service Department. How may I help you?

Caller: I have invented a new game that my mother-in-law and her bridge group feel is better than bridge, better than Monopoly, better than Trivial Pursuit. They told me that I should try to get the game produced so it can be sold at all the toy stores. I have a sample that was made by the industrial arts teacher at the high school, and I would like to send it to Total Play for evaluation so you can buy the idea from me and produce it. I am certain everyone in your company will agree with everyone in Paducah who has played the game.

TPCSD: Sorry, sir, but you cannot submit your game to us. We have a very large R&D department working with our marketing people to give us all the new toys and games we need. We do not accept unsolicited new game ideas—even one that may be the rage in Paducah.

Caller: But you will miss the next great best-seller. There is nothing like it and it is much better than anything on the market. I just know your company could make millions of dollars with this great game.

TPCSD: Sir, I'm afraid I can't change our policy. Our people tell me that just because something isn't on the market doesn't mean they or someone else hasn't thought of it. They tell me that for every toy or game on the market there are ninety to a hundred ideas that didn't make it. You may have that one-in-a-hundred winner, but we just cannot accept your unsolicited idea at Total Play.

Caller: If Total Play won't take a look, what am I supposed to do with my blockbuster idea? Help me . . . please.

TPCSD: You might call the Toy Manufacturers of America in New York City. Or you might keep calling other companies until you find one interested in looking at ideas from first-time inventors. Or you may find an agent who will try to sell your idea around the industry. Or you might produce it yourself. Or, if all else fails, you might just be happy letting your friends play your one sample in Paducah. Have a good day!

Never Say Die

Ben Kinberg can empathize with the fledgling inventor from
Paducah. He was in the same position twenty years ago when
trying to place his James Bond Attaché Case. He recalls,
"Times were different then. I merely picked up the telephone
and called the largest toy and doll company in New York—
Ideal Toy Company—and asked for an appointment. It was
much easier to get through to key people then than it is today.
As a matter of fact, today it is highly unlikely for a person to
do what I did then. For the uninitiated, the amateur, the
housewife, or the letter-carrier who is absolutely certain that
he or she has invented the world's new Monopoly, getting
through the front door of a toy company today is for all practical purposes impossible."

Getting a corporate executive on the telephone is difficult
enough. But establishing credibility as a reputable inventing
source and introducing a revolutionary product concept in
thirty seconds requires very precise, attention-getting statements. However, when most amateurs call, if they are fortunate enough to get an executive on the line, they dwell on their
personal resume and provide a coy, veiled description of a
product that often includes highly unrealistic promises of benefits.

One corporate inventor relations executive says about inventors trying to whip up interest in a concept, "It is amazing
how many callers insist their hot invention is similar to or better than some product with sales on the descend. All that shows
me is that the invention is too late and the inventor does not
know the marketplace. To get a marketer's attention, emphasis
should be on new and unique features, not on similarities to a
dying product."

As hard as it is to make headway with a phone call, it is
even harder to see manufacturers in person. "I forced my way
in," says Abraham Torgow, part-time inventor, when asked

why he was showing new concepts to Galoob product manager Patricia Ann Tura, on his knees, in the middle of the company's reception area, at the height of the 86th Annual American International Toy Fair. Standing above the inventor, clipboard in hand, Tura watched as he pulled item after item from his suitcases. She admitted that her company did not usually see inventors under these conditions, but she said Torgow insisted, since there was no time on the schedule to fit him in for a formal meeting.

"I'll present it [new product] anyplace that somebody will listen to me, because I don't have the connections to get in to where I want to go," explains Torgow, who claims to have been inventing and trying to license action games for more than twenty years and whose business cards read, "Patented Action Games & Inventions."

A Long and Lonesome Road

Remember the old saw that if a man builds a better mousetrap, even though his house is in the woods, the world will beat a path to his door? Maybe this was the case back in 1889 when Ralph Waldo Emerson penned the thought, but it is not true in the world of amateur toy inventing. For the most part, it's just the opposite. Toy and game developers must be prepared to beat a path to the manufacturer's door. And often, after a long, hard journey, newcomers will find the door locked.

To those attempting to develop and sell concepts as a part-time endeavor, that path Emerson spoke of will be especially hard, if not impossible, to clear. The consensus among the pros is that successful toy development and licensing works out to about 10 percent creativity, and 90 percent marketing skills. Creativity is a natural gift; either you have it or you don't. Marketing talents, on the other hand, while intuitive to a great extent, are learned through experience. Amateur toy and game

inventors become pros the same way amateur athletes do—
through training and competition.

A Dillar, a Dollar, a Ten o'clock Scholar

Few toy inventors, if any, have had formal training, because
until recently, there has been no college or university degree
program in toy design. The Fashion Institute of Technology
(FIT), in cooperation with the Toy Manufacturers of America,
is out to change this situation.

FIT says that its toy-design curriculum will emphasize conceptual and technical design development, supported by a thorough grounding in safety and regulatory requirements, child
psychology, production, packaging, marketing, and consumer-
motivation fundamentals—along with a general overview of
the toy industry itself. A strong liberal-arts component is included to broaden the designer's perspective as an interpreter
of cultural trends as reflected in the design of toys. Industry
internships with major toy manufacturers are also an important part of the program.

FIT graduated its first class of seventeen students on May
31, 1991. Judy Ellis, chairman of the Toy Design Department,
says the institute's goal is to graduate between thirty-five and
forty-five students annually.

"It's the first real training ground for the design of toys,"
says George Dunsay, a former senior vice president of R&D
at Hasbro and the master planner of the FIT curriculum. Asked
if he feels the toy industry has suffered for not having had such
a program, the industry veteran responds, "I don't think we've
necessarily suffered because we've gotten bad ideas. I think
we've suffered because it has taken longer to teach people how
to do toys. There is just no way of stepping in and becoming

a toy designer. When you hire someone, the first year is pretty much a training program, so it isn't very efficient.''

Realizing that many in-house designers either choose to go the independent route at some point in their career or find themselves in senior management, Dunsay, a consultant to manufacturers, wrote a business course into the FIT curriculum. He feels that to be well rounded, it is also important to understand how to write and negotiate contracts.

Applicants for FIT's Bachelor of Fine Arts program in toy design should have at least an associate's degree in an art- or design-related area, and they must exhibit a strong talent for drawing and an ability to conceptualize, besides having an understanding of and an appreciation for play. Scholarships will be made available to eligible students. For more information: Professor Judy Ellis, chairman, Toy Design (212-760-7810), or Michael Weingarten, assistant director, Admissions (212-760-7675), Fashion Institute of Technology, Seventh Avenue at 27th Street, New York, NY 10001.

It's a Hard Day's Night

''You must approach it as a business,'' responds veteran inventor Jay Smith when asked what advice he would have for amateurs. ''You must have the things that a business has—marketing and sales, finance and operations. I think that's the key to success. And no small part of that is, of course, being very good at what you do—being clever, being creative—but it has to be a business. If you're going to have one great idea and sell it and that's it, that's luck or opportunity knocking, but if you're going to do it over a long period of time, it has to be a business.''

How tough is it? Says Smith, ''If you have 1,000 ideas, you put 100 into sketch form and ten into prototype and one may get sold. You have to recognize those odds.''

Hank Atkins, inventor of Razzle (Parker Brothers), says that inventing games can be fun and satisfying, but that it should be done as a hobby. "Don't count on much money even if you sell a manufacturer," he advises.

Inventor Bruce D. Lund says the new kids on the block can expect two years without any income. He adds, "You have to be crazy to think you can make a living in this business." Tony Morley, inventor of Nerf Fencing (Parker Brothers), agrees, saying that would-be inventors first better make sure they have an eighteen-month supply of money to live on.

"Don't expect wealth overnight. Be prepared to struggle," warns Elliot Rudell. "And if you go bankrupt, it doesn't mean you're not creative."

And even when the amateur scores, it still does not guarantee financial freedom. Manuel Garcia of Houston, Texas, a prolific inventor of strategy games, is a perfect example. Out of the more than thirty games he has invented and prototyped, only two have been licensed—Triangoes and Holes in the Wall. Triangoes, sold to Kadon Enterprises, a small mail-order game company in Maryland, even made the *Games* magazine "Best New" list in 1988. Still, neither has made enough money to enable him to quit his job as an all-night computer programmer for a local oil company.

Nothing to Fear but Fear Itself

There seem to be two kinds of amateur inventors—the paranoid and the more paranoid. By profile they tend to trust no one and hesitate to reveal their ideas, even to their own patent attorneys, for fear of being cheated. Such an attitude is more pernicious to an inventor's situation than the actual hazards inherent in the affairs of licensing intellectual property. Sure, people get ripped off; it's a risk that goes with the territory.

But too much caution can kill an idea by depriving it of life-giving exposure.

The Legal Buffer

Every inventor dislikes rejection of a budding idea—and loss of a potential income source. In a business where only one or two concepts in a hundred make it to market, turndown is the rule. The pros use rejection to transform a concept into something new, hoping to gain acceptance of an idea in any form.

The casual or amateur inventor, however, is usually stung by the reality that a once-in-a-lifetime creation is among the rejections. Unable to turn a negative into a positive, the amateur all too often retaliates with litigation at the remotest hint of an infringement or overlap by a manufacturer's subsequent introduction.

The threat of a strike-back legal action is what keeps the doors of some companies firmly closed to amateur inventors. It is often impossible for casual inventors to accept two key points that should temper their dash for legal action: (1) Just because an item is not in a manufacturer's line is no evidence that the manufacturer does not have it in development; and (2) similar concepts can originate from two sources. This is known as parallel development.

When amateurs insist, ''They haven't seen anything like it on the market,'' it usually means two things: (1) The inventors haven't searched beyond a cursory review of current toy company catalogs or beyond a quick run through a local toy store; and, more important, (2) they judge that absence from the market can only mean that a manufacturer never had a similar idea. Never do they consider that the company merely judged the idea as not strong enough to survive market conditions.

With the flurry of concepts swirling around the industry, there is always a strong likelihood of overlap and duplication.

Much "invention" borders on reinvention or the use of a slight nuance of a previous play format. How much can an inventor do with a game board, spinner/dice, and pawns other than change themes, rules, or artwork? How many parts of a toy dog can wag, flap, roll, or strut without a special gear or microprocessor to add animation or sound?

Although pros do not like rejection any more than the amateurs do, they live with the reality that only so much product can be done in any single year. They may not like it that their concept was only a smidge different from an item ultimately selected for market, but they regard that as better execution of a similar concept rather than an infringement. And they may not like it that a manufacturer is now getting around to marketing a concept similar to one of their past ideas, but they know that the toy market is largely a matter of timing and salesmanship.

Pros know that their business relationships with manufacturers are based, among other things, on trust and ethics. They are in the business of living off their ideas, not living off legal settlements. As Phil Orbanes at Parker Brothers says, "There is a greater legal risk [for manufacturers] in having an inventor come in cold."

Mike Meyers at Milton Bradley expresses a similar reservation based upon legal issues. "Unfortunately, we live in a litigious society," he says, "and we have to be very, very careful not only to protect what we're doing inside, but also to protect the professionals we're working with, because as soon as someone opens up a case, opens up a box, opens up a letter, you begin to be in a compromised situation. Milton Bradley is a big company, and when you have size, it's assumed you have big pockets. There have been some suits. There are always threats of suits. There is no satisfaction in a successful defense; even when the company wins, there can be a tremendous financial loss. Nothing is gained by a moral victory that isn't greatly eroded by lost time and expense."

Lawsuits are an ongoing problem at the major toy and game companies. Some firms each year spend hundreds of thousands of dollars defending themselves against a wide variety of complaints. Some suits are valid, others are not. For example, there are many so-called paper-patent inventors, who get patents on concepts they never even prototype or attempt to sell in hopes of one day finding an infringer to hold up.

One of the most sweeping cases we found was the civil action brought by inventor Solomon Sperber of Deerfield, Florida, against sixty-five defendants, including a range of companies from Milton Bradley, Pressman Toy, West End Games, and The Games Gang to NFL Properties, Zayre Corp., R. H. Macy, Paramount Pictures, and Children's Television Workshop. Plaintiff Sperber issued a complaint against the defendants for the infringement of his U.S. Patent No. 3,643,958, duly issued on February 22, 1972. He charged that each defendant made, used, and/or sold board games that fell within the scope of his patent. His attorneys, Cobrin & Godsberg of New York City, listed some 120 games as infringing their client's patent. Sperber's patent covered the printing of questions on game cards.

Sperber's patent was awarded for a game "simulating aspects of society." Its U.S. Patent Abstract reads:

A game board, a first set of cards stating numbered issues, a recording set of cards, a second set of numbered cards stating laws, and having indicia identical to the issue numbers whereby one's opinion relating to the laws are correlated to the issues, a third set of cards stating cases and bearing indicia to the numbered issues and law cards whereby one's opinions as to the cases are correlated to the laws and issues, a fourth set of cards allowing players to advance, and a set of chance cards stored in and used in conjunction with a game accessories container. 9 Claims. 18 Drawing Figures.

On October 28, 1988, the U.S. District Court, Southern District of New York, ruled against Sperber and dismissed the complaint in its entirety.

Inventor Jerome Lemelson of Princeton, New Jersey, a man who claims to have been awarded more than 400 patents, took Mattel to court for infringing his 1969 patent for a flexible plastic track. The self-described "tinkerer" claimed he was damaged by sales of the track on which Mattel's popular Hot Wheels cars operate. Between 1972 and 1986, Mattel reportedly sold $545 million worth of Hot Wheels, 6 percent of which ($32.7 million) was for the sale of track.

On November 7, 1989, a federal court jury in Chicago awarded Lemelson $24.8 million in damages. If the damages are tripled and assessed interest, the final penalty could earn the inventor more than $100 million. (In 1977, the inventor had selected Chicago as the venue for his case because of its history of finding in favor of inventors over companies.) Upon hearing the verdict, Mattel attorney Sheldon Karon, according to wire-service reports, said to U.S. District Judge Charles Kocoras, "This man is entitled to be compensated for his damage, not to be given a windfall." Gerald Hosier, attorney for Lemelson, countered with the fact that no one purchases Hot Wheels "to run on a floor or the dirt, but on the trackway."

In spite of the risks, when asked whether he is afraid he may be missing a potential blockbuster by not seeing everything, Mike Meyers confidently responds, "There's no proof that we will. If we wanted to, we could see 10,000 products a year, but how do you process 10,000 products? How do you keep the sanctity of those products? How do you separate them? It's not practical. It can't be done." To illustrate his point, Meyers says that one agent to whom Milton Bradley recommends amateurs needing representation told him that in the twenty years he has been seeing Milton Bradley's referrals, he has never found a single worthwhile product among them.

Legal issues and the time to filter ideas notwithstanding,

there are still many companies that will review the work of amateurs. One is TSR, the $30 million-a-year manufacturer best known for Dungeons & Dragons. Michael Cook of TSR says, "I understand that it is very difficult to deal with the hundreds of things that come across the transom, but there is still always that one item, and dealing with closed lists tends to stagnate and develop a holier-than-thou attitude on behalf of the manufacturer. At TSR we make every attempt to at least look at the item in one way or another. We try to play-test it, we try to get it concept-formed, we don't simply say that we don't deal with outsiders."

International Games, best known for Uno products, also welcomes amateur submissions. "We're one of those companies—and there are not that many of them—that openly solicit to the unknown inventors. We have a very open-door policy, although we have an extremely rigid and strict legal submission system. However, from a public relations standpoint, we like people to think of us as a very approachable company," says Jeff Conrad, vice president of R&D. Nevertheless, he admits that the vast majority of his company's new product comes from a small core within the professional inventing community.

Every professional inventor seems to have a story about an idea that was misappropriated or at least a close call. "You go to an executive's birthday party on a Sunday, and on Monday your good friend says, 'So sue me,' " laments one prominent developer who asked not to be named. But, on the whole, toy-company executives are honorable professionals who value their relationships with independent developers and do everything possible to maintain the balance in the flow of ideas between in-house and outside development sources. They also know that if they intentionally cheat inventors, the pipeline would soon be empty.

"We play hardball with our developers. And we'll take advantage of whatever situation we can, just as I would expect them to do vice versa. After all, business is business, and we're all experienced professionals," admits the senior vice president for R&D at a major manufacturing company. "But the last thing we want to do is rip off an inventor," he hastens to add. "Word would spread like wildfire and all of our sources would dry up instantly. There is nothing to be gained, and everything to be lost."

When Tyco Toys was developing its electronic Data Race 500 in-house, Jim Alley, senior vice president of marketing, was advised by his R&D people that if they continued along the path they had taken, they were likely to infringe on a patent owned by Jay Smith, a veteran of twenty-six years in the industry. Alley said his decision was immediate. There would be no attempt to end-run Smith's patent; Tyco would address the possible conflict at once. He called Smith and within five days, a licensing arrangement was hammered out to both parties' satisfaction.

Earlier in the year, Smith, at Tyco's request, had provided the manufacturer with a copy of his patent. "My guess is that their people, as designers will do, were designing independently and thought that they had something that was quite unique. Jim Alley recognized the results—and recognized that there was a problem. I think it was a great example of being honorable about a situation. I don't mean to pretend that dishonorable things don't happen," says Smith, "but they did call and they did make a deal. This makes me feel good about Tyco and good about the industry in general. And I think that Jim Alley, in particular, deserves a lot of praise for that."

Smith feels that an inventor's best protection is to be good: "If people want to deal with you again and want the results of your work, they are not going to rip you off."

The Golden Rules

Never take yourself too seriously. Keep your ego out of projects; it
can be a major cause of failure. Regardless of who has the
original idea, every product becomes a team effort at some
point. In this way, development is no different from the kinds
of collaborative efforts and dynamics required to produce feature films, recordings, ad campaigns, and theatrical productions. Successful toys and games are the by-product of
numerous creative and business forces that cross-pollinate and
energize each other.

Never take your product too seriously. It is sobering to realize that
the world will survive without your product. The manufacturer
will probably survive without your product. You might need
it to survive, but no one else will!

Keep your eye on the ball. The main objective of the outside
developer is to get product to the most influential executives
and sold under the most favorable conditions. This mission
must always be kept foremost in mind. There are all kinds of
minor problems along the way that could, if permitted, get you
off course. Simply put—never respond to pygmies chewing at
your toenails.

Agents: The Pros

"It is physically impossible for us to see everybody who wants
to see us. We have to cut it off. The way you get around not
being accessible to somebody is to refer them to an agent,"
suggests Steve D'Aguanno of Hasbro's toy division. "Agents
are absolutely critical. A good one can help advance the career
of an amateur."

Agents are, indeed, the surest way for amateur inventors to
have their products reviewed by R&D or marketing departments at major toy-and-game companies. Agents understand

their important role in bridging the gap between the less-established part-time inventors and the industry manufacturers. Agents also recognize that individuals in the nonprofessional inventing community are often no less creative than people in the larger design groups, but they merely lack time, experience, or the resources to learn the business and fully develop and sell ideas themselves.

"I am not saying that we should discourage the guys off the street, but I think the guys off the street could do well to speak to an agent. The agent is going to guide them in the right direction, he's going to finesse their product, and in the long run he's going to save them money," says Lowell Wilson of The Ohio Art Company.

It is best to deal with an agent who comes highly recommended by a well-known manufacturer or a satisfied client. Agents are as varied as the people and products they represent. The toy companies know who the best ones are, and many will gladly share their list of favorites.

Agent Michael Kohner, who admits to having the toy industry in his blood from his family ties to the Kohner Brothers Company, actually coinvents with his group of inventors, who create exclusively what he sells. Kohner uses his family name, long recognized on such industry classics as Trouble, Headache, and Busy Box, to gain entry to sell manufacturers his new product ideas. Kohner and his "captive corps" of developers each year generate an average of thirty concepts, which he takes to some fifty manufacturers worldwide. Says Kohner, "The odds in my case of making the sale are better than average because I select a company where I feel the need is strongest for a particular concept." That inside knowledge helps create a convincing sales argument.

Bob Fuhrer, president of R. B. Fuhrer Enterprises, also feels he brings more than new concepts to his sales presentations. "I have aligned myself with several leading foreign developers with manufacturing facilities. I am offering 'one-stop shopping,' since we do everything—conceptualizing, prototyping, engineering, and tooling—everything but distribution. That's what we seek from the manufacturers and marketers," says Fuhrer. He claims access to 500 concepts a year through his inventing and product sources, but he takes only 8 to 10 percent of them to the prototype stage. "Only five or so items may actually sell, but we try to make each of those concepts into a mini line—that is, one item with several versions," says Fuhrer, who has placed, among other items, T.H.I.N.G.S. (Milton Bradley), Pocket Rockers (Fisher-Price), Super Crayons (Random House), Bongo Kongo (Tyco Toys), and Thin Ice (Pressman).

"I not only place toy and game concepts originating with American inventors, but I look for good existing product from markets in other parts of the world that may not as yet have a home in the U.S.," says Jim Becker, president of the Anjar Company. "My search includes the Japanese and European Toy Fairs in my annual itineraries," adds Becker. For Anjar, the search has paid off handsomely, with the U.S. placement of such popular playthings as Othello and Sliders (Japan), and Flipsiders (Spain).

A new player in the toy-and-game brokering business is Cactus Services, Inc., the firm responsible for the placement of Scattergories at Milton Bradley. "We do not restrict ourselves to toys and games, although more than 50 percent of the submissions we see fall into this category," explains Cactus's director of marketing, Thomas R. Ryan III. Ninety-five percent of the products submitted to him do not pass a phase-one review. Ten to 20 percent do not even make it through the initial telephone or mail screening. But those products that do make it are brought in-house for three to four months of a three-phase evaluation that he says can cost his company a minimum of between $10,000 and $12,000.

The very first product to pass his evaluation in 1988 was Scattergories. The inventor, Gunther Degen, paid Cactus several thousand dollars as a retainer—what Ryan describes as a "get-serious fee"—plus something in the range of 30 percent of any advances and royalties.

Technical Game Services (TGS) is another toy-and-game screening facility. It filters out those ideas that have little chance of making it in the marketplace and gives the inventor an objective recommendation on possible alternative actions. TGS then represents the strongest candidates to major manufacturers.

"Independent inventors are crucial to the toy-and-game industry," says Tom Braunlich, a principal in TGS and one of the developers of Pente (Parker Brothers) and Scratchees (Decipher). "Companies know this, but already suffer idea overload from the hundreds, even thousands, of submissions they get every year. It is a major task to keep track of them all," he adds, "not to mention the time needed to evaluate each submission properly. Also, manufacturers have a hypersensitivity to the possibility of a coincidence of similar ideas from in-house designers and inventors causing legal conflict. The manufacturer will make the final decision, but we help them with many of the preliminaries, such as play value, layout, graphics, and instructions on the concepts we offer for sale on their behalf."

Jim Becker, who placed his first item in 1970 and shows some 100 concepts to manufacturers in a year, says, "I believe everything I show has a chance to make it through, although it may be only a one-in-ten chance that I can sell it at the first stop. I may show an item to as many as five manufacturers before I get a hit. Certainly they must all be taking in many of the same considerations when making choices. It's hard to say why four places turn an idea aside and another makes the commitment."

Whereas many professional inventors spend 20 percent of their time selling their own ideas, hardworking agents may spend 50 to 60 percent of their time in aggressive efforts to place the works of a stable of creative sources. Often the relationship between the inventor and the agent becomes a true partnership. Both parties have strong vested interests in the property. The inventor or the agent may have the original idea; the inventor has the ability to make the product, the agent has the wherewithal to sell it. There is no standard royalty split between agent and inventor. Most agents work on a 50/50 split. But the split could be 40/60, with the higher percentage going to the agent, who is given the task of making the idea a reality.

Jeff Conrad of International Games feels that the amateur must be willing to take a little less money in return for the agent's talent in getting products placed with the major manufacturers—a shared percentage is infinitely better than 100 percent of nothing. But many amateurs balk at the business arrangements between themselves and agents. They may be missing a key point. Just because an agent decides to represent a product is no guarantee of placing it. The agents may do months or years of work before succeeding with a product, if they succeed at all. They are earning their percentage.

Some independent inventors feel dissatisfied by agent representation, despite having had product placed. Robert Carignan, a former Hasbro designer who was associated with an agent for years, says, "The problem of being represented by a broker is that you don't usually have the feedback that you would get if you went in directly. Also, you never develop any clout; the agent develops the clout. I feel that I would have done probably three to four times better if I had represented myself."

And there are also some executives who prefer not to work with agents. For example, Jack Daniels, senior vice president of R&D at Matchbox Toys (USA), says that his preference is to work one-on-one with professional inventors, who know more about their products than do their agents. Sometimes,

Daniels explains, his outside inventors are required to do up
to 75 percent of the development work on their items.

Invention Marketers:
The Con Game

Do not confuse agents and brokers with another, quite different
breed of middlemen, the invention marketing firms. There are
numerous horror stories about unsuspecting amateur toy and
game inventors being taken advantage of by these companies
who take hungry inventors for a joyride on their own money.
The majority sign up lots of product and place nothing, except
their hands in the pockets of trusting inventors. Like other
vultures, invention marketers kill for food, seeking to capture
inexperienced, frustrated casual inventors through slick advertising on late-night radio shows, midday television movies, and
via direct mail. Attorney generals in dozens of states are trying
to make these predators an extinct species. The U.S. Federal
Trade Commission has retired several of them for good.

As positive as executives were about the efficacy of using
professional agents, not a single one had anything positive to
say about invention marketing services. Most of their contact
appears to be through unsolicited mailings. "Usually it's form
letters and it's junk," says Loren T. Taylor at Nasta International. "They're just throwing things against a wall and seeing what sticks." Michael Lyden, vice president for business
development at Tyco Toys, says, "I have no use for them."
When their envelopes arrive at Tyco, they are not opened.
"We just save the envelopes and when we have a box full, we
send them back."

"Invention marketers scare the living daylights out of me,"
says James Kubiatowicz, director of product development at
Spearhead Industries. "They're leeches. They prey on nov-

ices." Then, pulling open his desk drawer, he holds up a handful of cards he has received from invention marketers. He adds,
"I've got thirty-two return-postage-paid postcards from these
guys and I am saving the stamps. One of these days I'll steam
them off and put them into a retirement fund. Anybody who
is breathing and has a dollar can get strokes from these companies. They treat each idea as if it were the golden cup of
creativity. "About 80% of all people claiming to help inventors
build a business, market their product, or raise capital, are con
men, beggars, thieves, or incompetents. Finding the other 20%
is damn tough."

The Law's on the Inventor's Side

To register a complaint against an invention marketer at the
federal level, or to learn whether or not there has been an
action against a particular person or company, write to Federal
Trade Commission, Complaint Division, Room 692, Washington, DC 20580 (202-326-2418).

Some states—California, Illinois, Minnesota, North Caro-
lina, Ohio, South Dakota, Tennessee, Texas, Virginia, and
Washington—reportedly have protective legislation for inventors. Both Minnesota and Virginia were more than willing to
send us free copies of their legislation after a simple telephone
request to their respective State Houses. If you want to know
your rights, it would be worth the effort to read one of these
state laws. The two we've seen are both clearly drafted and
very enlightening.

Whether you're dealing with a professional agent or an invention marketer, you are entitled to ask questions about their
track record. Their success should be measured in the number
of products placed and the money they have earned from royalties, not through service fees charged the inventor to compensate the marketer or agent for his time.

Homework Means More Effective Work

If you want to do the selling yourself, the first question to answer is, Where will a product have its best chance of fit and success? A rule of thumb is to have submissions follow a company's category direction and marketing goals. No two companies have the same needs. The easiest way to get a feel for the kind of product a company normally sells is to visit the nearest Toys R Us stores, or a similar toy supermarket. You will generally find a company's complete product line represented there. It is probably not worth contacting a manufacturer whose toys and games are not carried by a major chain.

Jeff Conrad of International Games advises, "If I were an amateur inventor, I would get on an airplane, go around the country, and visit major retail stores and just look at what's there." He complains that because the amateur does not do any homework and operates in a vacuum, "eighty percent of what we get from them has been done before." In fact, he uses their submissions as a bellwether for tracking trends. When amateur inventors begin sending him a groundswell of products in a particular category, that usually marks the last year of a particular phase or craze. "This is because they are hearing about it way down the line," Conrad concludes.

"The thing that bothers me most is that inventors think any toy company can do any idea," says Anne Pitrone, director of product development at View-Master/Ideal. She suggests that an inventor look at a company's line first to see if his or her product makes sense for it. When inventors don't do that, it wastes a lot of time for both inventor and manufacturer.

Yet, as necessary as it is that inventors follow product lines with their submissions, it can be a double-edged sword. Neil Werde, Tyco Toys' director of marketing, feels that outside inventors have a big problem because "They go with what they feel a company wants to see and not with what they feel would be a hit product." Adds Jim Kubiatowicz, "You don't have to be brilliant to show a predictable product." He thinks that the inventors who have done best are those who do not edit their work down to where it's so narrowly focused it can fit only one company.

The Lowdown Can Lead to the High Ground

Information is power. Armed with the right information about the industry, a particular company, its executives, and its product, an inventor can enhance the chances of making a sale. Visiting toy stores to find out who makes which product is an important step. But while the information gathered on such sojourns is critical, it becomes more effective when combined with industry and corporate background intelligence.

The Industry

To obtain the most up-to-date information on the industry as a whole, the best bet is Toy Manufacturers of America, Inc. (TMA). Founded in 1916 and based in New York City, TMA is the trade association for U.S. producers and importers of playthings. TMA's 250 members account for an estimated 90 percent of total domestic wholesale toy sales. In 1984, an associate membership category was added in order to include professional toy inventors, design firms, and toy testing laboratories.

The association is recognized by government, trade, media, and consumers as the authoritative voice of the U.S. toy industry. Among its major activities and services are: management of the annual American International Toy Fair in New York City; working with government agencies and legislators on issues relating to the industry; engaging in an ongoing toy safety program; providing counseling in such activities as logistics, import/export, and management; compiling industry statistics; and conducting a full consumer and educational communications program. The association is located at 200 Fifth Avenue, New York, NY 10010 (212-675-1141).

Public Companies

In the case of public companies, the best source of information is the United States Securities and Exchange Commission (SEC). All companies whose securities are registered on a national securities exchange, and, in general, companies whose assets exceed $3 million, with a class of equity securities held by 500 or more persons, must register such securities with the SEC. This registration establishes a public file containing financial and business information on the company for use by investors and others (such as inventors) and creates an obligation on the part of the company to keep such public information current by filing periodic reports.

The most useful form for independent inventors is the Form 10-K, an annual report that provides the best and most comprehensive overview of the registrant's state of business. Let's take the Form 10-K issued by the Tonka Corporation for the fiscal year ended December 31, 1988, as an example of what such reports reveal:

The form says that Tonka Corporation, a Minnesota corporation, was organized on September 18, 1946, and that the company designs, manufactures, markets, and distributes a broad line of toys and games. Tonka's primary markets are shown to be the United States, continental Europe, Canada, the United Kingdom, and Australia. For almost forty years, Tonka's principal toy products consisted of a traditional line of trucks. Then, between 1984 and 1986, it experienced significant growth in sales and earnings as a result of two highly successful lines, Gobots action figures and Pound Puppies plush toys. In late 1987, Tonka acquired Kenner Parker Toys, Inc., an acquisition that brought Tonka a wider base of staple products and, with the addition of Kenner Parker's extensive foreign operations, greater access to offshore markets. The company had 1988 revenues of approximately $908 million. The report further explains that Tonka is composed of four operating units—the Tonka Products, Kenner Products, Parker Brothers, and International divisions. Tonka Products and Kenner Products are both under the management of the U.S. Toy Group, which provides "unified strategic management" of the two divisions.

The company outlines its principal products: Tonka trucks and vehicles; Parker Brothers' Monopoly, Risk, Sorry!, Clue, and Trivial Pursuit board games and Nerf foam toys; and Kenner Products' The Real Ghostbusters action figures and play sets, Starting Lineup sports figures, and Play-Doh modeling clay.

Tonka shows tables for the previous three fiscal years in which the growth (read: net revenues) of its principal products is tracked. Then each category is broken down by individual products and described. About Play-Doh, for example, it says that it was introduced in 1955 and has been updated yearly. Its 1989 Play-Doh accessory is Make-a-Meal, a molding, cutting, shaping, and decorating toy with a cooking theme.

Under the subheading "New Product Development," Tonka explains how it develops new product. This section reads, in part, "To generate new products, the Company employs various approaches to drive the creative process, including the following: internal development groups following clearly laid-out product direction, key independent inventors working with specific category assignments, internal staff pursuing ideas they believe worthwhile, and constant contact with a broad spectrum of inventors and licensors." This paragraph indicates that Tonka is receptive to outside ideas.

Tonka claims to have more than 1,000 accounts worldwide, with approximately 18 percent of its 1988 sales derived from one account, Toys R Us. No other single account did over 10 percent of net revenues in 1988. The form also gives the name, title, age, and professional background of each of its executive officers. Information on executive compensation is also a matter of public record. The form includes a potpourri of other information, such as patents, trademarks, and copyrights; legal proceedings; financial statements; any disagreements with accountants on accounting and fiscal disclosure; plus myriad stockholder items.

How to Obtain SEC Documents

For the most up-to-date information on how to obtain copies of SEC documents such as the Form 10-K, contact the commission's public reference branch (202-272-7450). The commission will also send copies of documents in response to a written request. Such requests should list the documents and information needed and indicate a willingness to pay copying and shipping charges. Send requests to: Securities and Exchange Commission, Public Reference Branch, Stop 1-2, 450 Fifth Street, NW, Washington, DC 20549. (Include a daytime telephone number and allow approximately two weeks for processing.)

Such reports provide a great deal of useful information upon which to base an approach to a particular manufacturer and may even suggest a negotiation posture should a selling opportunity arise.

Private Companies

There is no open book on private companies. No agency such as the SEC sets regulations and guidelines for their operation, so it is much more difficult to get any meaningful information on them.

The best way to approach private companies is to ask questions of both corporate officers and the trade. Try to formulate a clear picture of the company's business profile, products, manufacturing capabilities, distribution system, customer base, and advertising and promotion budgets.

A View from the Top

Michael Langieri, vice president of creative development at Milton Bradley, has been on both sides of the conference table in the selling/buying arena. His experience includes years as an "inside" designer with various R&D departments, as well as time outside at his own firm, Design America. Langieri, who has reviewed or presented thousands of concepts, offers a perspective for inventors on the meeting between the inventor and the manufacturer:

1. Arrange for a personal review of your idea. Never send in a model or a prototype unless it's absolutely impossible for you to be there. A special relationship could circumvent this, but products are best demonstrated by the inventor, and questions can be answered readily.

2. Deal with the highest-ranking product reviewer you can, and, if at all possible, one-on-one. That way, attention is focused on the product, not lost in the distraction of a large group.

3. If a reviewer doesn't know you well, or doesn't know about your significant accomplishments, quickly refresh his or her memory before showing your new idea.

4. While every inventor loves his or her own idea, try to have some objective information about projected user(s);

relate the experiences of a meaningful sample of consumers exposed to it.

5. Make the presentation professional—from your knowledge of the categories to be discussed to your appearance and attitude. If you expect to sell an idea for today's market, you have to be in step with today's market in every way and in every action.

6. If the product idea you're suggesting doesn't fit the manufacturer's needs, probe the possibility of some "customizing" to make it more viable. The best thing you can do is to try to keep the project moving forward.

7. Suggest the possibility of working "on spec." Sometimes, if the representative/manufacturer has a special need, having a fresh outside approach can be positive. The fact that they also have a somewhat "vested interest" in the project might increase the likelihood of its being looked on more favorably.

8. Always close the meeting with some clearly defined action plan detailing what will happen next and by what dates. There are no "on-the-spot" sales, but there should be a beginning of commitments to move the selected idea into the manufacturer's product selection process. Inventors must not lose sight of the fact that if they have something unique, something magical, the manufacturer will respond in a buying mood.

"If a person doesn't have passion for his product, chances are we never will," says Randy Karp, senior vice president for sales and marketing at Monogram/Kidstar. "I would add to this, persistence and an ability to be open-minded enough to listen to the manufacturer's input on helping shape the product."

"Any inventor making a presentation is in the 'hook' busi-

ness," says Jerome L. Houle III, president of Bliss House and
a former corporate vice president of licensing at Milton Bradley. "There's a nuclear core to every idea. That's the hook.
That premise is either valid or invalid. It should take no longer
than ten seconds to articulate. If it does, he's in the wrong
business."

Many manufacturers have offices charged with inventor relations and/or new-product acquisitions, which screen new inventors and their products. This is where to make the initial
query.

Prototypes

"The execution of an idea is as important as the idea itself,"
says Bernie Loomis, former president of Kenner Toys. A
working prototype will help convey to corporate executives the
feeling you are striving to achieve with your product. In order
to have any chance at all of a sale, there must be a bonding
process between the item and those considering it. Consumers
purchase products by emotion, not logic. Prototypes should be
as sophisticated as necessary to make the toy understandable.
Parker Brothers, for example, wants to see prototypes that are
play-testable, according to Chris Campbell. "It has to be such
that the game can be given to a group of people who have
never seen it before and they can experience it without a life-
support system provided by the inventor."

Anne Pitrone at View-Master/Ideal says, "If somebody is
trying to sell me a mechanism, I want the mechanism proved
out. I don't see why I have to spend the time doing that.
However, if it is a design concept or a fashion concept, marker
renderings are fine enough."

The Spoken Word Dies, the Written Word Lives

Before a product is taken in to a manufacturer, it is a good idea to have available the information listed below. In addition to serving as talking points for the product presentation, it can be left behind should the item be retained for serious consideration.

1. *Instructions.* Write a step-by-step instruction sheet for the toy or game. Take nothing for granted. The worst thing that can happen is that someone at the company forgets how to operate or play your item. If appropriate, do not hesitate to make an instructional videotape.

2. *Marketing.* Highlight your item's advantages over existing product; explain what makes it unique and suggest where it might fit into the market scheme from the standpoints of pricing, competition, and "hook." Don't tell manufacturers how many millions of dollars it will make, however, since you have no factual basis for such projections.

3. *Play Value.* Present the results of any independent testing you may have conducted. Include photographs or videotapes. A picture is worth a thousand words. Use strangers. Never support an idea with the testimony of someone who loves you, because you will never get the truth.

4. *Names/Trademarks.* If you have done a trademark search (a search of registered marks at the Patent and Trademark Office to make sure the suggested trademark is available), include the results.

5. *The Future.* Through the use of marker drawings and explanatory text, illustrate potential accessories, line extensions, and future directions for your item.

6. *Patents.* Share with the manufacturer the status of any patent actions you may have taken, i.e., searches, applications, or issued patents.

Trading Places

Trade shows are a must for taking the pulse of the industry and making contacts. There you will see all the new products exhibited, and you can obtain catalogs, price sheets, show directories with corporate addresses, telephone/fax numbers, and the names of executives. Such shows or fairs are not, however, the time or place to present new product ideas without a previous appointment.

The easiest trade shows for amateur inventors to visit are the regional toy shows, which begin after the New York fair and are held in such places as Dallas, Atlanta, and Los Angeles. A complete schedule of domestic and foreign trade fairs appears in the appendix.

The annual American International Toy Fair, which occurs the second week of February, is the biggest domestic sales show and the most difficult to attend. At 200 Fifth Avenue (aka The Toy Center) in New York City, showrooms are open only by appointment. While a business card will get you a badge that allows you to walk the hallways, badges don't guarantee showroom access. Individual showroom security is very tight. Across town, at the Javits Convention Center, with accreditation, it is possible to roam among exhibition booths set up by the smaller toy and game manufacturers. This runs concurrently with the New York Toy Fair.

The Licensing Agreement

"If it's not on the page, it's not on the stage," says game inventor Sheryl Levy. Once a manufacturer decides to move ahead on an outside submission, it will offer the inventor a licensing agreement. Every manufacturer has a boilerplate contract drafted by its lawyers. But nothing is as temporary as that which is called permanent. Toy companies are usually flexible within certain parameters.

It is wise for any inventor to be represented by an attorney or agent. Prolific toy inventor Howard Wexler says that in his early days in the business, "I never felt that I needed a lawyer. Now it's gotten uglier. Hard times have set in, and very often hard times bring out the ugliness in people. I find myself having to be more a businessperson than I ever wanted to be."

In licensing negotiations between inventor (licensor) and manufacturer (licensee), the inventor has to realize that two plus two does not always equal four. Deal-making tends to be fluid and wide open. In the final analysis, terms are rarely hammered out between lawyers representing both parties, but rather between the inventor and a senior R&D or marketing executive. Lawyers do not understand the product or the market. They are not hired to authorize business risks, just to point them out. Exceptions always outnumber the rules if a manufacturer wants an item badly enough. And by the time an inventor learns the exceptions, no one remembers the rules to which they apply.

Terms of Endearment

It all begins with the word *advance*. To a professional inventor, the advance signifies the money a manufacturer is willing to commit up front for the rights to produce a particular item. It is a magic number, one that means different things to different people. To some inventors it may represent a giant step forward and perhaps even a meal. To the more prosperous inventors, advances are the way that manufacturers display commitment to their product, a barometer by which the inventor can gauge the importance of his product to the company. The pros know that the higher the advance, the less the likelihood that a product will be dropped in the face of development problems or new submissions. In addition to reflecting the kind of support a company will give the project, the size of an advance also often indicates what a manufacturer requires of the inventor in the form of further development. Six-figure advances, for example, typically require further development work by the inventor and are paid out in stages.

Advances usually are nonrefundable and offset against future royalties. For board games at small manufacturers, advances range anywhere from $1,000 to $5,000. Major board-game publishers pay in the $25,000 range. Adult social interactive games, such as Adver*teasing* and Noteability, and injection-molded skill and action games, such as Pass the Trash and Hungry Hungry Hippos, can bring in more than $25,000. Electronic games can easily have much higher advances, depending upon the technology and development work the inventor has done or must do.

Toy advances usually begin in the $10,000-to-$15,000 range and can go into six figures, depending upon the potential return on investment and the development work the inventor may be asked to perform.

The standard royalty for toys and games is 5 percent of the item's net wholesale price. (The net wholesale price is generally defined as the seller's price less freight allowances, commissions, trade discounts, and returns that are accepted and credited by the manufacturer.)

Protecting Your Ideas

Unlike in many industries, in the toy industry it is normally not required that a concept be protected before it is reviewed by a toy or game manufacturer. Nevertheless, the federal government provides several ways to protect ideas, and it is wise to pursue them: (1) patents; (2) trademarks; and (3) copyrights.

What Is a Patent?

A patent is a grant of property right by the U.S. government to an inventor, acting through the Patent and Trademark Office (PTO). It gives the inventor the right to exclude others from making, using, or selling an invention. But take note: What is granted is not the right to make, use, or sell, but the right to exclude others from doing so. The term of a U.S. patent is seventeen years from the date of issue, subject to the payment of maintenance fees. The right conferred by the patent grant extends throughout the United States and its territories and possessions.

There are two kinds of patents. *Utility patents* are granted to any person who has discovered or invented any new and useful process, machine, manufacture, or composition of matter, or any new and useful improvements thereof. *Design patents* are granted to any person who has invented any new, original, and ornamental design for an article of manufacture. The design patent protects only the appearance of an article, and not its structure or utilitarian features.

A patent cannot be obtained for a mere idea or suggestion. A complete description of the actual device or other subject matter sought to be patented is required.

A prototype is not required to secure a patent. The Patent and Trademark Office does not require inventors to submit working prototypes with their applications.

While the government says that an inventor may prepare

his or her own patent application and file it in the Patent and Trademark Office and conduct the subsequent proceedings, an inventer who is unfamiliar with such matters could get into considerable difficulty. And, even if you are able to get a patent on your own, there is no guarantee that it will adequately protect your invention. The Patent and Trademark Office maintains a register of patent attorneys, who must comply with the regulations prescribed by the office, which requires evidence not only that the person is of good moral character and of good repute, but also that he or she has the legal, scientific, and technical qualifications necessary to enable him or her to render patent applications. Some of these qualifications must be demonstrated by passing an exam. The PTO insists that those admitted to the register must have earned a college degree in engineering or science, or the equivalent of such a degree.

For specific questions about the patenting process, contact the Commissioner of Patents and Trademarks, Washington, DC 20231 (202-557-5168).

Do Patents Matter?

Opinions are mixed about the value of patents. Every manufacturer's licensing agreement requires that the inventor attempt to secure a U.S. patent, and at no expense to the corporation. On the other hand, the lack of patent protection is not a valid reason for a manufacturer to reject an item. The general attitude of a promotional toy company is that it will protect its market share through aggressive marketing, not patents.

"Yes and no," says Saul Jodel of Lewis Galoob Toys, when asked whether patents are critical. "I've been beaten on patents. I find them one of the more frustrating things in the industry. A company takes a stand, invests money to bring out a proprietary product, and then someone knocks you off; on top of that, the retailer supports it, and that's bad business. We can't keep affording to do that. Yes, patents are important, but even with a patent there are ways around it."

"Patents are just about meaningless," says Hasbro's Steve D'Aguanno. "If you look at the major successes in the marketplace, over the history of the promotional toy business, almost none have been based on a patent. I have no prejudice against the inventor for not having one. I don't care."

"Patents are better than a nail in your foot, as they say in Texas," jokes Chris Campbell of Parker Brothers. "In general, we place a high priority on the proprietary nature of products. The more difficult it is for somebody to knock off, either on the basis of design protection or major tooling investment, the better we like it." Practically speaking, he feels, patents act more as a deterrent than they do as a substantial lever for legal protection or as the basis for a legal action.

Tyco Toys' Michael Lyden says that the patentability of a product is often what will determine the royalty rate his company will pay, and the amount of an advance.

"Patents are extremely valuable," says Larry Jones, inventor of Baby Secrets (Matchbox Toys USA), a sixteen-inch doll that "talks" when its hand is pressed. "I pay my patent lawyer about $5,000 a month for services," he reveals. "It's one of my major business expenses."

A helpful reference on the subject of patents is *General Information Concerning Patents*, published by PTO. It is available from the Superintendent of Documents, U.S. Government Printing Office, Washington, DC 20402.

Trademarks

G.I. Joe. Scrabble. Barbie. Adver*teasing*. Etch-A-Sketch. Scruples. Nerf. Micro Machines. Hot Lixx. Super Mario Bros. Gnip Gnop. Othello. Play-Doh. Catchy trademarks are important tools in selling toys and games to manufacturers. A good trademark helps create immediate product identification. It helps tell the product's story. Just as trademarks are used by manufacturers to sell consumers, so can they be helpful to the inventor in giving the total product picture to the manufacturer.

A trademark is any word, name, symbol, or device, or any combination thereof, adopted and used by a manufacturer or merchant to identify his goods and distinguish them from those manufactured or sold by others. It is not generally necessary for a toy developer to register a suggested product trademark before presenting it for review. Most of the time manufacturers do not use trademarks suggested by outside developers. However, if you believe the trademark is of special importance to your item, it might be worth a trademark search to see if it has been used before.

For answers to questions about trademark filing requirements call (703) 557-INFO. On November 16, 1989, new regulations went into effect that let inventors obtain trademarks on an "intention-to-use" basis. Written requests should be directed to: the Commissioner of Patents and Trademarks, Washington, DC 20231.

Patent and Trademark Depository Libraries

There are seventy Patent and Trademark Depository Libraries (PTDLs) located throughout the nation in prestigious academic, research, and public libraries. Their purpose, according to Carole A. Shores, director of PTDL Programs, is to "bring more information and help to all the people out there that need it and can't afford to pay big money to get it. We really listen to inventors and when they bring requests in to us, we try very hard to give them what they want."

PTDLs receive current issues of U.S. Patents and maintain collections of earlier issued patents. The scope of these collections may vary from library to library, ranging from patents of only recent years to some issued as far back as 1790. They have extensive trademark lists as well. Open to the general public, the PTDLs have all the official publications on patents and trademarks from the Patent and Trademark Office.

Copyrights

Copyright protection covers the form of expression rather than the subject matter. For example, the rules of the game could be copyrighted as a piece of writing, but this would only prevent others from copying the rules. It would not prevent them from writing another set of rules of their own or from making and using the game. Copyrights taken out today last until fifty years after the death of the author.

The process of securing copyright protection is frequently misunderstood. In years past, it was necessary to fill out special forms and send them to the Library of Congress, together with a check and copies of the original work. Under the current law, no publication or registration or other Copyright Office action is required to secure copyright. Today, copyright is secured "automatically" when the work is created, and the work is "created" when it is fixed in a copy or phonorecorded for the first time.

Notice of Copyright

Before you publicly show or distribute your work, it is your responsibility to put a notice of copyright on it. The notice should contain the following elements:

1. The symbol © or the word *Copyright,* or the abbreviation *Copr.*

2. The year of first publication of the work. In the case of compilations or derivative works incorporating previously published material, the year of first publication of the compilation or derivative work is enough. The year may be omit-

ted where a pictorial, graphic, or sculptural work, with accompanying text, if any, is reproduced in or on dolls or toys, or any useful articles.

3. The name of the owner of copyright in the work, or an abbreviation by which the name can be recognized, or a generally known alternative of the owner. Example: © 1990 Richard C. Levy and Ronald Weingartner. Affix the notice prominently enough to provide "reasonable notice of the claim of copyright."

The above notwithstanding, it is still prudent to submit a formal application to the Library of Congress. This establishes a "public record" of your claim and entitles you to a certificate of registration (required if you have to go into court over infringement).

For the most up-to-date information on obtaining copyrights, or for specific information on copyrights, contact a copyright information specialist at (202) 479-0700, between the hours of 8:30 A.M. and 5:00 P.M., Eastern time. You can also send a written request to the Copyright Office, Library of Congress, 101 Independence Avenue, SE, Washington, DC 20559.

Supplemental Reading

The Inventing and Patenting Sourcebook, published in 1990 by Gale Research, is one of the best and most comprehensive books on the subject of patents, trademarks, copyrights, and invention marketing, and it is available at most public libraries. The 920-page book contains a step-by-step guide to the various methods of protecting ideas, including all the government forms required for submitting patents and copyrights, as well as a listing of the 12,000 patent attorneys registered to practice before the Patent and Trademark Office. To order, call 1-800-877-GALE.

Thomas Register is an excellent resource for product and corporate profiles. Available in most public library reference rooms, the distinctive green-covered encyclopedia contains alphabetical listings of 120,000 U.S. firms, including addresses and phone numbers, asset ratings, names of company executives, locations of distributors and plants, plus sales, service, and engineering offices. To order, call 1-800-222-7900.

Standard & Poor's Register of Corporations, Directors, and Executives is another excellent library resource. Its volumes carry data on more than 45,000 corporations, including zip codes; phone numbers; and names, titles, and functions of approximately 400,000 officers, directors, and executives. A separate volume offers biographical sketches, including home addresses as well as dates and places of birth for 70,000 key executives. The third volume contains a classified industrial index. To order, call 1-800-221-5277.

Business Strategies for Toy Designers and Inventors is a newsletter published quarterly by Royalty and Property Management Incorporated. In addition to reporting on issues affecting the industry, it also provides current information on copyrights, trademarks, and management of intellectual properties. It reports the results of annual surveys of TMA members on their policies and procedures regarding submissions by outside inventors. To order, call (201) 822-1177.

A number of trade publications highlight the products, events, tone, and marketing moves of the industry. If you are going to create for this business, you should keep up to date by reading these periodicals.

Playthings (monthly). Geyer-McAllister Publications, 51 Madison Avenue, New York, NY 10010. (212) 689-4411.

Toy & Hobby World (monthly). International Thomson Retail Press, 345 Park Avenue, New York, NY 10010 (212) 741-7210.

The Toy Book (monthly). Adventure Publishing Group, 264 W. 40th Street, New York, NY 10018. (212) 575-4510.

Discount Store News (biweekly; monthly in Dec.). Lebhar-Friedman, 425 Park Avenue, New York, NY 10022. (212) 371-9400.

Games (bimonthly). PSC Games Limited Partnership, 810 Seventh Avenue, New York, NY 10019. (212) 246-4640.

Chain Store Age (monthly). Lebhar-Friedman, 425 Park Avenue, New York, NY 10022. (212) 371-9400.

P.O.P. Times (bimonthly). Hoyt Publishing, 2000 N. Racine, Chicago, IL 60614. (312) 281-3400.

Small World (monthly). Earnshaw Publications, 225 W. 34th Street, New York, NY 10122. (212) 563-2742.

Some Final Thoughts

Unless you are out there every day, knocking around the toy-and-game industry, you will never get the proper feeling for the soul of the business or its character, nuances, subtleties, golden rules, and personalities. *You will never get what* you *want unless you can help them to get what* they *want.* And you won't know what *they* want unless you are on the alert, networking daily through phone contacts and personal visits.

Amateurs often have trouble handling rejection. They would rather hang onto the dream of success than be told that their item has a problem that must be corrected or eliminated. They are extremely defensive where their creations are concerned, and this can be a fatal error.

The most important point to remember is that as an inventor, you are always selling two things—yourself and your concept. Personal credibility is critical. If you cannot sell yourself, you will never command enough respect from corporate executives to champion your product. Do it right the first time and you will be welcome anytime, whatever the concept. You cannot put a value on the ability to make an encore. Ninety-nine percent of what is sold happens in Act II. Leave a poor impression and you may never be able to return. Therefore, the way you get through the proverbial door deserves considerable thought and reflection. It is during this time that you set the tone for further contact. First impressions are lasting impressions.

Back to the Future

As for the future of independent toy and game development, most pros agree with Elliott Rudell, who says, "It'll always be hard. It'll always be frustrating. It'll always be a crapshoot. It'll always be exhilarating. There will always be knockoffs and ethically questionable companies to work around. But there will always be a need for great product."

It is that need for great product that weaves the creative fiber of the independent toy inventor inextricably into the toy industry. Inventors are a remarkable, renewable natural resource that satisfies the industry's insatiable appetite for novel and innovative product. Without the continuous and nutritious supply of new concepts provided by external inventing sources, the toy business as we know it today would not exist. Invention, after all, is the fount of all sales and the economic future of the industry. It is what provides the "new" in a business that is always asking the question, "What's new?"

Inventor Profiles

The following profiles cover over seventy key professional inventors active today in the toy-and-game industry. We based our list upon a consensus of several senior R&D executives, plus our own experiences. We knew from the start that we could miss some key people, but these inventors are representative of the professionals upon whom the industry depends, people on corporate VIP lists and, in some cases, names on executives' speed dialers. In a few instances, inventors to whom we sent questionnaires elected not to participate in our survey. Some answers were edited to fit space requirements, but not for conformity of style or alteration of content or meaning.

Several inventors profiled are mentioned elsewhere in the book as agents because they wear those two hats. All of these highly gifted men and women are dues-paying members of the so-called inventing community, people who live the roller-coaster profession described in the preceding pages. Their creative skills could launch new companies; their past creations, indeed, sustain many of today's industry giants.

The inventors described in these vignettes are a resilient, dedicated, specialized group who represent longevity in a demanding, consuming, highly competitive business; the business of new toy and game ideas. These inventors have been in the business an average of just under nineteen years and represent a composite of more than 1,000 years of searching, analyzing, perceiving, conceiving, and defining new playthings—the activity we have chosen to call "inventing."

Throughout these profiles is a shared view of "the inventor" more as an artist/orchestrator than as a scientist/researcher. Many of the definitions of the word *inventor* refer to the importance of responding to unmet needs and the application of known solutions in a unique way. This is a group whose inventiveness can spark virtually anytime, anywhere. Clearly, toy inventing, like so many other demanding professions, is not a nine-to-five endeavor. Some inventors admit to creative sparks during fitful sleep or a refreshing shower, or while sunbathing *au naturel* on an isolated tropical beach.

These profiles offer inspiration to aspiring inventors, wisdom from industry professionals who have earned through firsthand experience their roles as sages and soothsayers. Perhaps the most succinct message of them all is Julie Cooper's advice to would-be inventors: "Don't give up—don't grow up!"

Inventors: Judy and Arthur Albert

Company: Alberts Design Company, Inc.

Years in toy and game business: 35   **Yrs. inventing:** 8

Typical year: New concepts: 8–10; concepts presented: 4–5; concepts sold: 1–2

Most successful toys and games: Some Cabbage Patch Kid accessory items; Puffalumps; Honey Comb; Dress 'n Dazzle

Favorite toys and games as kids: None special

We think an inventor is: Someone who can originate a new idea or do an advanced version of an old one.

What sparks original ideas: No one way. Stimulation can come from anywhere, anytime, either consciously or through serendipity.

Advice to would-be inventors: If you have the guts and luck, you will enjoy it. If not, you will need a job with a steady salary.

Inventor: Randice-Lisa Altschul

Company: Dieceland

Years in toy and game business: 5   **Yrs. inventing:** 18

Typical year: New concepts: 100–200; concepts presented: 50; concepts sold: 1–2

Most successful toys and games: Miami Vice: The Game; Clay to Win; Just for Girls

Favorite toys and games as a kid: Boys and boys' toys

I think an inventor is: A person who has the ability to create an item out of thin air—one who displays creativity, ingenuity, and originality.

What sparks original ideas: It can be contact from an R&D person asking me to create something to fill a certain need. You never know exactly what will trigger an idea. It could be an object, a conversation, anything.

Advice to would-be inventors: If you can't take criticism, you don't belong in this business. If you can, and you've got talent, go for it! You'll never know until you try.

Inventor: Alan Amron

Company: Talk to Me Programs, Inc.

Years in toy and game business: 7   **Yrs. inventing:** 20

Typical year: New concepts: 5; concepts presented: 5; concepts sold: 1

Most successful toys and games: Battery-operated water guns

Favorite toys and games as a kid: Cowboy guns and rifles; tools for building things

I think an inventor is: A person who does not use instructions to assemble something but uses imagination.

What sparks original ideas: When I see a need or the existence of a problem.

Advice to would-be inventors: Go for it! If you have an idea, draw it, make it, develop it, sell it, just do it!

Inventor: Hank Atkins

Company: Atkins Associates
Years in toy and game business: 15   **Yrs. inventing:** 18
Typical year: New concepts: 100; concepts presented: 10; concepts sold: 1
Most successful toys and games: Razzle
Favorite toys and games as a kid: Erector Set, Lincoln Logs, Monopoly
I think an inventor is: Anyone who purposefully tries to think of new ideas and then builds a prototype or has one made.
What sparks original ideas: I make lists in categories such as types of playing pieces, types of playing surfaces, types of play action. I select an element from each category and brainstorm what may be done in a play setting. This starting point usually leads me to something totally different.
Advice to would-be inventors: If you enjoy inventing games, then by all means do it. It can be fun and satisfying. Do it as a hobby. Don't count on much money even if you sell an item to a manufacturer. In some corner of your mind, keep the fact alive that with a lot of perseverance and luck you may defy the odds and make a small fortune.

Inventor: Gordon Barlow

Company: Barlow-Rehtmeyer Design
Years in toy and game business: 30   **Yrs. inventing:** 30
Typical year: New concepts: 40–50; concepts presented: 15; concepts sold: 8–12
Most successful toys and games: Mouse Trap; Stay Alive; Pivot Pool; Time Bomb; Gnip Gnop; Sureshot Hockey and Baseball; Power Blaster Motorcycle; Magic Hat

Favorite toys and games as a kid: Marbles, roller skates, tops, toy soldiers, bike, bat and ball

I think an inventor is: A person who originates an idea that the world has never seen.

What sparks original ideas: Free association, watching children, conversations, or daydreaming.

Advice to would-be inventors: If you are not very, very good and very tenacious—FORGET IT.

Inventor: Jim Becker

Company: Anjar Company

Years in toy and game business: 44   **Yrs. inventing:** 30

Typical year: New concepts: 25; concepts presented: 100; concepts sold: 20

Most successful toys and games: Othello; Nerf Ping-Pong; Pony Bop; Got a Hunch; Fire Ball Island; Go for Broke: Flipsiders; Sliders

Favorite toys and games as a kid: Toy soldiers and cars

I think an inventor is: Someone who develops ideas into working prototypes.

What sparks original ideas: Something I see or hear.

Advice to would-be inventors: Keep trying harder; always check the stores for the kind of product you want to design.

Inventor: Andrew Bergman

Company: James Wickstead Design Associates, Inc.

Years in toy and game business: 17   **Yrs. inventing:** 17

Typical year: New concepts: 100; concepts presented: 40; concepts sold: 3–5

Most successful toys and games: Sesame Street Clubhouse; JWDA projects: Etch-A-Sketch Animator; Etch-A-Sketch Animator 2000; PXL2000 Camcorder

Favorite toys and games as a kid: Scrabble, Erector Set, jigsaw puzzles, J. Fred Muggs hand puppet

I think an inventor is: One who looks at what exists in a unique way and recombines elements to create something new.

What sparks original ideas: In a very organized fashion, studying a company's product lines, reviewing marketing strategies, evaluating economic conditions. Once an area of opportunity has been identified, then the sparks ignite.

Advice to would-be inventors: Spend several years at a major toy company as an in-house designer to gain knowledge of the industry, meet key industry people, and convince yourself that this is something you like doing and that you can support yourself doing.

Inventor: Judy Blau

Company: J. Hope Design, Ltd.

Years in toy and game business: 10 **Yrs. inventing:** 10

Typical year: New concepts: 50; concepts presented: 50 + ; concepts sold: 1–8

Most successful toys and games: Sweetie Pops; Crib Sitters; Billy and Bellie Button; Abacus Turtle; Letter Lion; Bedkins

Favorite toys and games as a kid: Barbie, Lego, Monopoly

I think an inventor is: Someone who brings into existence an original product, feature, or concept.

What sparks original ideas: Everything feeds the creative process. Stimulation comes from my own fantasy world, verbal expressions, trends, music, movies. Observation of children at play, their current interests.

Advice to would-be inventors: Persevere, constantly reevaluate directions, the climate of the times, and the marketplace. Accept rejections as a fact of life. Have a backup skill or other means of support to help through slow periods. Remember, there is no recipe for a hit or everyone would do it. Even though a hit is the major goal, creating solid product that enhances play time for children through skill development, emotional growth, and imagination is a worthwhile goal too!

Inventor: Tom Braunlich

Company: Technical Game Services, Inc.
Years in toy and game business: 10   **Yrs. inventing:** 3
Typical year: New concepts: 100 + ; concepts presented: 10–15;
  concepts sold: 2–4
Most successful toys and games: Pente; Scratchees
Favorite toys and games as a kid: Bas-Ket, Monopoly, chess
I think an inventor is: An artist. A person with a "talent" for
  play who knows the classics, develops intricate design skills,
  and brings them together to create something unique. The
  best inventors are those who can combine mass commercial
  appeal with innovative play designs.
What sparks original ideas: The unusual and the insignificant.
Advice to would-be inventors: Have a good knowledge of all
  aspects of the industry, plus a good "feel for what's fun."
  Plug ideas into the competitive industry where they have a
  chance in the marketplace. Ally with as many experts as possible, and be open-minded to the suggestions and opinions of
  others.

Inventor: Jeffrey Breslow

Company: Breslow, Morrison, Terzian & Associates
Years in toy and game business: 22   **Yrs. inventing:** 22
Typical year: New concepts: 800; concepts presented: 150; con-
  cepts sold: 40
Most successful toys and games: Always next year's. Who cares
  about the past?
Favorite toys and games as a kid: Tops, yo-yo, and basketball
I think an inventor is: Someone who creates something out of
  something that already exists, who puts together in a new
  form familiar objects that in this new combination create the
  "AHHHH" factor—as in, Ahhh, why didn't I think of that?
What sparks original ideas: The spark for new ideas always
  comes from interaction with other people. I never wake up in

the middle of the night with an idea. The spark always comes
when you are looking for it. You must be ready for opportunity and constantly be alert for ideas.

Advice to would-be inventors: Keep playing with toys and never
grow up.

Inventor: Ernie Bridge

Company: Yankee Ingenuity
Years in toy and game business: 12   **Yrs. inventing:** 3
Typical year: New concepts: 20; concepts presented: 6; concepts
    sold: 1–2
Most successful toys and games: Einstein; I See You Dolly
Favorite toys and games as a kid: Chemistry sets, Erector Set,
    toy and real guns
I think an inventor is: Someone who devises new, cost-effective
    uses of existing technology, usually in support of a marketing
    concept.
What sparks original ideas: Usually I define a product category
    that I think represents an opportunity, and then I think about
    it while driving alone (on selling trips) and/or discuss it with
    colleagues. It's more problem-solving than open-ended "in-
    venting."
Advice to would-be inventors: You don't win very often, but it
    doesn't take many wins to do very well. So, it's a long time
    coming, but worth the wait.

Inventor: Paul L. Brown

Company: Paul L. Brown Development
Years in toy and game business: 18   **Yrs. inventing:** 26
Typical year: New concepts: impossible to estimate; concepts
    presented: varies; concepts sold: varies
Most successful toys and games: WIZ·Z·ZER; Tune Tops

Favorite toys and games as a kid: Erector Set, model planes, chemistry sets, crystal radio sets

I think an inventor is: A person possessed with a unique ability to tune in on thoughts, sights, and sounds for a new idea. Thinking about unknowns and trying to offer solutions.

What sparks original ideas: Seeing the familiar and being able to create it into something new. One creation triggers another.

Advice to would-be inventors: Learn the language of the inventive process. Do not entertain thoughts of instant wealth. Research your idea *before* investing. Avoid up-front money agents. Make face-to-face contact with other inventors. Use discretion, but remember that your idea is worth nothing if you do not stop somewhere and trust somebody.

Inventor: Dane Coe

Company: Dane Coe Design

Years in toy and game business: 24   **Yrs. inventing:** 20

Typical year: New concepts: 8–10; concepts presented: 2–3; concepts sold: 0–1

Most successful toys and games: Dressy Bessy; Dapper Dan; Baby's First Doll; all kinds of plush animals

Favorite toys and games as a kid: Paper dolls, coloring books, drawing pictures, making things

I think an inventor is: Someone who comes up with a new concept for a toy or a new way to present an old concept.

What sparks original ideas: To have a company come to me with a need. That usually starts you thinking. Or going to a toy store. You will often see something that you think is interesting but what they have done with it is terrible. That will lead to redesigning. So many concepts have been done a million times with a different twist or interpretation. Or you'll see a kid playing with something that will suggest something else. I look critically at the *old* ideas to see *new* ideas.

Advice to would-be inventors: Don't put all your eggs (or energies) in one basket; stick with the major toy companies.

Inventor: Cal Cook

Company: Cook, Lantzy Corp.

Years in toy and game business: 42   **Yrs. inventing:** 30

Typical year: New concepts: 10–12; concepts presented: 5–6; concepts sold: 1

Most successful toys and games: Big Wheel

Favorite toys and games as a kid: Handmade toys, models and kits

I think an inventor is: Someone who sees a need or has an idea for an item and racks the brain to come up with a solution.

What sparks original ideas: A lot of times, going through toy stores and catalogs or just watching children play.

Advice to would-be inventors: Keep plugging, but be sure you have other income.

Inventor: Julie Cooper

Company: Cooper & Kunkel

Years in toy and game business: 43   **Yrs. inventing:** 39

Typical year: New concepts: 20–30; concepts presented: 10–15; concepts sold: 1–2

Most successful toys and games: Beat the Clock; Buck-A-Roo; Crossfire; Rebound; Joe Palooka Baby Doll; Ka-Boom; Stock Market; Gunsmoke; Price Is Right; To Tell the Truth; Beatle Wigs; Candid Camera; Twenty-One; $64,000 Question; Total Control Racing; Sunset Strip; Evel Knievel Motorcycle; Baby Talk—The First Electronic Talking Doll

Favorite toys and games as a kid: Mechanical motor boat race, electric football, checkers

I think an inventor is: A person who can think and bring to fruition a device or process that is totally new and original.

What sparks original ideas: Sometimes it is deliberate concentration on a subject. Other times, it is something I see or hear or just comes out of the blue, and I put it into an idea for a new toy or game.

Advice to would-be inventors: Don't give up—don't grow up.

Inventor: Garry Donner

Company: Random Games and Toys

Years in toy and game business: 15   **Yrs. inventing:** 15

Typical year: New concepts: 24; concepts presented: 6; concepts sold: 1–2

Most successful toys and games: Pocket Trivia; Uno Dice; Wizard's Quest; Sproing; Travel Memory

Favorite toys and games as a kid: Monopoly, checkers, chess, Aggravation, Stratego

I think an inventor is: Someone familiar with his/her field to the point of being an expert so that he/she can apply new ideas or combine old ideas in new ways, within the field, to create something new.

What sparks original ideas: It seems to lurk in my subconscious, and pops out, usually when stimulated by my conscious, and often in a relaxed moment. I try to combine different things in different ways and think of things in opposite ways.

Advice to would-be inventors: Don't do it unless you love it, and don't expect to make much money for a few years. Get a good agent. Study the market, become an expert, and target your products.

Inventor: Ron Dubren

Company: Dubren & Associates

Years in toy and game business: 10   **Yrs. inventing:** 10

Typical year: New concepts: 50; concepts presented: 10; concepts sold: 2

Most successful toys and games: Rich Little's VCR Charades; Quink; Letter Ring; Tetris (the board game)

Favorite toys and games as a kid: Chess, magic items, sports

I think an inventor is: Someone who has conceived, developed, and sold a product to a manufacturer.

What sparks original ideas: Observing things going on in the culture and when there is an application in the business, a light bulb goes on above my head. If the idea works, it gets brighter; if not, it flickers and goes out.

Advice to would-be inventors: Learn all you can about the industry for which your invention is targeted. Listen to feedback, especially constructive criticism. Don't be paranoid—at least, not too paranoid—most people will not rip you off.

Inventors: Julius Ellman and Steven Ellman

Company: Lernell Company

Years in toy and game business: (J) 40; (S) 16   **Yrs. inventing:** (J) 40; (S) 16

Typical year: New concepts: 20–25; concepts presented: 10–15; concepts sold: 3–5

Most successful toys and games: In conjunction with my former partner, George Lerner, and my present partner, Steven Ellman, we have had more than 150 items marketed, about 20 percent of which had a market life of five years or more. Among products: Whip Stick Flyers; High Chair Activity Set; Trap Tennis; Chain Reaction; Pig Out

Favorite toys and games as kids: Julie: glider planes, water guns, yo-yos, Monopoly, electric trains, playing cards, balls; Steve: Stratego, Shenanigans, Risk, Winky Dink TV coloring kit, and street ball games

We think an inventor is: Someone with the ability to recognize a need through observation and/or "gut" feeling and then execute this need with a practical, creative approach. An inventor is someone who "stops to think" and can isolate thoughts while exploring the horizons and the basics of an idea.

What sparks original ideas: Anything!

Advice to would-be inventors: Make a working prototype or explicit illustration of the concept. Don't hide in a closet. Take some risks and show your concepts to interested parties after checking them out. Don't submit ideas by mail or messenger. Present concepts in person. Don't go broke pursuing patents. Make sure you have at least a five-year plan before expecting meaningful income return. Avoid getting into your own manufacture of the concept. Pursue royalty compensation. Don't sell your concept for a flat amount. And, finally, lighten up, don't take yourself too seriously. Don't go overboard on any one item. Accept criticism from professional reviewers, and try to be objective.

Inventor: Norman Fabricant

Company: Fabricants Associates
Years in toy and game business: 20 **Yrs. inventing:** 20
Typical year: New concepts: 100; concepts presented: everything; concepts sold: 4
Most successful toys and games: Dr. Drill'n'Fill; Tumble Tower; Animal Smackers; Boomin' Busy Box
Favorite toys and games as a kid: A ball and all kinds of "runaround" games
I think an inventor is: A person who creates new and unique products.
What sparks original ideas: I rarely get a brainstorm. I keep making notes and have filled many books. I keep reviewing my notes and adding to them. When something seems complete, I do model work or have a rendering made. Perhaps 10 percent of my ideas are complete enough to go directly to model-making at the time of conception.
Advice to would-be inventors: Don't quit your job.

Inventor: Mike Ferris

Company: Mike and Eddie, Inc.
Years in toy and game business: 20 **Yrs. inventing:** 20

Typical year: New concepts: 15–20; concepts presented: 8–10; concepts sold: 4–7

Most successful toys and games: Mickey Mouse Telephone; Masterpiece; SSPs

Favorite toys and games as a kid: Chess, backgammon

I think an inventor is: A creative assembly of apples and oranges—a bunch of unlike things.

What sparks original ideas: Usually from skuszoos of past failures.

Advice to would-be inventors: Have a good time.

Inventor: Bob Fuhrer

Company: R.B. Fuhrer Enterprises

Years in toy and game business: 12   **Yrs. inventing:** 12

Typical year: New concepts: 500; concepts presented: 40–50; concepts sold: 5

Most successful toys and games: T.H.I.N.G.S.; Pocket Rockers; Backwords; Super Crayons; Loco-Motion; Bongo Kongo; Rattle-Me-Bones; Flying Pirates; Thin Ice; Record Breakers

Favorite toys and games as a kid: Matchbox cars, toy soldiers, baseball, football, chess

I think an inventor is: Creator and conceptualizer of original ideas, or original approaches to common ideas and products.

What sparks original ideas: I've had sparks in my sleep, in a museum, during brainstorming sessions, on vacation.

Advice to would-be inventors: Align yourself with an accomplished agent; be patient, persistent, and original. Do thorough work and start by trying to create simple, inexpensive products that are easy to manufacture. Don't expect to get rich, but devote yourself to the endeavor.

Inventor: Derek Gable

Company: West Coast Innovations
Years in toy and game business: 21   **Yrs. inventing:** 21
Typical year: New concepts: 30–50; concepts presented: 30–40;
  concepts sold: 2–8
Most successful toys and games: Silly Dillys; active concept and
  design involvement on Mattel toys while director of prelimi-
  nary design for more than ten years, including accessories for
  Barbie and Hot Wheels, Masters of the Universe line, Star
  Guitar, Chatty Patty, Baby Grows Up, Baby Cries for You,
  Jingle Babies, Dancerella, Baby Magic, Galactica Ships, and
  Splash Happy
Favorite toys and games as a kid: Making models, flying planes,
  construction toys, Erector Set
I think an inventor is: A person who conceives of an original
  idea or concept (can be and most often is a combination of
  old elements) and puts together a new twist.
What sparks original ideas: Usually by being in a constant state
  of alert and awareness open to stimulation from all life experiences. Seeing a kitchen gadget can spark an idea for a game!
  Studying the market and its direction and need and concen-
  trating on filling those needs.
Advice to would-be inventors: Don't expect to make a living by
  it. Rather get steady income some other way and use the
  highly speculative inventing as a hobby or form of rolling the
  dice. It can make you a fortune, but don't bank on it! Be very
  selective on what you spend your speculative time on. Per-
  sist—Enjoy the process every day and don't make your success and happiness dependent on getting lots of money.

Inventors: Charlie and Maria Girsch

Company: Girsch Design Associates
Years in toy and game business: 18 (Charlie); 11 (Maria)   **Yrs.
  inventing:** 18 (Charlie); 11 (Maria)

Typical year: New concepts: 75–100; concepts presented: 60–
   80; concepts sold: 6–8
Most successful toys and games: Wrist Racers; People Magazine
   Game; Tubtown; Fun House Game; Funwich Factory; Cookie
   Monster Shape Muncher
Favorite toys and games as kids: Clue, Lincoln Logs, Sorry!,
   Erector Set, Monopoly
We think an inventor is: Charlie thinks an inventor is someone
   who can create a marketable opportunity. Maria thinks an
   inventor is someone who wakes up at 3 A.M. with a good idea
   when she'd really rather be sleeping; who steals parts from
   her kids' toys when they are at school in order to prototype
   said good idea; who hopes and prays there will be no ortho-
   dontia needed while said good idea is "under consideration";
   and who, when said good idea is returned five months later
   in a dusty box on which someone has fingered, "Wash me"
   (with a note tucked inside saying the concept does not fit the
   company's present marketing plans), has the grace and com-
   posure to simply wipe off the dust, send it out again, and go
   to bed an hour earlier in case another idea should happen to
   go bump in the night.
What sparks original ideas: Charlie walks stores, toy departments, hardware, gift/stationery. Maria says, "I have absolutely no set formula. I wish I knew of one. I try to read as
   many popular general-interest publications as I can and am
   probably more aware of trends as a result. Of course, I observe my children and their friends, but frankly, I don't think
   that they're as much a source of inspiration as they are of
   testing. Finally, because I am so very nonmechanical, I tend
   to be more "blue sky" oriented. I probably look less for a
   "new and revolutionary" idea (especially if the revolutionary
   part involves technology) and more for the "new and improved" idea or the new way to look at or position a "basic."
Advice to would-be inventors: Know that this is an industry of
   delayed gratification. Be sure you can survive for about two

years from other sources. Even if you sell your very first concept, it will be about 1½ to 2 years before you will be bringing royalty checks to the bank on a regular basis. The lifespan of the average toy is very short. The optimum situation is to have a promotional novelty at the same time you have a "kinder, gentler" long-term basic.

Inventor: A. Eddy Goldfarb

Company: A. Eddy Goldfarb & Associates

Years in toy and game business: 46   **Yrs. inventing:** 46

Typical year: New concepts: 150–200; concepts presented: 80–90; concepts sold: 12

Most successful toys and games: Yakity Yak Teeth; Stompers (with Del Everitt); Battling Tops; Kerplunk; Vacuum Form; Quiz Wiz; Shark Attack!, and many others using some 300 patents

Favorite toys and games as a kid: Electric motor kit, Erector Set; my favorite "game" was inventing something

I think an inventor is: Someone who can come up with a plaything out of the blue that is completely different, not just an improvement on an existing item.

What sparks original ideas: Sparks can come anywhere from dreams to anywhere there is a relaxed situation, like concerts, travel, etc. I read a lot, pursue interests in many subjects, and am generally curious.

Advice to would-be inventors: If you are a general inventor and want to be successful, stop shooting in all directions. Specialize. Get a creative offspring into the business. . . . My son, Martin, has come up with many great ideas.

Inventor: Perry Grant

Company: "Garage"

Years in toy and game business: 25   **Yrs. inventing:** 25

Typical year: New concepts: 8; concepts presented: 6; concepts sold: 0–1

Most successful toys and games: Hide'n Thief; Hang on Harvey; Bash; Whosit; Smess; Bird Brain

Favorite toys and games as a kid: Kick the can, tops, Monopoly

I think an inventor is: A person with free time and an itch.

What sparks original ideas: Whenever I am not trying to think of a game.

Advice to would-be inventors: Don't listen to early want-list ideas from manufacturers. They will be dead when you get there with your concepts.

Inventor: Larry Greenberg

Company: Larry Greenberg Associates

Years in toy and game business: 14   **Yrs. inventing:** 17

Typical year: New concepts: 6–8; concepts presented: 4–5; concepts sold: 0–1

Most successful toys and games: Alphie; Little Maestro Electronic Piano/Organ

Favorite toys and games as a kid: Monopoly, electric trains, toy soldiers

I think an inventor is: Someone who has the ability to transform an idea into a three-dimensional object and know when to stop.

What sparks original ideas: Usually in conjunction with another person (who is a codeveloper). We set up parameters/goals and then start "noodling" (free association) concepts and ideas. We attempt to limit discussion to set categories or areas (e.g., in the game area, we might go after adult, interaction, nonintellectual, games that retail for $15 or less).

Advice to would-be inventors: This isn't original with me, but it's appropriate: "Try not to come up with a solution for which there is no problem."

Inventor: Paul Gruen

Company: Gruen Studios
Years in toy and game business: 24   **Yrs. inventing:** 24
Typical year: New concepts: 20; concepts presented: 8; concepts sold: 2
Most successful toys and games: Payday; Caper; Scandal; Powerball
Favorite toys and games as a kid: Gilbert Erector Sets, Lionel trains
I think an inventor is: One who rearranges and expands upon existing data to create something new and unique.
What sparks original ideas: Primary ideas (the start of a project) come from any number of stimuli, about half within the industry and half from without. Secondary ideas (next level after the primary brainstorm idea) are actually of greater importance and separate professional from amateur.
Advice to would-be inventors: Get an MBA.

Inventor: Doug Hall

Company: Ha-Ha, Inc.
Years in toy and game business: 3   **Yrs. inventing:** 5
Typical year: New concepts: 24; concepts presented: 6; concepts sold: 2
Most successful toys and games: Octopus; Once
Favorite toys and games as a kid: Basketball, Risk, magic set, Monopoly
I think an inventor is: One who creates new-to-the-world concepts that are either useful or entertaining.
What sparks original ideas: It just comes. You can't force the process, although sipping white wine in a hot tub doesn't hurt.
Advice to would-be inventors: Be honest with yourself. Before taking out a second mortgage, test your concept on some people in an independent setting. Friends and family will never be honest.

Inventor: Ed Holahan

Company: Mike and Eddie, Inc.

Years in toy and game business: 16   **Yrs. inventing:** 16

Typical year: New concepts: 20–30; concepts presented: 15; concepts sold: 4

Most successful toys and games: Assorted Nerf items (airplane, train, etc.); Punt, Pass & Kick Machine; Ride-Through Car Wash; Trap Door; Sting; Dino Bones; Jolly Green Giant Farm/Factory

Favorite toys and games as a kid: Slinky, Silly Putty, Candy Land, Monopoly, Carom, Skilly, Erector Set

I think an inventor is: Someone who imagines "new" and makes new "real."

What sparks original ideas: Usually seeing something in the world and having it turn over sideways in my mind, e.g., kids love baseball—but what if Martians played it?

Advice to would-be inventors: Give yourself time to succeed/fail. Go with your instincts. Don't get too attached to yesterday's notion. Keep in touch with your contacts.

Inventor: Greg Hyman

Company: Greg Hyman Associates

Years in toy and game business: 16   **Yrs. inventing:** 33

Typical year: New concepts: 50–60; concepts presented: 30–40; concepts sold: 0–6

Most successful toys and games: Alphie; Alphie II; Major Morgan; Smart Alec; Lullabye Songbird; Electronic Musical Phone; Little Maestro Electronic Piano/Organ

Favorite toys and games as a kid: Whistle-controlled space vehicle, RCA radio kit, electronic worm getter

I think an inventor is: "Me."

What sparks original ideas: Waking up at night. Driving in a car. Talking to R&D person as he/she is rejecting my current idea. Lying on the nude beach in St. Martin (most often).

Advice to would-be inventors: Have enough money to sustain yourself while you invent and present full-time for minimum of two years. If you don't license anything in that time, get a job. There's a fine line between persistence and stupidity.

Inventor: Leonard Israel

Company: Leonard Israel
Years in toy and game business: 25 **Yrs. inventing:** 10
Most successful toys and games: Heart Throb
Favorite toys and games as a kid: Construction toys of any kind, and card games
I think an inventor is: The person who sees a need for an item and then creates it.
What sparks original ideas: Many start when I'm out walking or I dream about the idea.
Advice to would-be inventors: Have enough working capital or marry money.

Inventor: Larry Jones

Company: Cal R&D, Inc.
Years in toy and game business: 27 **Yrs. inventing:** 20
Typical year: New concepts:1969—463; 1988—6; concepts presented: 1969—463; 1988—6; concepts sold: 1969—4-6; 1988—6
Most successful toys and games: Cricket; Bucky, The Wonder Horse; Micronauts; Geodesic Dome Climber; Karate Chop
Favorite toys and games as a kid: Monopoly and sports
I think an inventor is: A person who reduces his ideas to practice and consequently onto the marketplace.
What sparks original ideas: Ideas can come at any time or place and are usually worthless. It is only when you combine them with the market needs that they truly become useful. Understanding the market, combined with weekly communication with the manufacturer, will often define a hole in the market. Then, research all historical data that is pertinent

and then create the new idea to "fill the hole." Actually, it is very easy.

Advice to would-be inventors: Root behind the obvious "creating-of-ideas" syndrome and treat the needs of the marketplace as a business that requires research, planning, and funding. Then you will be on the road to success.

Inventor: Benjamin Kinberg

Company: Benjamin Kinberg & Associates
Years in toy and game business: 30   **Yrs. inventing:** 20
Typical year: New concepts: 10–12; concepts presented: 100–125; concepts sold: 4–6
Most successful toys and games: James Bond Attaché Case; Glo-Doodler
Favorite toys and games as a kid: We had none in those days. I substituted books, which were abundantly available in libraries.
I think an inventor is: In the pragmatic sense, an individual who conceives of a commercial product that has never been done before, or never been done in quite the same way, or revives an old idea that was before its time and then successfully negotiates its acceptance (the hardest part) by a manufacturer.
What sparks original ideas: Difficult question. It could be a chance remark, a newspaper item, a movie. (My most profitable toy product came from an idea that popped into my head five minutes after my wife and I exited from a theater showing "From Russia with Love" with James Bond.) Ideas for toys, games, dolls, etc., have been instigated by museum visits, books, other toys, opera and theater shows, photographs, visits to foreign countries and visits to the corner store, looking in the shop windows on Fifth Avenue, in bed, and in the bath.
Advice to would-be inventors: Take up taxidermy. Seriously, I would ensure a steady income first and then try to break into

toy invention with the knowledge that my next meal is forth-coming even if my toys do not sell.

Inventor: Reuben Klamer

Company: ToyLab (SM)
Years in toy and game business: 30 +   **Yrs. inventing:** 30 +
Typical year: New concepts: difficult to answer; concepts presented: 15–20
Most successful toys and games: Originator and an inventor of The Game of Life; Roller Skates (Fisher-Price); Zoo-it-Yourself; Busy Blocks
Favorite toys and games as a kid: Basketball, baseball, football, tennis, Ping-Pong
I think an inventor is: One who creates something out of nothing.
What sparks original ideas: Memories. Seeing children at play. Reading newspapers/magazines; TV/movies; observing nature—without purpose. Going through toy stores regularly. Seeing one thing and visualizing another.
Advice to would-be inventors: Work for a toy/game company or a well-financed independent toy invention company that needs your talent. Don't mortgage your house to finance an idea.

Inventor: Michael Kohner

Company: The Michael Kohner Corp.
Years in toy and game business: 24   **Yrs. inventing:** 14
Typical year: New concepts: 30; concepts presented: 30; concepts sold: 20
Most successful toys and games: Trouble; Headache; Busy items; Ginny-O
Favorite toys and games as a kid: Model trains and all ball sports
I think an inventor is: Someone who has the ability to create

new ways of doing things or create something that to the best of his knowledge hasn't been done before.

Advice to would-be inventors: Don't fall in love with your concept, because you might chase an unattainable goal for too long. Try to learn manufacturers' capabilities. Learn model-making skill, i.e., forming plastic, gluing plastic, box-making, game boards. Don't quit. Rejection happens more often than not.

Inventor: Fred Kroll

Company: Shelbud Products Corporation.

Years in toy and game business: 51 **Yrs. inventing:** 29

Typical year: New concepts: 2–3; concepts presented: 1–2; concepts sold: 2–3

Most successful toys and games: Trouble; Busy Pop 'n Pals; Busy Faces; Hungry Hungry Hippos (via Japan); Busy Choo Choo; Leap Frogs; Play 'n' Go Rider

I think an inventor is: One who comes up with an original idea for a new product that has the potential to be marketed, used, or licensed to a manufacturer. Sometimes an inventor is just an idea man; other times, he may be a technical person.

What sparks original ideas: Observing life. Deciding on concepts that will sell to a manufacturer first and to the public second.

Advice to would-be inventors: Be able to recognize what will sell and not what the inventor's (your) family likes. I apply a high quality of exclusivity and selectivity so I only associate with firms and products that will be successful 90 percent of the time.

Inventors: Wayne Kuna and Ralph Kulesza

Company: Wayne Kuna & Associates

Years in toy and game business: 17

Typical year: New concepts: 80; concepts presented: 65; concepts sold: enough!

Most successful toys and games: Wayne: Finger Racers; Big Zoom; Omni Helicopter; Ralph: Big Foot (Playskool); Flex; Laser Attack, Melvin.

Favorite toys and games as kids: Wayne: Winky Dink Screen; Hopalong Cassidy gun and holster; Ralph: Made my own toys.

We think an inventor is: Wayne: The question is "Invent*or* what?" It must be "Invent*or* starve." Ralph: The Big Bang Theory in miniature. Together: One who exercises the unique ability to create, as it has been placed in him or her by the Almighty Creator, whether they would recognize that fact or not.

What sparks original ideas: We pray, observe, and the Lord blesses.

Advice to would-be inventors: The Four Don'ts: Don't fall in love with your ideas; don't be afraid to throw a bad idea in the garbage; don't throw yourself in with it; and don't stop trying.

Inventor: Andy Kunkel

Company: Cooper & Kunkel

Years in toy and game business: 25   **Yrs. inventing:** 25

Typical year: New concepts: 20–30; concepts presented: 10–15; concepts sold: 0–2

Most successful toys and games: Chips Are Down; Jitters

Favorite toys and games as a kid: Monopoly

I think an inventor is: An individual who truly believes the old saying, "Creativity begins with 90 percent perspiration and 10 percent inspiration."

What sparks original ideas: One can germinate anytime or anywhere. I usually write it down and never let it get away. If it's an object, I try to place it where I will see it a number of times, thus drawing my thoughts back to it again and again.

Advice to would-be inventors: Never give up, and if it isn't fun, don't do it.

Inventor: Stephen Lane

Company: Compass New Product Development
Years in toy and game business: 2   **Yrs. inventing:** 4
Typical year: New concepts: 75; concepts presented: 30; concepts sold: 15
Most successful toys and games: Flounder Pounder; Car Seat Circus
Favorite toys and games as a kid: Lego, Mr. Potato Head
What sparks original ideas: My best ideas come to me in just that form—a spark. There is usually no correlation between what I happen to be doing at the time and that particular new idea. One thing for sure—I've got to be relaxed. "Ideas under pressure" would not be a good tag line for my business card. Sleeping (dreaming), driving, and people-watching have proven to be as successful a "design process" as I've been able to identify for myself.
Advice to would-be inventors: Just do it. Probably 80 percent of people I talk with about jobs or careers will tell me how they would love to be an inventor. Everyone has ideas. It is only a question of committing to a career of ideas. Give yourself a year. Life is just a long education that sometimes you pay for and sometimes you don't. Other than time, some pocket change, and a few blows to the ego, there's not a lot to lose. There is, however, a tremendous amount to gain—and fast. Start small. In the beginning, approach smaller companies that appear to have a degree of integrity. They are usually more receptive to new ideas, they move faster, they allow you to see the internal workings, and they are less apt to rip you off. The money won't be as good, but they are excellent training grounds. Hit the bigger companies when you have your act together.

Inventor: Paul Lapidus

Company: Together Group
Years in toy and game business: 13   **Yrs. inventing:** 20
Typical year: New concepts: 25; concepts presented: 25; concepts sold: 2
Most successful toys and games: Smokin Shakers; Modifiers; BMX Helmut
Favorite toys and games as a kid: Model kits and toy guns
I think an inventor is: A person who recognizes an unfulfilled need in the marketplace and has the vision and skill to create something of value to fulfill that need.
What sparks original ideas: A perceived market need, seeing an area of opportunity, hearing a neat name, seeing a poorly done concept and knowing it can be improved, extensive reading, listening to people carefully.
Advice to would-be inventors: Be smart. Learn the market. Don't give up. Keep creating. Be independently wealthy.

Inventor: Roger Lehmann

Company: Lehmann & Satten
Years in toy and game business: 21
Most successful toys and games: Sweet Secrets; Army Gear; Powerods; Bathing Beauties; P. J. Sparkles doll; Hot Wheels Car Go Carrier; Sports Starters Baseball Glove.
Favorite toys and games as a kid: Erector Set, Lionel trains, Aurora slot cars, roller skates, Roadmaster bicycles, Monopoly, baseball
I think an inventor is: A combination of talents acquired through association in the toy industry; able to creatively take the germ of an idea, blend in the understanding of children's play patterns, toy-company marketing philosophy, a sensitivity for design and aesthetics, the realities of mass production, and the management talents of a business executive.

What sparks original ideas: Identifying a need in the market-place, changing fashions, and play patterns all promote thinking to find the solution to the problem. Solving existing problems leads to new creative ideas.

Advice to would-be inventors: Handling rejection must be part of your regular diet, and success your occasional dessert.

Inventor: Richard C. Levy

Company: Richard C. Levy & Associates

Years in toy and game business: 13   **Yrs. inventing:** 13

Typical year: New concepts: 40; concepts presented: 20; concepts sold: 1–6

Most successful toys and games: Adver*teasing;* Noteability; Screen Challenge; Hot Lixx, Jell-o Popcycle; Crest Fluorider; Tune Tops

Favorite toys and games as a kid: Dinky toys, plastic model kits, War, Go Fish

I think an inventor is: A person to whom the elves still whisper.

What sparks original ideas: Most everything, and, above all, my daughter Bettie.

Advice to would-be inventors: Understand that rejection is no more than the shakedown phase before the big event. If you hear hoofbeats, expect a horse. Know your market. Get a great permanent partner like my wife, Sheryl, a creative lady who also knows how to manage a three-ring circus.

Inventor: Ray Lohr

Company: Lohr Designs

Years in toy and game business: 56   **Yrs. inventing:** 56

Typical year: New concepts: 20; concepts presented: 8–10, concepts sold: 1

Most successful toys and games: Big Wheel, Electroshot; Magic Shot; Marvel the Mustang; Krazy Kar; Guide-A-Scottie

Favorite toys and games as a kid: Velocipedes, B.B. guns

I think an inventor is: One who thinks up and constructs new items of use or improves on old ones.

What sparks original ideas: Studying toys and children playing with them. Looking over toys in stores and manufacturers' catalogs; always analyzing. Seeking to improve on classic toys.

Advice to would-be inventors: Just keep working hard, test models well with children, keep in contact with potential customers to find out what types of product they want.

Inventor: Bruce Lund

Company: Lund & Company

Years in toy and game business: 9   **Yrs. inventing:** 9

Typical year: New concepts: 400; concepts presented: 50; concepts sold: 3–4

Most successful toys and games: Fireball Island

Favorite toys and games as a kid: Estes rockets, Bulldog Tank, Vertibird

I think an inventor is: One who conceives of what doesn't exist. One who answers needs that others don't realize they have.

What sparks original ideas: Usually in idea meetings with co-workers or searching through newspapers, magazines, catalogs, etc., for new directions.

Advice to would-be inventors: You have to be crazy to think you can make a living in this business. Expect two years without income.

Inventor: Patrick MacCarthy

Company: MacCarthy Products

Years in toy and game business: 7   **Yrs. inventing:** 10

Typical year: New concepts: 10; concepts presented: 5; concepts sold: 1

Most successful toys and games: Kaleid-A-Sketch; Ribbon Yo-Yo

Favorite toys and games as a kid: Kaleidoscopes, spinning tops, jigsaw puzzles

I think an inventor is: One who invents—that is, creates products previously unknown to that person.

What sparks original ideas: Generally, the idea does not just come in a flash. Usually my thinking is directed in a particular direction by a perceived need in a certain area. For example, I might say to myself, Here is a need for a new sketching-type toy. Now I will concentrate on this for days or weeks, contemplating it from all angles, like individual brainstorming. This may go on intermittently for more than a year. Here, generally, ideas do come to me in a flash, almost from the subconscious, but I have been making my mind receptive to such flashes by thinking deeply on the subject for a long time.

Inventor: Ron Magers

Company: Products For Children

Years in toy and game business: 18   **Yrs. inventing:** 15

Typical year: New concepts: 5–10; concepts presented: 5; concepts sold: 0–3

Most successful toys and games: Clik-Claks; Clean-Up Truck; Steer Crazy Truck; Attach-N-Go Stroller Toy; Story Scope; Freedom Force Helicopter; Flip Flop Frog; Vampire Bat

Favorite toys and games as a kid: Boomerang, Slinky, airplanes, cars

I think an inventor is: Someone who can make something out of nothing—and sell it.

What sparks original ideas: I look for a void, a hole if you will, and get out my designer's shovel and try to fill it.

Advice to would-be inventors: S.C.A.N. his or her idea: It should be *simple* in its form and under stability, *clean* in its presentation, *and neat* as in Wow! Fantastic!, etc. It also helps to make it cheap.

Inventor: James McMurtry

Company: Play Value Designs
Years in toy and game business: 3 **Yrs. inventing:** 20
Typical year: New concepts: 100; concepts presented: 3; concepts sold: 1
Most successful toys and games: Game of Dragons; Oreo Cookie Factory Game
Favorite toys and games as a kid: Monopoly, Canasta, toy soldiers
I think an inventor is: A right-brain person who creates things of practical, artistic, or entertainment value.
What sparks original ideas: They may originate as a format idea for which I must then develop a game system, or occur the other way around. Many good ideas grow out of my files of previous ideas that at some point fell short of full development. I think one builds up a critical mass of ideas, then it's possible to begin combining these into fully developed product ideas that have currency and completeness. A good title idea may also lead to a good game invention.
Advice to would-be inventors: Have a backup profession.

Inventor: Burton C. Meyer

Company: Meyer/Glass Design
Years in toy and game business: 35 **Yrs. inventing:** 50
Typical year: New concepts: 50–100; concepts presented: 10–15; concepts sold: 5–10
Most successful toys and games: Mr. Machine, Lite Brite, Tip-It, Toss Across, Tin Can Alley, Popza Ball, Mouse Trap, Rock'em Sock'em Robots, Inchworm, Smarty Bird, Bop the Beetle, Odd Ogg, King of the Hill, Big Parade, Tigeroo, Clean Sweep, Toot-L-oo-Loco, Golfarino, Mickey Mouse Telephone. (Note: Most of the foregoing items, as with all inventions, are cooperative efforts and there is not a single one

that would have been created if it were not for at least some contribution from others.)

Favorite toys and games as a kid: Erector Set, Tinkertoys, Lincoln Logs, airplane kits, Monopoly, "Spike," and heavy sports

I think an inventor is: Someone who pursues the world around themselves and reassembles the observed elements to form a new or different concept, system, or device.

What sparks original ideas: Being a full-time receptive observer. R. Buckminster Fuller, one of the greatest inventors of all time, said, "There are no failures, only unexpected results." His attitude is one of the most useful in invention success.

Advice to would-be inventors: Find an organization. Don't be a loner. Don't be afraid to come up with bad ideas. Don't just think up ideas. Make time and discipline yourself to spend X number of hours per week in the workshop or studio making something. Have faith in yourself and your ideas. Be generous with recognition of the contributions of others to your items. Be willing to dump 100 fair ideas to find one good one. Don't accept mediocrity. Study the toy market and its history, then think two or three years ahead of it. Don't preconceive.

Inventor: Donald Miffitt

Company: Venture Technologies

Years in toy and game business: 10   **Yrs. inventing:** 25

Typical year: New concepts: 80–90; concepts presented: 25; concepts sold: 1–3

Most successful toys and games; Luminations

Favorite toys and games as a kid: Homemade toys, car racing sets, basketball, Tinkertoys

I think an inventor is: An individual or group that creates new product to solve a problem or meet a market need.

What sparks original ideas: A product category, technology, market need, price, or combinations of these. Most ideas are triggered by a comment or suggestion of one partner, which generates a new or unique direction, not necessarily in the same direction as the comment/suggestion.

Advice to would-be inventors: Understand the market. Be persistent.

Inventor: Ron Milner

Company: Applied Design Labs, Inc.

Years in toy and game business: 15   **Yrs. inventing:** 40

Typical year: New concepts: 50; concepts presented: 10; concepts sold: 1

Most successful toys and games: Atari 2600; A.G. Bear; Hot Lixx

Favorite toys and games as a kid: Erector Set, Monopoly, chemistry set

I think an inventor is: Totally nuts. Someone who doesn't immediately discard new ideas as ridiculous.

What sparks original ideas: Easiest spark is an unfilled need.

Advice to would-be inventors: Sell your concept first before you put a lot of money into it. We have a $15,000 self-balancing bicycle on the shelf from before we learned that lesson.

Inventor: Tim Moodie

Company: Girsch Design Associates

Years in toy and game business: 6   **Yrs. inventing:** 6

Typical year: New concepts: 60–80; concepts presented: 40; concepts sold: 3–6

Most successful toys and games: Fun House Game; Trivia Bingo

Favorite toys and games as a kid: Helium-filled blimp, Mr. Machine, Matchbox cars

I think an inventor is: Somebody who thinks stuff up for somebody else to execute.

What sparks original ideas: It could happen any time, but it's usually while I'm driving or in the shower. This makes writing down the ideas very difficult.

Advice to would-be inventors: If you don't like to starve or if you haven't salted away enough money for two or three years, consider driving a bus.

Inventor: Tony Morley

Company: Red Racer Studio
Years in toy and game business: 9   **Yrs. inventing:** 3
Typical year: New concepts: 30–35; concepts presented: 20–25; concepts sold: 2
Most successful toys and games: Nerf Fencing (with associate external developer)
Favorite toys and games as a kid: Johnny Reb Cannon, Careers, Stratego, toy soldiers, kites, Sno-Cone Machine, Erector Set, gas airplanes, trucks
I think an inventor is: Somebody who creates a new technology, mechanism, character, play pattern, game scenario, or who finds a new application for any of the above.
What sparks original ideas: A gizmo. A new application of an old idea. Some "neat" material may interest me. A problem presented by a company.
Advice to would-be inventors: Make sure you have eighteen months of money to live on first.

Inventor: Betty Morris

Company: K & B Innovations, Inc.
Years in toy and game business: 17   **Yrs. inventing:** 17
Typical year: New concepts: 100s; concepts presented: 10; concepts sold: 5–6
Most successful toys and games: Shrinky Dinks; Zip-N-Stick; Chumpkins
Favorite toys and games as a kid: Blue steel railroad engine, yo-yo, Erector Set, jacks, pickup sticks, Uncle Wiggily, Monopoly, chess, card games

I think an inventor is: Someone who has the mental ability to "step" outside the square of existing products or ideas.

What sparks original ideas: An idea may come at any time. Watching my grandchildren at play, reading gadget books, thinking how neat it would be if . . . Taking away what already exists, brainstorming, expanding on a concept to see how many different products can be created. Solutions or ideas are often generated while in bed. Problem-solving, evaluations of the difficult, simplifying, etc. Referring to past toys and games and applying modern technology. Taking a concept or material from another industry and applying it to toy ideas. Combining several toy/game concepts to create a new product. A toy company's interest or need.

Advice to would-be inventors: If you want to make money from your idea, you are really going to have to do your homework. The industry is very complex. Read everything you can. The library is packed full of books relating to all the necessary steps to take and think about as it relates to getting your product idea to market. If you can make your toy or game and establish a trademark name, you probably have the best chance to interest a large manufacturer. A publication called *Playthings* will allow you to get a feel for what various toy and game manufacturers are doing, trends of the industry, etc. Read and reread as many current publications as you can.

Inventor: Henry Orenstein

Company: Toy Builders
Yrs. Inventing: 36
Most successful toys and games: Suzy Homemaker; Dawn dolls; Johnny Lightning (and cars); Johnny 7; Baby Magic; Dolly Surprise; Transformers (numerous); Suzy Smart
Advice to would-be inventors: Be patient.

Inventor: Charles Phillips

Company: Game Systems

Years in toy and game business: 14   **Yrs. inventing:** All my
life—45

Typical year: New concepts: 150–200; concepts presented: 10–
15; concepts sold: 3–4

Most successful toys and games: Advance to Boardwalk; Casino
Card Games; Clue, Jr.; I Vont to Bite Your Finger; Vegas
Nites

Favorite toys and games as a kid: The ones I could make for
myself, toy cars, toy trucks, etc. A hammer, nails, pieces of
wood, and wheels; checkers

I think an inventor is: An individual who recognizes the product
cycle, can define an idea fully, and knows the details and steps
to complete an idea.

What sparks original ideas: Everything around me; when I talk
to people, I get ideas; when I read magazines, I get ideas;
when I watch TV, I get ideas. The problem is not sparking
with ideas; I can get twenty to twenty-five a day. The issue is
filtering out the ones valuable enough to work on.

Advice to would-be inventors: Get a fix on the marketplace. See
what people are looking for—either consumers or manufacturers. Put that need into the least expensive and most exciting form and package you can. Get the best graphics you can
on your prototypes. Remember to think excitement and experiences—you are trying to get the most in a box. Try to get
a manufacturer (yourself); avoid an agent if at all possible.

Inventor: Gary Piaget

Company: Piaget Associates

Years in toy and game business: 20   **Yrs. inventing:** 40

Typical year: New concepts: 50; concepts presented: 20; concepts sold: 4

Most successful toys and games: Alexander's Star; Crest Fluorider; One-Piece Jigsaw Puzzle; Jell-o Popcycle

Favorite toys and games as a kid: European military vehicles,
firecrackers, model kits, gas airplanes

I think a toy inventor is: The strangest, most complex form of
humanity; a person of diverse creative ability, one who can
wear many hats in this arena of chance.

What sparks original ideas: Stimulation is the key to a hardworking, creative mind. I try to feel stimulation in everything
I do.

Advice to would-be inventors: I would stress the need for a
profound entrepreneurial spirit, an understanding of what this
spirit means in dedication and just plain hanging in there,
and how to apply this spirit to your best advantage. The inventor must generate his own power. He is his only man, he
is the ship. He learns to draw on everything around him, from
the natural to the very synthetic.

Inventor: Douglas Polumbaum

Company: DHP Company

Years in toy and game business: 15 **Yrs. inventing:** 6

Typical year: New concepts: 30; concepts presented: 10; concepts sold: 3

Most successful toys and games: Keypers; Just Girls/Hair Flair;
Blabber Mouth Talking Radios

Favorite toys and games as a kid: Toy cowboys, rubber balls,
Slinky

I think an inventor is: One who originates an invention, design,
or marketing concept and is motivated to develop and refine
the idea into a specific product or product-line execution.

What sparks original ideas: Having an immediate and instinc-
tive perception of what will delight a child as a toy or game,
and then applying reason and experience to qualify and refine
the uniqueness of the creative insight.

Advice to would-be inventors: Believe in yourself, but be willing to modify your ideas based upon professional feedback from the toy companies. In other words, be a good listener so that you can isolate what is truly unique about your invention; and don't be afraid to incorporate that uniqueness into a modified version of your initial concept.

Inventor: Vic Reiling

Company: Victor G. Reiling Associates
Years in toy and game business: 20   **Yrs. inventing:** 20
Typical year: New concepts: 100–150; concepts presented: 40–50
Most successful toys and games: Fisher-Price Airport, Play Desk, Circus Train (as staff designer). Hand Command; Hot Potato; Hit Stix (with Bryan Dean); Hit Guitar; Hit Strings; Super Sax; Horn Magic
Favorite toys and games as a kid: Trains, soldiers, construction sets, play sets
I think an inventor is: A combiner of elements—some old, some new—in such a manner as to be appealing to children of an appropriate age, thus insuring a profit for both originator and client.
What sparks original ideas: From a spoken word or phrase; from a visual, sometimes fleeting, sighting; from a suggested need; from an experience; from something created for an entirely different purpose; and from flashes in the mind, the origin of which I cannot fathom.
Advice to would-be inventors: Think of the Frisbie Pie Company pie plates (five cents deposit) and the workers who threw them about during breaks. Think of the Navy man who dropped a spring down a ship's ladder and then called it Slinky. And, in the words of Langston Hughes, "Hold fast to dreams, for if dreams die, life is a broken-winged bird that cannot fly."

Inventor: Larry Reiner

Company: Larry Reiner Associates
Years in toy and game business: 28   **Yrs. inventing:** 30
Typical year: New concepts: 50; concepts presented: 25; concepts sold: varies
Most successful toys and games: 12-inch G.I. Joe; Skittle; Obsession; Star Trek (various toys); Dress 'n Dazzle. Started game division for Ideal Toy Company
Favorite toys and games as a kid: Soldiers, Monopoly, Scrabble
I think an inventor is: A creator who comes up with an innovation of a new idea or the adaptation of an old idea with a new and innovative twist.
What sparks original ideas: A new idea can happen at any time. It can happen while I'm talking to someone or driving a car or just walking through a store. A new and brilliant idea cannot be forced. Once an idea comes to you, that is the time it must be nurtured and expanded upon.
Advice to would-be inventors: Find a need, then learn the marketing and psychological needs of the group you are aiming your product at. Make the product appeal both visually as well as with its play value. Make products that are not complicated.

Inventor: Jim Routzong

Company: Joynt Ventures
Years in toy and game business: 10   **Yrs. inventing:** 35
Typical year: New concepts: 25-50; concepts presented: 25-50; concepts sold: 2-5
Most successful toys and games: Spit Balls; Willoughby Weebok; Sturdy Wall Pool
Favorite toys and games as a kid: Lincoln Logs, Erector Set, cars and trucks; playing ''army'' and building things with found objects.

I think an inventor is: A person who is constantly thinking of
new ideas or new ways of doing things.

What sparks original ideas: I eat, sleep, and live thinking about
new ideas. Ideas originate as a result of being constantly aware
and observant of "things" around me. The seed of an idea
originates as a result of a spontaneous reaction to my observations.

Advice to would-be inventors: Be prepared. Have an inventory
of fully developed ideas before starting on your own. Know
that you will be able to get "in the door" to sell your stuff.
Establish contacts. Understand the process of taking an idea
from concept through to the consumer.

Inventor: Elliot Rudell

Company: Rudell Design

Years in toy and game business: 19   **Yrs. inventing:** 14

Most successful toys and games: UpWords; Word Rummy;
Playskool Express; Weebles; Shuffletown; Attach 'n Go; Oh,
What a Mountain; Minnie Mouse Sidewalk Bike; Mickey
Machine Tricycle; Force Field

Favorite toys and games as a kid: Pink rubber ball, slot cars,
bicycles

I think an inventor is: Someone who creates, conceives, or con-
cocts something new or unique or at least convinces himself
or others that he has the potential to do so.

What sparks original ideas: Any number of things. I'll see a
new consumer product that sparks an idea, notice a child's
play pattern or play pattern deficit, brainstorm a particular
category and analyze past successes and failures. Prayer—
several major ideas have just been given to me.

Advice to would-be inventors: Be honest. Be prepared to struggle. Trust your own feelings. Don't expect wealth overnight.
If you go bankrupt, it doesn't mean you're not creative. If
you make it, don't get puffed up. The race is not to the swift,
and the battle is not to the warrior (strong), and neither is

bread to the wise, nor wealth to the discerning, nor favor to men of ability; for time and chance overtake them all.

Inventor: Sid Sackson

Company: Sid Sackson (Guru of Games)

Years in toy and game business: 30   **Yrs. inventing:** 60

Typical year: New concepts: varies; concepts presented: varies; concepts sold: 2–6

Most successful toys and games: Acquire, Can't Stop

Favorite toys and games as a kid: Uncle Wiggily, Lotto, Monopoly

I think an inventor is: Someone who comes up with new ideas for useful or pleasant ideas—and makes them work.

What sparks original ideas: Most of the games I work on now are in answer to specific assignments, or suggestions, from various sources. Before arriving at this point (and still, when I get a little spare time), my ideas came in many different ways: helping my children with their homework; an interesting tile pattern on a bathroom floor; dissatisfaction with a game on the market—"of course I can do it better"—and ending up with something very different. (In this connection, I am occasionally asked to come up with a minor variation of a standard game, which paradoxically I find quite difficult. So I go my own original way, sometimes losing the assignment as a result.)

Advice to would-be inventors: Love it very very much—or forget it.

Inventor: Michael Satten

Company: Lehmann & Satten

Years in toy and game business: 18

Most successful toys and games: Sweet Secrets; Army Gear; Powerods; Bathing Beauties; P. J. Sparkles doll; Hot Wheels Car-Go Carrier; Sports Starters Baseball Glove

Favorite toys and games as a kid: Action figures and playsets, Tinkertoys, Monopoly, paint-by-numbers

I think a toy inventor is: Some are designers, some marketers, others salesmen. Many are combinations of all three. Toy inventors are people who can see where something is not, visualize what that something might be, and execute it in a way that is magic in the eyes of a child.

What sparks original ideas: First, the fear that I have wasted a year. We work on many programs in a year, and when February Toy Fair comes around, you either have items in the marketplace or you don't. Ideas are everywhere, you just have to look for them. Take a shower—think of water toys. Drive your car—what would you love your car to be able to do? Life's experiences help originate much of what you create.

Advice to would-be inventors: Practice staying in the lines, but occasionally go over them. AND DON'T GIVE UP!

Inventor: Marc Segan

Company: M.H. Segan & Company, Inc.

Years in toy and game business: 11   **Yrs. inventing:** 11

Typical year: New concepts: 50–100; concepts presented: 60–120; concepts sold: 5–30

Most successful toys and games: Musical greeting cards; musical Christmas ornaments; Horn-A-Plenty; Kawasaki musical instruments

Favorite toys and games as a kid: Blocks, electronic kits

I think an inventor is: As much a stylist and synthesist and follower of fashion as a creator. Indeed, there is quite a bit of authentic invention in the business, but much of what is considered invention is really deal-making.

What sparks original ideas: Anytime, anyplace. Favorites are in the car and sleeping, although during the workday, conversations and reading stimulate a lot of good material.

Advice to would-be inventors: That absolutely no one knows all the answers and so one "expert's" hit is another one's "dog."

Keep producing as many concepts as you can; stay close to clients and the marketplace; no deal's done until the check clears the bank (probably).

Inventor: Jay Smith

Company: Western Technologies
Years in toy and game business: 23   **Yrs. inventing:** 20
Typical year: New concepts: 50; concepts presented: 15; concepts sold: 5
Most successful toys and games: Microvision; Vectrex; Baby Talk
Favorite toys and games as a kid: Full-size U-drive truck cab built by my dad, Tinkertoys, Erector Set
I think an inventor is: A creative designer who has this year's answer to next year's question.
What sparks original ideas: Identifying our customers' needs and matching our visions to their needs.
Advice to would-be inventors: Know your customers and give them what *they* want, not just what you want.

Inventor: Rollie Tesh

Company: Technical Game Services, Inc.
Years in toy and game business: 10   **Yrs. inventing:** 3
Typical year: New concepts: 100–200; concepts presented: 20–30; concepts sold: 3–5
Most successful toys and games: Pente; Scratchees
Favorite toys and games as a kid: B.B. guns, chess
I think an inventor is: Someone with good ideas who can take full advantage of resources, can do research to find if anything like this idea has been done before, can find the experts who can assist with the idea, and find trends on where the market is heading. Research can help greatly to turn raw concept into reality.
What sparks original ideas: Sparks come with accumulated ex-

perience. The more "needs" a person comes across, the greater the likelihood that research, creative thinking, or even an offhand remark will trigger an "ah-ha."

Advice to would-be inventors: Perseverance! Overcome luck through diversity! The more good ideas, the less the need to be lucky.

Inventor: Joe Wetherell

Company: Wetherall Associates

Years in toy and game business: 28   **Yrs. inventing:** 45

Typical year: New concepts: 200; concepts presented: 25; concepts sold: 2-3

Most successful toys and games: Dolly Surprise; Jem; Pretty Cut & Grow; Nerf (baseball); Nerf Man; Giggley-Jiggley; Green Ghost Game

Favorite toys and games as a kid: Erector Set, trains, models, checkers, Monopoly, punch ball, knucks, bike, roller skates

I think an inventor is: Anyone who observes a need or unfulfilled desire, develops a concept to fill that need or desire, and executes that concept so that it fills the need in a universal enough way.

What sparks original ideas: Ideas are a function of observation, experience in problem-solving and openness. An idea is simply the result of allowing your observations and experience to whirl around chaotically in your brain and leaving openings to allow all combinations to come out.

Advice to would-be inventors: Get a good idea, believe in it, make it work, test it thoroughly—with strangers if possible (Mom always will like it). If you cannot make a contact directly with the companies, use a reliable professional inventor to help. Be open to share. The professional inventor might also add something to the product—half of something sold is better than all of something in your closet.

Inventor: Howard Wexler

Company: Interplay Inc.

Years in toy and game business: 20   **Yrs. inventing:** 20

Typical year: New concepts: 40; concepts presented: 40; concepts sold: 10

Most successful toys and games: Connect Four; 3-D coloring books; Wilson Stuffs

Favorite toys and games as a kid: Construction and sports toys

I think an inventor is: A creator of unique materials and methods of play.

What sparks original ideas: Observing and studying what people like to do at leisure play; knowing what manufacturers need to improve lines; analyzing marketplace needs.

Advice to would-be inventors: Know very well what it takes to sell an idea.

Inventor: Bruce Whitehill

Company: Bruce Whitehill

Years in toy and game business: 6   **Yrs. inventing:** 6

Typical year: New concepts: 12; concepts presented: 2; concepts sold: 1

Most successful toys and games: Ripley's Believe It or Not

Favorite toys and games as a kid: Go to the Head of the Class, Stratego, Careers, Racko, Mr. Potato Head, Cootie, Go Fish, Pickup Sticks, Scrabble, Numble, Troke, Jotto

I think an inventor is: One who creates a new idea or concept or develops a new application for an old idea.

What sparks original ideas: From something I see around me, something somebody says, or something that just seems to pop into my head. Often, when creating "on assignment," I am given a basic starting point so that I develop a menu of things that will go well with the basic concept; sometimes I look at "mathematical" possibilities.

Advice to would-be inventors: The quality of your idea or prod-

uct is one of the least important factors pertaining to its potential success—selling the best possible product is still a long
shot. You are not inventing games for the general public—
you are inventing games for the head buyer of Toys R Us.
Don't forget the old adage about who you know, not what
you know—if you're not going to manufacture and market
your game yourself, who is going to look at your product or
idea? Determine in advance whether you are going to manufacture and market your own product ($50,000 minimum re-
quired), or whether you hope to sell it to a company (you give
up 95 percent). Most important piece of advice: Make sure
you have another income.

Inventor: Ted Wolf

Company: Ted Wolf

Years in toy and game business: 35   **Yrs. inventing:** 20

Most successful toys and games: U-Drive-It, Max machine, To-
bor and Thundercats

Favorite toys and games as a kid: Erector Set, wooden blocks,
steam shovel

I think an inventor is: In the strictest sense, one who creates a
device that was previously unknown. In the toy industry, one
who adapts previously known devices to previously unknown
products.

What sparks original ideas: Something I read or hear—then
sweat and toil, and sometimes a subconscious thought (spontaneous combustion).

Advice to would-be inventors: Better be pretty damned sure of
yourself. There used to be a handful of us, now there are
hundreds.

Glossary

PLAY ON WORDS

If you step off an airplane onto foreign soil and speak or attempt to speak the language of that country, the nationals tend to pay more attention to you, warm up a little faster, understand you better, and, in general, want to please you more than those who don't try to communicate in their lingua franca.

So it is when your flight (of fancy) arrives in toyland. Marketing and R&D executives, the first natives you are most likely to encounter as an outside developer, have their own idioms, too. Communication will be a lot smoother if you understand the toymaker's tongue.

Knowing the appropriate "buzzwords" also ensures exact answers to your queries and helps avoid potentially embarrassing semantic ruptures. For example, if a sales executive complains about dating problems, don't try to ingratiate yourself by offering an introduction to a single friend. In the toy industry, dating refers to the way manufacturers bill customers for merchandise.

When someone wants you to "polish up a thumbnail," you'll do nothing to the value of your personal stock by reaching for an emery board. Chances are the person is requesting that a rough pencil drawing of a new concept be tightened and colored with markers.

If the task is for you to "cannibalize" a doll, don't grab the next flight to the Amazon. Chances are you just have to go to the nearest Toys R Us and bring back an existing doll that they can use for parts.

In the toy industry, a "J-hook" is not a shot made by basketball superstar Dr. J; "tissues" are not used to wipe a runny nose; "choke factor" has nothing to do with the Heimlich maneuver; "SKUs" are not deviations from straight lines; "noodling" is a far cry from making pasta; and a "Glass item" does not mean some amorphous inorganic transparent product formed by the fusion of silica.

We hope you'll enjoy and make use of this glossary, which contains some of the most commonly used words, expressions, and abbreviations in the toy industry.

A

ABS: Strong, long-wearing, stain-resistant thermoplastic widely used in toy components where extra strength is required. Expensive.

Accessory: Companion item, adornment, or other piece developed for use with a particular toy or game, the number of which usually broaden an inventor's royalty base substantially.

Accumulation games: Object is to be the first player to collect a quantity of objects like marbles, tokens, or money. Examples include Monopoly, The Game of Life, Hotels.

Action figure: "Doll" for boys, usually partially or fully *articulated*—e.g., G.I. Joe, He-Man—whose main purpose it is to stimulate the sale of complementary accessories such as clothing, playsets, vehicles, and weapons.

Add-on: *See* Accessory.

Adult Social Interaction Games (ASI): Games, usually for adults, that reveal information about themselves and fellow players.

Advance: Negotiated sum of money given to an inventor against future royalties. It is normally nonrefundable.

Age grading: Labeling of products for the appropriate age level of users.

Agency: Manufacturer's advertising agency.

Agent: Person who represents independent inventors. Also called a broker.

Airbrush: Atomizer for spraying paint onto models and/or prototypes; used to achieve soft gradations and merging of tones on original artwork.

A-price: Manufacturer's wholesale price to the trade as reflected on the company's price sheet.

Archives: (1) Collections of product that an inventor has not yet sold; (2) library of old toy catalogs.

Articulated figure: Doll or action figure with jointed parts such as legs and arms.

Associate: One of two or more inventors who works in partnership part or full time.

Atomic: Refers to a product the likes of Trivial Pursuit that sells way beyond anyone's expectations and jumps suddenly well into the millions of units. *Trivial Pursuit went atomic in its second year.*

Audit: Examination of a manufacturer's books of account by an inventor and/or his appointed representatives for the purpose of confirming the veracity of royalty reports.

B

Backstory: The storyline developed by a manufacturer or developer to set the stage for a toy, action figures, or dolls; sometimes the basis for an animated television series.

Back to basics: Signifies a return to uncomplicated products, usually heard every time the industry has a bad year and wishes to support a move away from heavily promoted product.

Ball-and-paddle game: Type of video-game format.

Bar code: Universal Product Code symbol, or UPC seal.

Beauty shot: Product image used on packaging that shows the consumer what is actually being purchased and captures the product in its most exciting form. *Let's use a photo of the real airplane on the front panel, and put the beauty shot on the back.*

Big Pond: Pacific Ocean. *I'm going over the Big Pond for a couple of weeks.*

Big Wheel: Distinctive style of tricycle, made famous by Louis Marx, that has a large, 16-inch front wheel and two smaller back wheels.

Blank check: What toy companies never give inventors.

Blank space: What inventors have to fill with creative output.

Blister: *See* Clam shell.

Blister-card package: Four-color printed card that holds and sells a product. Generally displayed hanging on a hook. *See* J-hook; Delta hook.

Blow molding: Manufacturing process that consists of forming a tube and introducing air or gas that causes the heated tube to expand against a mold for forming hollow objects such as bottles or toys.

Blow off the shelves: To sell extremely well. *Barbie continued to blow off the shelves at retail even at the height of Cabbage Patch fever.*

Blue-skying: *See* Noodling.

Board game: Game played on an illustrated, printed playing field.

Bow wow: Lousy product.

Brain death: Shutdown of an executive's central nervous system caused by an overambitious developer showing too many products at one sitting.

Breadboard: (1) To make an experimental arrangement of a mechanism or electronic circuit on a flat surface; (2) a model that demonstrates to R&D how something will work. *Let's breadboard the circuit and demo it.*

Breakeven: Point at which a product makes back its initial investment and begins to pull its own weight in the marketplace.

Bridge, The: Ninth-floor passageway that links 200 Fifth Avenue and 1107 Broadway; a favorite meeting place for inventors during the New York Toy Fair. *I'll meet you on The Bridge at three o'clock.*

Broker: *See* Agent.

B-sheet: Preliminary sketch. *Get me some B-sheets on the concept.*

Build-upper: Someone who hypes a product for the purpose of selling it to a manufacturer.

Busy Box: Infant activity toy that typically incorporates multiple actions—e.g., clicking dials, squeaking bulbs, spinning wheels, rattles—and is designed for use in crib, playpen, or on floor.

Buyer: Decision-maker for toy retailers who selects and purchases items from manufacturers that will appear on store shelves.

Buzz: Sensation that a good product delivers.

C

Calendering: Manufacturing process that produces thin plastic sheets and films by squeezing melted resin between sets of rollers. It can best be compared to the spreading of butter.

Cannibalize: To use parts from an existing product for the purpose of making a prototype.

Casting: Manufacturing process whereby a molten substance (e.g., zinc for miniature vehicles) is poured—not squeezed—into a mold and takes shape as it cools. This process is best compared to baking a cake.

Category: General class to which a particular product belongs—e.g., hobby, action figure, skill and action, doll, preschool, etc.

CES: Abbreviation for Consumer Electronics Show.

Chain: Group of three or more retail stores involved in the business of merchandising toys and games.

Champion: Corporate executive who advocates and defends a product throughout its development process.

Chance games: Games that require no skill, no strategy, or no general knowledge; player action is entirely dependent on random movement of dice, cards, or spinner.

Character licensing: (1) Imprinting of a character, image, logo, signature, design, personality, or property on an existing

product for the purpose of heightening awareness and sales;
(2) reproduction of a character, image, logo, signature, design, or property in and of itself as a viable commercial entity.

Child test: Formal or informal hands-on testing of a product by
kids.

Chip: (1) Small piece of semiconductor material, typically silicon, on which electronic components are formed; (2) playing
piece in certain games of chance.

Chipboard: Heavy paper board used for packaging and for appropriate parts of prototypes.

Chotchke: Toy; a little plaything.

Christmas: What it's all about.

Chromalin: Four-color, one-of-a-kind proof on plastic substrate;
used to check artwork before going ahead with a full press run.

Clam shell: Packaging of clear plastic that has been molded to
an item's physical profile, hinged in the middle, and snapped
around the product, for point-of-sale display.

Classic: Any product that has been popular with millions of people for more than twenty-five years—e.g., Barbie, Monopoly,
Mr. Potato Head.

Closeout: Industry heartbreak. Toy or game that has been a major disappointment at retail and is being reduced in retail price
to get rid of remaining inventory.

Collectible: Assortment of product with a common design or tie-
in that encourages multiple purchases.

Comp: Shortened version of ''comprehensive''—a drawing or
model that shows what a product will look and/or work like
when it is finished.

Confidential disclosure: Agreement between two parties that an
idea is being reviewed, with an understanding that information about it will not be shared with others.

Consumer: End-user of a toy or game; someone who has selected
the product at retail with the expectation of great entertainment and play value.

Consumer research: Studies with consumers to determine their unmet needs, their buying patterns, their attitudes toward existing products on the market, reactions to packaging and commercials, and other factors related to marketing toys and games. *See also* Focus group.

Control drawing: Drawing with specifications, from which model-makers can produce working samples.

Copyright: Exclusive legal right to reproduce, publish, and sell the matter and form of a literary, musical, or artistic work.

Corrugated: Protective paper packaging material used on many outer cartons; when decorated with four-color printing, used for individual packaging structures.

CPSC: Abbreviation for Consumer Product Safety Commission, the federal watchdog agency for established safety standards.

Crafts: Activity category comprising products that require manual dexterity or artistic skills.

Cross-marketing: Promotion of one or more company products on the back panel of another company product.

Cross-sell brochure: Insert placed in manufacturer's boxes showing consumers other similar or accessory products available from the same source.

Customer: Most important person in the business.

Cut steel: To produce a mold. *They're cutting steel for our gizmo next week.*

CYAWP: Acronym for "cover your ass with paper." Refers to the advisability of documenting everything that is said and done between the outside inventor and the manufacturer vis-à-vis the development of product.

D

DAL: Acronym for "dumb ass luck," a factor responsible for many sales of new products to toy and game manufacturers. *The guy's got DAL.*

Dating: Esoteric form of billing in which the trade receives its merchandise as early in the year as possible but doesn't have to pay for it until after Christmas dollars are received from consumers.

Deferred: Marketing euphemism that means a product has been dropped but marketing won't tell R&D until next year.

Delta hook: Opening in the top of a blister card that takes the form of a delta wing. With this design the consumer cannot get to any card without removing all of the cards in front of it on the hook.

Demographics: Statistical studies relating to human populations, especially with reference to size, density, distribution, and vital statistics.

Designer: Person who creates, executes, or builds a product according to plan.

Design patent: Protection for the appearance of an item, and not its structure or utilitarian features.

Die-cast: Metal toy, generally a vehicle, that is cast from zinc.

Die-cut: To cut sheet material—whether paper, plastic, or cardboard—into unique forms and shapes using a steel rule die mounted onto heavy press equipment for mass-production purposes.

Disclosure form: *See* Nondisclosure form.

Dog-and-pony show: Elaborate presentation of new product by its creator.

Doll: Small-scale figure of a human being.

Double tooling: Expanding production output to meet demand. The wish of every inventor.

Dough: (1) Any of numerous soft modeling compounds; (2) inventor royalties.

Drop paper: Act of giving firm purchase orders for product. *Has the trade dropped any paper on this item?*

Dropped item: Product that has been withdrawn from consideration or from the line.

E

Edutain: To educate through entertainment; usually used for science toys or other discovery toys and games.

Eighty/twenty formula: 80 percent of the business is done by 20 percent of the manufacturers.

Electronics: Toys or games using microcircuitry in their function, as opposed to mechanical action.

End cap: Best display space a product can get in a toy store; shelves that occupy the ends of aisles.

Engineer: Person assigned to transform approved concept, design, and model into specifications and tolerances leading to mass-producible pieces.

Engineering drawing: Detailed and accurate drawings of all parts needed to manufacture a new toy; these become the blueprints for ultimate tooling and production of parts.

EPS: Abbreviation for expandable polystyrene, which, with the addition of various agents, can assume a variety of densities.

Ergonomics: Science of making the buttons and controls on a toy or game fit the product within the limitations of its design.

Errata sheet: Message inserted in packages to alert consumers of changes in information affecting game play and/or assembly.

Extension: Independently marketed product that trades on the name of another product.

Extrusion: Manufacturing process in which solid resin pellets fluidize while being pushed continuously through a heating chamber by a large screw. It can best be compared to the squeezing of a toothpaste tube. Different openings are used to shape the resulting mass.

F

Face panel: The front or main panel of a package that usually faces the aisle when on retail shelves.

Fair, The: Shorthand for the annual American International Toy Fair held in New York City.

Family board game: Parlor game for ages ten to adult that offers some strategy or theme to keep the interest of older children and parents.

Fantasy quest: Video-game format.

Fashion doll: Usually partially or fully articulated—such as Barbie, Maxie; its main purpose is to stimulate sales of complementary accessories, such as clothing, playsets, and vehicles.

Federal Express: The quickest and most expensive way to get an inventor's prototype to the key marketing and R&D executives just as they leave on vacation.

First-handshake item. Fisher-Price marketing term for a product that captures the attention of a new mother with her first child. A successful first-handshake item will be one that's instrumental in building brand loyalty.

Flashing: Excess plastic not trimmed off during the molding process; caused by poor tool match. Easily removed with X-acto blade or pen knife.

FOB: Abbreviation for freight on board, which is generally used to signify a purchase plan whereby the trade can pick up product at its foreign point of manufacture for a lower price than in the United States.

Focus group: Formally organized testing of a product by volunteer or paid consumers.

Folding carton: Packaging structure (usually of die-cut chipboard) that, when folded into dimension, anchors and displays product.

Forecast: Projection of number of units of a toy or game that will sell within a given period, such as one month or one year; sometimes called a guesstimate.

Free: "Magic" word with some strings attached.

Free-standing insert (FSI): Newspaper supplement in which retailers announce sales for toys and games, usually during the major consumer buying time, e.g. Thanksgiving to Christmas.

G

Game: Organized contest with rules, opposing interests, and goals; a real-life situation in miniature.

Gamer: Player of non-mass-market games, such as role-playing formats.

Glass: At one time the industry's leading independent toy and game development company; named for its founder Marvin Glass.

Glide rate: The distance a product goes after it has been *jump started;* usually occurs in a product's second year.

Glossies: Black-and-white photographic prints used for advertising and publicity.

Go South: Inventor's idea dropped by manufacturer. Idea is free to go "south" to another company, or country.

Grabber: Any visual or verbal element associated with a product that will "grab" the consumer's attention; may be special price, name, claim, etc.

Graphics: Artwork on a toy, game, or package.

Green sheet: Manufacturer's wholesale price list.

Gremlins: Obstacles designed into games to create problems for players.

Guarantee: Minimum sum of money that a manufacturer assures an inventor he will earn on a product, even if it is dropped or performs poorly.

H

Hairplay: Brushable hair, an important and popular feature in dolls.

Handhelds: Miniaturized portable games, usually electronic.

Hard cost: A product's full cost to manufacture, including materials, labor, and packaging (if offshore, add duty and freight).

Hero's powers: What you can do to your enemies in video games.

Hero's weaknesses: What your enemies can do to you in video games.

Ho-hum: A product that causes boredom, discomfort, and overall dissatisfaction.

I

Imaginative play: Make-believe, fantasy play.

Infant: In age grading for a variety of toys and activity items, a child under eighteen months.

Inflatable: Any indoor/outdoor, hollow vinyl toy that requires inflation with air. Primary cause of hyperventilation among parents.

Infringement of patent: Unauthorized making, using, or selling for practical use, or for profit, of an invention covered by a valid patent.

Injection molding: Manufacturing process in which machines pressure-inject molton plastic granules into relatively cold molds, where they solidify and take the shape of the mold cavity. It can best be compared to making waffles.

Insert: Packaging element added to a box to anchor the product so it stays in a predetermined position.

In stock: Manufacturer's inventory of product ready to ship.

Intellectual property: Ideas or concepts that are subject to ownership.

In the loop: Involvement with the internal corporate product development of one's product. *I've been in the loop from presentation to Toy Fair.*

In the mail: Inventor's prototype, contract, or check, which hasn't yet been sent, but will be now.

In the pipeline: (1) Product that is being prepared, processed, or worked on by a manufacturer; (2) product that is being distributed to retail outlets.

In review process: Often means the secretary hasn't sent out your rejection letter yet.

Introduction: Launch of a new plaything, usually at Toy Fair and always with great fanfare and ballyhoo.

Inventing community: Industry catchall term for professional inventors.

Inventor relations: Department at a manufacturer that deals with outside developers.

Inventory: List of goods on hand.

Item: single product.

J

Javits: Shortened reference to Jacob Javits Convention Center in New York City, where part of the annual American International Toy Fair takes place.

J-hook: Opening in the top of a blister card that takes the form of the letter J. This design allows the consumer to remove product from anywhere on the rack without disturbing other blister cards hung in front of and behind it.

Joystick: Type of hand control for video games that players use for moving images on the screen.

Jump-start a product: To throw a lot of television dollars behind an item in hopes of getting strong consumer *sell-through*.

K

Keeper: New product that a manufacturer wants to hold for further review.

Key account: Major customer—determined by number of retail stores and sales history.

Kidvid: Saturday-morning television programs, usually animated.

Kitchen research: Informal research conducted in a casual manner to get reaction to the play of an item.

Knockoff: (1) Stealing of another person's or manufacturer's product by copying it so closely that it embodies the spirit of the original; (2) nonpromoted copy of a best-selling product at a lower price.

L

Labor-intensive: Manufacturing that requires large amounts of handwork that cannot be automated.

Lawyers: The only individuals in the toy industry who consistently turn a profit.

LC: Abbreviation for *letter of credit.*

LCD: Abbreviation for liquid crystal display; a type of screen that gives scoring or playing fields in a visual form.

Legals: Corporate shorthand for patent, trademark, and copyright notices that appear on packaging and product.

Letter of credit: Letter addressed by a banker to a correspondent (usually refers to an offshore manufacturer) certifying that the person or company named is entitled to draw a certain amount of money upon the completion of a specific performance—e.g., the production of a quantity of toys or games.

Licensed property: Unique character, event, or personality that has proven consumer appeal, which manufacturers incorporate into their products for a royalty.

Licensee: Term used in licensing agreements to designate the manufacturer.

Licensing: Act of contracting for the rights to manufacture and market an item or concept. *How many items did you license last year?*

Licensing agreement: Authorization to manufacture and market a piece of intellectual property—e.g., a toy, game, or design.

Licensor: Term used in licensing agreements to designate the inventor.

Life support: Where a product goes just before it is dropped. *The product's on life support awaiting the decision as to its final disposition.*

Line: Family or series of toys or games tied together by a common design or theme; always better than a single item.

Line art: Drawing made in solid lines as copy for a linecut.

Linecut: Letterpress printing plate photoengraved from line art.

Line review: Periodic conference to review line development.

Load-'em-up-and-bust game: Game in which players fill something until it overloads and bursts.

Looks-like: Three-dimensional model that looks exactly like the production model of an item will look, although it need not be made from the ultimate materials.

Loss leader: Selling technique used by retailers in pricing a popular item at or below cost to attract consumers in hopes they will buy that item and more. *Pampers are a loss leader for Toys R Us.*

M

Majors, The: Large manufacturers, such as Hasbro, Mattel, and Tyco.

Margin: Amount of profit made on a toy or game based upon the difference in manufacturing and other costs versus manufacturers' selling price.

Markdown: Reduction in an original selling price.

Marker rendering: Illustration done with Magic Marker.

Market: (1) Price offered for a particular product; (2) area of demand; (3) organized coming-together of buyers and sellers.

Marketer: A person masterful in marketing.

Marketing: Process of selling or offering something for sale based upon a plan.

Marketing plan: Business objectives that include: (a) merchandising (product policy), (b) pricing, (c) distribution channels (the route products take between manufacturer and consumer), (d) personal selling, and (e) advertising.

Market share: Portion of a particular category "owned" by a particular product.

Markup: Percentage added by the retailer, above what was paid to the manufacturer, to reach a shelf price.

Mass marketer: Large chain operators such as K mart, Walmart, and Toys R Us, which have the capacity to purchase and sell the largest number of SKUs to the greatest number of consumers.

Mature market: The major market segment of senior citizens; toy industry has yet to come to grips with this phenomenon.

Mechanical: Artboard with layout of typesetting and art placement positioned according to specifications for the production of printed pieces.

Media plan: Advertising program that delivers effective messages to the greatest number of target consumers at the lowest possible cost.

Metalize: To give a toy a lustrous metallic veneer. Often a signal to pros that an item is on its last legs. *They've taken that item about as far as they can; I guess the next move will be to metalize it.*

Me-too product: Close copy of another item; usually a knockoff of something successful.

Microcontroller: Brain of an electronic game; a small integrated circuit that processes the information entered by the player.

Mockup: Two- or three-dimensional representation of an idea to translate the verbal into the visual.

Model: Clear and detailed prototype of an item.

Model-makers: Personnel who handcraft prototypes/models.

Mold: Cavity in which a substance is formed.

Multicavity mold: Mold with multiple cavities for increased production; often these cavities produce multiple copies of a single component.

Multiple submission: Submission by an inventor of the same concept simultaneously to several companies.

N

Nailed to the shelf: Stiff product; one that doesn't move at retail.

NES advantage: Nintendo super-joystick controller.

Net wholesale price: Manufacturer's billed price to his customers, less cash and trade discounts and allowances.

New product review: Periodic conference to consider new product submissions.

NIH: Abbreviation for not invented here, a term used to describe companies that do not consider outside submissions from inventors.

No-brainer: A toy or game that is easy to explain or use, something obvious.

Nondisclosure form: Agreement between an inventor and a company that makes it possible for both parties to share and review new concepts in confidence. Weighted in the favor of the manufacturer.

Nonpromoted item: Toy or game with no advertising or publicity budget.

Noodling: Mental exercise by which developers create new product.

Novelty: Small, inexpensive manufactured item usually sold on blister cards.

Nürnberg: Site in Germany of the largest European toy fair.

O

Objective: Brief summary of the object of a board game or the storyline of a video game.

OEM: Abbreviation for original equipment manufacturer; used to describe an element in a product that can be purchased ready-made from a source. *We can get OEM sand timers for the game from a factory in Singapore.*

Offshore: Placed or made abroad.

On the water: A product that has been made and is en route via freighter to the United States.

Option: Agreement allowing a manufacturer to hold a prototype for a designated period of time.

Original: Product that has been done before, but in a different way.

Overpackaged: (1) Far too little product for the size of the box; (2) too much air.

P

Package structure: Physical package design.

Paddle controls: Type of hand controller for video games that players use to move the images on the screen.

Paper: Customer order to purchase merchandise. *The customer likes the product but hasn't passed the paper yet.*

Parallel development: Similar products from two different inventing sources.

Patent: Grant of property right by the government to the inventor; it confers the right to exclude others from making, using, or selling the invention throughout the United States for seventeen years from the date of issue, subject to the payment of maintenance fees. *See also* Infringement of patent.

Patent attorney: Lawyer who specializes in writing patent applications.

Patent pending: Notice to the public that an application for patent on a particular item is on file in the Patent and Trademark Office.

Pawn: Playing piece or token used in games to represent individual players.

Payoff: The reward at the end of a game.

Perceived value: Worth of a product as reflected in its components, its packaging, and its ad campaign.

Pips: Markings on each side of a die cube, from one to six; dice can also have other markings, such as colors, letters, geometric designs, etc.

Plastic: Synthetic material produced from chemicals that can be molded into almost any form. It may be any color or colorless. Some have the hardness of steel, others the softness of silk.

Plastic by the pound: Basic, inexpensive playthings sold primarily by mass marketers, often unpackaged. Commodity business.

Play environment: Line of accessories that complement toys, such as houses, forts, garages, etc.

Play pattern: The way in which children use a toy.

Play value: Lasting fun and amusement inherent in a toy or game.

Plush: Stuffed animals or toys.

Polyethylene: Lightweight, flexible thermoplastic that has a wax-like feel—e.g., beach bucket and shovel.

Polypropylene: Lightweight, strong, heat-resistant thermoplastic used to mold many popular toys; will bend but not break.

POP: Abbreviation for manufacturers' point of purchase or sale—that is, advertising displays positioned near the product on the shelf.

Preliminary design: (1) R&D department, a think tank charged with offering suggestions to product managers; (2) the breadboard stage of a product under development.

Prepricing: Price printed on product by manufacturer to designate a suggested retail cost.

Preschool: In age grading for a variety of toys and games, three to six years old.

Presell: To sell a product to the trade before its introduction at Toy Fair.

Presentation: Meeting to show product; for the inventor, the belief that if he/she spends $1,000 on a plane ticket, rental car, and hotel room a concept will sell itself.

Pre–Toy Fair: Product presentation period a few months ahead of New York Toy Fair during which manufacturers pitch product to their largest accounts.

Price point: Price at which a product is offered for sale to the trade.

Print campaign: Advertising schedule of ad placement in magazines or newspapers versus other media, such as radio and/ or TV.

Product description: The only verbiage that is read less often than assembly instruction.

Product manager: Marketing person charged with seeing a product through from its initial stages to completion, positioning, packaging, and promotional campaign. Responsible for bottom line. His or her word has become law in many companies.

Profit: Dollar return over and above all expenses to develop, produce, and market a product.

Progression games: Object is to be the first player to reach a goal, such as the end of a path; moves are typically determined by chance.

Promoted item: Toy or game that has an advertising and publicity budget.

Promotion: Product hype, usually involving a combined campaign of print, television, trade displays, and public relations.

Proof: Test applied to articles or substances to determine whether they are of standard or satisfactory quality. *This afternoon we're going to see the package proofs.*

Prototype: (1) Original model on which something is patterned; (2) to create an original model. *Let's prototype it and see what we have.*

PTO: Abbreviation for the Patent and Trademark Office in Washington, DC.

Purchase intent: Indication by consumers during product testing that if product is available in a particular form, at a specific price, then, in all likelihood, they would buy it.

PVC: Polyvinyl chloride.

Q

QA: Abbreviation for quality assurance.

QC: Abbreviation for quality control.

Quarterly reports: (1) Statements from manufacturers to inventors that tell how many of any particular licensed item have been sold. Royalty checks, inventors hope, also accompany such reports; (2) financial report to stockholders on condition of business during previous three-month period.

R

R&D: Abbreviation for research and development.

Rack jobbers: Wholesalers specializing in blister-carded rack toys.

Random generator: Dice, spinner, or other device for randomizing moves in a game.

R/C: Abbreviation for radio-controlled toys, such as cars, boats, and aircraft, that are either gas- or battery-powered and steered by means of handheld transceivers.

Red light: New product that stops traffic.

Reflective art: Original art created for packaging or product.

Rejection letter: A regular happening; standard communication between manufacturer and inventor.

Research and development (R&D): Careful and diligent investigation that companies conduct into products they contemplate manufacturing; the process of creating new products.

Returns: Products that have been on sale at retail, have not sold through, and are being shipped back to the manufacturer by the retailer.

Roller ball: Type of hand controller for video games that players use to move images on the screen.

Rotational molding: The heating of finely ground vinyl plastisols in a rotating mold until melting or fusion occurs. When the mold is cooled, a hollow part is removed. This is a relatively cheap, scrap-free process, especially popular for the production of large plastic items.

Royalty: Payment made to an inventor by a manufacturer for each piece sold, calculated at a negotiated percentage of net wholesale receipts less all allowances.

S

Sand timer: Instrument for measuring the time of gameplay that consists of a plastic hourglass vessel in which sand runs from the top into the lower section.

Schematic: Diagram of an electronic circuit.

Schlock: Of low quality or little worth. *The developer had a terrific item, but it died because of his schlock presentation.*

Sculptor: Artist capable of producing three-dimensional forms from verbal, sketch, and/or photographic guidelines.

Sell-in: Purchase of product by the trade.

Sell panel: Front panel on a package.

Sell-through: Purchase of product by the consumer.

Semiconductors: Conductors of electricity (typically made from silicon) that allow the design and manufacturing of very small, very complicated, yet very inexpensive electric circuits.

Separations: Lithographic process by which printers ''separate'' colors of artwork in preparation for making printing plates.

Set-up box: Common packaging structure in which there is a box top and a box bottom.

Shakers and rollers: Entrepreneurs or intrapreneurs. Both make toys and games happen.

Shelf space: Linear footage in a toy store that manufacturers can never get enough of and that retailers monitor for product movement.

Ship air: To pack a product improperly so that the package is oversized for the dimensions of the contents, thereby capturing excess space (i.e.,air); often referred to as slack packaging.

Shrink-wrapping: Tight plastic protective covering used to seal packaging.

Shut-up toy: Plaything given to a child to keep him or her quiet and occupied.

Skill-and-action game: Fast-paced three-dimensional game in which two to four players, ages five and up, race to complete the collection of certain pieces—e.g., marbles.

SKU: *See* Stock keeping unit.

Slot car: Electric toy racing vehicle that has an arm underneath fitting into a groove for guidance and metal strips alongside the groove for power.

Slot racing: Racing of slot cars.

Soft goods: *See* Plush.

Soft sculpture: Umbrella term that refers to stuffed animals or toys.

Soft-toy designer: Person experienced in soft sculpture, pattern-making, prototype construction.

Sourcing: Locating the supplier or manufacturer of component parts required to produce a particular toy or game.

Specifications: (1) Description of an invention for which a patent is sought; (2) detailed dimensions or list of components or processes for something to be manufactured.

Spinner: Movable arrow that is spun on its dial to indicate the number or kind of moves a player may make in a board game.

Split royalty: Situation whereby two or more inventors/licensors divide a royalty on a product.

Splurge ad: Full-page print advertisement.

Spot: Television commercial.

Staple: Product that sells year in and year out and is considered indispensable by the manufacturer.

Stiff: Product that does not sell-through at retail.

Stock keeping unit (SKU): Single toy or game inventoried by a retailer that occupies shelf space.

Storyboards: Sketches of pictures and their related narration or dialogue; used to plan a television commercial or animated program.

Strategy games: Games won through mental superiority. Formats include whodunits, war games, puzzles, and games of alignment, such as Stratego, Battleship, Clue, Lie Detector.

Sublicensing: Licensing of an inventor's product to one or more third parties by the primary licensee.

Submission form: *See* Nondisclosure form.

Suggested list price: Retail price suggested by the manufacturer.

T

Tag line: Slogan for a product, usually printed under the trademark.

Take-apart: Toy that kids can disassemble completely or partially.

Tasteless cake and beautiful frosting: A product that has great form but little substance.

Telegenics: Characteristics necessary for a product to deliver a message via television.

Thumbnails: Rough pencil or charcoal sketches of a concept. Also called tissues.

Time line: Schedule showing a planned order or sequence of a product's development and introduction.

Tissues: Rough pencil sketches of a concept.

TM: Abbreviation for trademark.

TMA: Abbreviation for Toy Manufacturers of America, Inc.

Toddler: Age grading that designates items as appropriate for children eighteen months to three years.

Tooling: Steel molds with which to manufacture plastic components for an item.

Toy doctors: Model-makers who repair broken prototypes for the manufacturers during New York Toy Fair or any other sales meeting.

Toyetics: Play values that make up a good toy.

Toy Fair: Largest American toy fair, which takes place each February in New York City.

Toys R Us: World's largest chain of retail toy stores.

Trade, The: Umbrella term used to refer to wholesalers and retailers.

Trade buyer: *See* Buyer.

Trademark: Any word, name, symbol, or device used in trade with goods to indicate the source or origin of the goods and to distinguish them from the goods of others.

Trades, The: Specialized magazines and newspapers dedicated to the industry—e.g., *Playthings, Toy & Hobby World.*

Transformers: Hasbro trademark that has come to represent any product that converts itself from one form to another through hand manipulation.

Triple tooling: Expanding production output to meet trade demand. The wish of every inventor.

Truncated cylinder: Device used by quality-control people to simulate the throat passage in children three years and under for the purpose of establishing the safety of small parts.

Try-me package: Design that permits the consumer to activate a product at a retail outlet without removing it from its package.

TV item: Product that the manufacturer will promote through television ads.

Two Hundred Fifth: Abbreviated reference to 200 Fifth Avenue, aka The Toy Center, site of the annual American International Toy Fair.

U

Umbrella: Theme for a major line of products.

Utility patent: Protection for the novel utilitarian features of an item.

V

Vac-forming: Manufacturing process in which a heated sheet of plastic is drawn into or over a mold via vacuum; used for prototyping and blisters.

Vendor: Supplier of products and/or services required by a manufacturer in the production and preparation of a toy or game for market.

Video game: Game played through a television monitor.

W

Wannabe: Product that is not fully or accurately defined—i.e., it wants to be something else.

Wheeled goods: Bicycles, tricycles, wagons, scooters, etc.

Word games: Games dependent on the players' understanding of words, spelling, and/or definitions. Examples include Scrabble, UpWords, Password, Wordsearch.

Word-of-mouth: Best form of advertising bar none; one consumer tells another about product satisfaction.

Works-like: Model that works exactly like the production model of an item will, although it need not be made from the ultimate materials.

Wow factor: Strongest and most promotable feature of a new toy or game—i.e., a remarkable and exciting point of difference.

X

X: The spot on the contract where the inventor signs.

Y

Yawn: Boring product.

Youngling: Slang for a child.

Yum-yum: Tasty, delightful new product. *Hold it for review; it's a real yum-yum.*

Z

Zapper: Handheld control unit for video games.

Appendix

TOY EVENTS CALENDAR

January

Las Vegas: Winter Consumer Electronics Show, Las Vegas Convention Center. CES, (202) 457-4919.

Hong Kong: Hong Kong Toys and Games Fair, Hong Kong Convention and Exhibition Centre. Hong Kong Trade Development Council, (212) 838-8688.

Harrogate, Great Britain: Harrogate International Toy Fair. Harrogate International Toy Fair, Ltd., 8/9 Upper Street, Islington, London N1 0PP, England.

Dallas: HIA Convention and Trade Show, Dallas Convention Center. HIA, (214) 794-1133.

London: British International Toy and Hobby Fair, Earl's Court. British Toy and Hobby Manufacturers Association, 80 Camberwell Road, London SE5 0EG, England.

Toronto: Canadian Toy Fair. Canadian Toy Manufacturers Association, Box 294, Kleinburg, Ontario, L0J, 1C0, Canada.

February

Paris: Paris International Toy Fair, Paris-Nord International Exhibition Center. Salon International du Jouet, 103 rue Lafayette, 75010 Paris, France.

Nürnberg, West Germany: International Toy Fair. International Schpielwarmesse, GmbH, 8500 Nürnberg-Messezentrum, West Germany.

New York: National Back-to-School Merchandise Show, Javits Center. Thalheim Expositions, (516) 627-4000.

New York: American International Toy Fair, 200 Fifth Avenue, 1107 Broadway, Javits Center. TMA, (212) 675-1141.

Valencia, Spain: Valencia Toy Fair. Feria del Juguete, y articulos para la Infancia, Llano del Real—Apartado 476, Valencia, Spain.

New York: MIAA Trade Show, Penta Hotel. Offinger Management, (212) 452-4541.

New York: Variety Merchandise Show, Javits Center. Thalheim Expositions, (516) 627-4000.

New York: Toytech, Penta Hotel. Robert P. Birkfield, (212) 513-7878.

Atlanta: The Super Show, Georgia World Congress Center. SGMA, (800) 327-3736.

Milan: Milan Toy Fair. E.A. Salone Internationale del Giocattolo, Via Petitti 16, 20149 Milan, Italy.

March

Las Vegas: Game Manufacturers Association Trade Show and Retailers Seminar, Tropicana Hotel. Howard Barasch, (214) 247-7981.

Dallas: Dallas Toy Show, Dallas Market Center. DMC Travel Services, (800) 634-2630.

Seattle: Pacific Northwest Toy Association Show, Seattle Trade Center. PNTA, (206) 441-8442.

Chicago: National Halloween and Costume Show and National

Party Show, O'Hare Exposition Center. TransWorld Exhibits, (312) 446-8434.

Pomona, California: Western States Toy and Hobby Show, Los Angeles County Fairgrounds. Phyllis St. John, (818) 442-1635.

April

Atlanta: Atlanta Toy Fair, Georgia International Convention and Trade Center. Adele Gilchrist, (404) 449-8444.

Seattle: The Child's Fair, Seattle Center Exhibition Hall. Linda J. Browne and Associates, (206) 441-1881.

New York: Premium Incentive Show, Javits Center. Thalheim Expositions, (516) 627-4000.

New York: New York Home Video Market, Javits Center. Knowledge Industry Publications, (914) 328-9157.

May

New York: National Stationery Show, Javits Center. George Little Management, (212) 686-6070.

Buenos Aires: National Toy Fair of Argentina, Exhibition Hall. Argentine Chamber of the Toy Industry, (920) 1537-0169.

Beijing: Toys China, Beijing Exhibition Center. Robert Yuan, China Association for Science and Technology, Dwight D. Eisenhower Building, Spokane, Washington 99202.

June

Chicago: Consumer Electronics Show, McCormick Place. CES, (202) 457-4919.

San Jose, California: Great American Family Expo, San Jose Convention Facility. Great American Family Expo, (415) 594-0452.

New York: Mid-Year Variety Merchandise Show, Javits Center. Thalheim Expositions, (516) 627-4000.

New York: International Licensing and Merchandising Conference and Exposition, Javits Center. LIMA, (212) 244-1944.
Tokyo: Tokyo Toy Fair. Japan International Toy Fair Association, No. 22–4, Higashi-Komagata 4-Chome, Sumida-Ku,
Tokyo, Japan.
Anaheim, California: Western States Craft Show, Anaheim Convention Center. HIA, (201) 794-1133.

July

Rosemont, Illinois: TransWorld Housewares and Variety Show,
O'Hare Exposition Center. TransWorld Exhibits, (312) 446-
8434.
Atlanta: Southeast Craft and Hobby Show, Georgia International
Trade Center. SECHA, (404) 252-2454.
Chicago: International Craft Exposition, Chicago Craft and Cre-
ative Industries Show, O'Hare Exposition Center. ACCI,
(614) 452-4541.
Lake Tahoe: Toy Wholesalers' Association of America Summer
Conference. TWA, (609) 234-9155.
Dallas: Southwestern Craft and Hobby Christmas in July Show,
Dallas Market Center. SWCHA, (614) 452-4541.

August

New York: New York International Gift Fair/Just Kidstuff, Javits
Center. George Little Management, (212) 686-6070.
Long Beach, California: Miniatures Industry Association of America, Long Beach Convention Center. Offinger Management,
(614) 452-4541.

September

Paris: Monde de l'Enfant Show, Paris Porte de Versailles. S.I.J.,
S.A., 103 rue Lafayette, 75010 Paris, France.
New York: American Games Fair, Roosevelt Hotel. CCE Ltd.,
(212) 867-5159.

New York: National Merchandise Show, Javits Center. Thalheim
Expositions, (516) 627-4000.

Dallas: Juvenile Products Show, Dallas Market Center. Juvenile
Products Manufacturers Association, (609) 234-9155.

Seoul, South Korea: SITOY. Korea Toy Industry Cooperative, 361-1,
2-ka, Hankang-ro, Yongsan-ku, Seoul, South Korea.

Hong Kong: Asian International Toy and Gift Fair, Ocean Ter-
minal, Tsimshatsui, Kowloon, Hong Kong. Cahners Exposition Group, 1507 Shun Tak Centre, 200 Connaught Road,
Central, Hong Kong.

Taipei, Taiwan: Taipei International Toy Show, Taiwan World
Trade Center. CETRA, (212) 532-7055.

Chicago: National Premium Incentive Show, McCormick Place.
Peter Erickson, (312) 850-7779.

October

Atlanta: Gifts International, Georgia World Congress Center.
Gifts International, (404) 394-1263.

Chicago: TransWorld's Housewares and Variety Exhibit, O'Hare
Exhibition Center. TransWorld Exhibits, (312) 446-8434.

November

New York: Spring and Summer Toy Preview, 200 Fifth Avenue,
1107 Broadway. TMA, (212) 675-1141.

Chicago: Chicago Model Hobby Show, O'Hare Exposition Center. Kerry Connelly, (312) 299-3131.

Dallas: Dallas Toy Preview, Dallas Market Center. DMC Travel
Services, (800) 634-2630.

December

New York: TMA Annual Meeting, 200 Fifth Avenue Club. TMA,
(212) 675-1141.

Index